DICTIONARY
OF
SPIRITUALISM

DICTIONARY
of
SPIRITUALISM

by

HARRY E. WEDECK

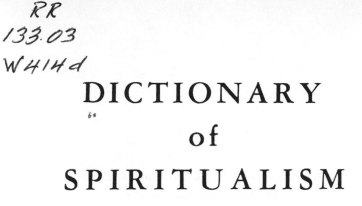

WITH THE ASSISTANCE OF WADE BASKIN

PHILOSOPHICAL LIBRARY

New York

INTRODUCTION

As human beings, we are bounded and constricted by certain acknowledged physical and material circumstances, by corporeal and mental and cosmic limitations that compel us normally to submit perforce to certain ascertainable conditions. We are confined within the periphery of our presumably inherent human characteristics. If by some chance or machination or suddenly discovered faculty we can transcend these rigid natural frontiers, these indurated laws, then we pass into experiences which we say are beyond the natural laws. These experiences cannot conform to human explanations of phenomena as they regularly occur, but pass, or appear to pass, into a zone that knows no such limitations and long accepted barriers. This is the domain of the supernatural. It is the region where what is impossible in human terms becomes possible and actual. It is the realm whose symbol is the paradoxical apothegm: Credo quod impossibile est.

The concept of the Supernatural embraces Heaven and Hell and all that is between. It deals with human beings, with the animate and the inanimate world, with impalpabilities and thoughts. It is easier, in fact, to offer an instance of what might be termed the supernatural than to define it by categorical prescriptions. In its literal sense, in its etymological essence, it denotes that which occurs beyond or above the normal consciousness of humanity. Yet by that very definition it creates a paradox. For one must first of all define what is normal. Normality is that which consistently and repeatedly occurs in the same manner, in a predictable situation, as the rising and the setting of the sun, the force of gravity, the opacity of certain materials. If I can see through a brick wall without interfering with the structure of the wall itself, as in H. G. Wells' story, with regard to that visual penetration, I should be actually, abnormally, outside the usual experience of human beings.

v

If I cannot explain this capacity of mine to pierce the opacity of a wall, I am achieving an act that is beyond the natural scheme of things, that is beyond nature, that is, in fact, supernatural.

Or again, as in another of Wells' tales, when the severed head of an African native goes rolling along, following an Englishman across country, across the sea, as far as London, that is a phenomenon within the realm of the supernatural.

It is obvious that the term embraces many varieties of phenomena in different situations and in a variety of circumstances. This book surveys, in a strictly academic and objective sense, phenomena, trends, attitudes and views and personalities associated through the sequence of human history with such supernatural facts as are unexplainable in terms of normal human experience. Beginning with antiquity and continuing into the present, the survey ranges over the continents, touching on a multiplicity of ethnic legends, beliefs, and supernatural situations that fall outside the periphery of man's experience.

H. E. W.

DICTIONARY
OF
SPIRITUALISM

AANROO   In theosophy, this celestial field is surrounded by an iron wall. The dead glean this field and can thus reach the blissful state. Other disembodied spirits proceed to lower zones.

AARON   In theosophy he is the Illuminated, the chief of the Hierarchy of the initiated seers.

AARON'S ROD   A magic wand adorned with an entwined serpent. When it was cast before the Egyptian Pharaoh, it turned into a serpent. Symbolically, the wand now represents the professional magician's skill.

ABARIS   In ancient Greek legend, an attendant to Apollo. He was endowed by the god with the power of transvection. In his travels he carried the golden arrow, the god's symbol. He lived without partaking of any food whatever. He helped the Spartans by performing sacrifices that eliminated all plagues thereafter. He was also believed to be the master of the philosopher and mathematician Pythagoras.

ABATUR   In mysticism, the Father of the Demiurge of the Universe, the Third Life.

ABBEN-RAGEL   An Arabian astrologer, generally known by the Latin name of Alchabitius. His tenth-century treatise on astrology was translated into Latin and printed in 1473, under the title De Judiciis seu fatis stellarum. Many of his predictions were fulfilled.

1

ABHAMSI In mysticism, a designation of the four orders of beings: gods, demons, pitris, men. Pitris are the ancestors of mankind.

ABIGOR In medieval demonology, the Grand Duke of Hell. He reveals himself as a handsome rider bearing a standard or scepter. He foresees the future, knows the secrets of war, and commands sixty legions.

AB-I-HAYAT In mysticism this term denotes the water of immortality that confers eternal life and eternal youth.

ABIRAM A Biblical character who, with Korach, conspired against Moses. He was swallowed by the earth.

ABODE OF LEARNING Centuries ago this was the headquarters, in Cairo, Egypt, of an Islamic sect. This sect of Shi'itesfi was opposed to the concept of Mohammed as a divinely inspired prophet.

ABOMINABLE SNOWMEN Creatures, half-human and half-animal, who are known as Yeti. The Sharpas believe that these creatures dwell in the Himalayas.

ABOU-RYHAN (MOHAMMED-BEN-AHMED) An Arabian astrologer credited with introducing judicial astrology. He is supposed to have possessed to a remarkable degree the power to predict future events.

ABRACADABRA A mystical word which, when written in the form of an inverted triangle and worn on an amulet, is supposed to ward off and cure disease.
It is one of the alphabetical and numerical experiments undertaken by Kabbalists.

ABRAHAM, THE JEW A German Jew who was at once an alchemist, magician, and philosopher. He is thought to have been born in Mayence in 1362 and to have received by word of mouth a number of secrets guarded by Abramelin, the Egyptian adept.

ABRAVANEL, JUDAH (c. 1460-1530) A notable figure in the transition between the Middle Ages and the Renaissance. Jewish physician and scholar. Born in Lisbon, died in Venice. Lived in contact with three cultures: Jewish, Spanish, Italian. He was interested in philosophy, mathematics, astronomy, and lectured at the Universities of Naples and Rome. He was a friend of Pico della Mirandola. His chief work is Dialoghi di Amore. The book was translated into Hebrew, Latin, French, Spanish, English. It was a synthesis of Jewish teachings and Neoplatonic mysticism, and influenced many writers and poets, among them Camoens and Cervantes. He maintained that love was the cosmic principle, inseparable from being. He also maintained that happiness is the 'union of the human intellect with the Divine intelligence.' Although there is an element of pantheism in Abravanel, he stressed his Judaic orthodoxy and tried to reconcile his pantheistic views with the Biblical concept of God.

ABRAXAS In the mysticism of the Gnostic sect, Abraxas was the divine name that was endowed with magic significance.

ABRED In Celtic cosmogony, Abred is the innermost of three concentric circles symbolizing the totality of being. Abred also represents the stage of struggle against Cythrawl, the power of evil.

ABSCISSION OR FRUSTRATION In astrology, when a planet is simultaneously forming an aspect to two other planets, the one that culminates first may produce an abscission of light that will frustrate the influence of the second aspect.

3

ABSENCE OF WAR   Among certain tribes in India and among Eskimo communities and South American native groups there is no concept of war. Some of these tribes, particularly in Eastern Asia, are so pacific that they refrain from killing insects or animals.

ABSENT TREATMENT   In a popular magazine absent or telepathic treatment is offered by means of which the organs of a sick person may be renewed.

ABSOLUTE   In occultism, the English form of the Latin word absolutum ('freed,' 'loosened') parallels the Sanskrit term *mukti*. A *mukta* is one who has obtained *mukti* or freedom. The Silent Watcher in theosophical speculation is a good example of one who can claim to be Absolute.

AB-SOO   In mysticism, this is the dwelling of the Father. The term denotes space itself.

ABULAFIA, ABRAHAM BEN SAMUEL (1240-1291)   A Kabbalist who lived in Safed, Palestine, Spain, Greece and Italy. He was reputed also to be a practicing thaumaturgist.

ABULIA   In the field of hypnosis, this term means loss or impairment of will power.

ACCIDENTAL ASCENDANT   A device employed by Evangeline Adams whereby to draw Horary interpretations from a natal Figure. In applying this method one determines the Ascendant for the moment the question is propounded, and rotates the Figure until the degree occupies the East Point.

ACHMETN   An Arab soothsayer who flourished in the ninth century A.D. He was the author of The Interpretation of Dreams.

4

ACOEMITES   This term means The Sleepless Ones. They were a religious body, grouped into three choirs in order to maintain prayers day and night. Instituted on the Euphrates and at Constantinople by St. Alexander, in 440 A.D.

ACOSMISM   In mysticism, the age of chaos, when the cosmos was still non-existent.

ACRONYCAL   This expression used in astrology stems from Greek, meaning: on the edge of the night. It is said of the rising after sunset, or the setting before sunrise, of a planet that is in opposition to the Sun: hence in a favorable position for astronomical observation. Acronycal Place: The degree it will occupy when it is in opposition to the Sun.

ACTIVE INFLUENCE   In astrology, the result of an aspect between two or more astrological factors or sensitive points, thereby producing the action that can materialize in an event.

ADAMANTIUS   A Jewish physician of Constantinople. During the reign of the Roman Emperor Constantine he produced a treatise on physiognomy, a branch of the occult arts.

ADAM KADMON   A Hebraic expression associated with the Aramaic Adam Kadmaah. It is of mystical significance. It denotes primal humanity, the prototype of primordial man.

ADEPTS IN THE OCCULT   In the Middle Ages manuals and treatises dealing with arcane subjects were often attributed to personalities who had acquired legendary fame. Among such putative writers on supernatural themes were Aristotle, Moses, King Solomon, Zoroaster, Alexander the Great, the Roman poet Vergil, St. Jerome the Church Father, and Mahommed.

5

ADJUSTED CALCULATION DATE   In astrology, a term used with reference to a directed or progressed horoscope, indicating the date on which the planet culminates. A variant term is Limiting Date.

ADLER, FELIX (1851-1933)   Rabbi and then professor of Oriental literature at Cornell University. Founder of the Society of Ethical Culture. He maintained that the idea of a personal God is unnecessary, that the social and ethical conduct of man constitutes the Godhead, and that man's personality is the central force of religion. The principle of the good life, he asserted, can be achieved independently of religious ritual and dogma.

ADRAMELECH   In the infernal Satanic hierarchy, a powerful archdemon. In antiquity, sacrifices of children were dedicated to Adramelech.

ADVANTAGE, LINE OF   In astrology, a term used with reference to the position of the Moon's Ascending Node in a Geocentric Figure. The line of advantage runs between the cusps of the third decanates of the Third and Ninth Houses. A position of the Node East of this line is judged to be favorable. Related to it are the Arcs of Increased and Dwarfed Stature. From the middle of the First House, clockwise to the middle of the Eighth House, is the arc of Increased Stature, with its peak at the cusp of the Twelfth House; and from the middle of the Seventh House, clockwise to the middle of the Second House, is the arc of Dwarfed Stature, with its peak at the cusp of the Sixth House.

ADVENTISTS   Religious sects that conceive a second, personal appearance of Christ. They also believe in the physical resurrection of the dead.

AEROLITE In mysticism, this is a symbol of spiritual life. Aerolites are regarded as virtual messengers or agents from the heavenly regions.

AEROMANCY A method of divination by observation of atmospheric conditions.

AETHROBACY In mysticism, this term is equivalent to levitation, that is, moving in the air without external support.

AFFINITY In astrology, this term means a binding by mutual attraction. The Sun is said to have an affinity with all the planets; Mars with Venus, in a magnetic or physical sense; Venus with Jupiter, in a philanthropic sense; Venus with Mercury, in an artistic sense.

AFFLICTED In astrology, unfavorably aspected. Loosely applied to any inharmonious aspect to a planet, or to any aspect, particularly the conjunction, parallel, square, or opposition to a malefic planet. Some authorities apply the term to a mundane or zodiacal parallel with, or when besieged by both Infortunes. Again, the sensitive degree on any House cusp can be afflicted, though such consideration must be confined to instances where the birth-moment is known.

AFRICAN BUILDERS' ARCHITECTS A mystical association founded by C. F. Koffen (1734-1797) for the purpose of supplying Egyptian, Christian, and Templar mysteries to the initiate. It had branches at Worms, Paris, and Cologne. Its several grades were designated as inferior (Apprentice of Egyptian Secrets, Initiate into Egyptian Secrets, Cosmopolitan, Christian Philosopher, Alethophilos) and superior (Esquire, Soldier, Knight).

AFRICAN CULT In the Cameroons, in Africa, there is a flourishing mystery cult known as Ekpe. It traces its origin back for hundreds of years.

AFTER-LIFE Greek and Roman antiquity was particularly concerned with the life on earth, but there was a general belief in survival after death. One of the earliest notions was that the dead live on in the tomb, but without human wants and desires. In entire communities, too, there developed a cult of dead heroes who were conceived as existing timelessly.

AG The natives of Hindustan use the ag, a red flower, to propitiate the congenial god Sanee. The flower is hung around the neck of the god in a nocturnal ceremony.

AGADA An Aramaic form of the Hebraic term Haggadah. It means a story, and it is used with reference to the Talmudic legends and mystical meditations. The Agadas discuss the mystical interpretations of Creation, the sacredness of the Sabbath, miracles, magic phenomena, and the future life.

AGAMAS The sacred writings to which certain Jains of India are dedicated. The Agamas advocate, among other concepts, non-injury to living things and sustenance by vegetarian means.

AGAPE A Greek expression meaning a love feast. In early Christianity such a festival had a devout and benevolent purpose. But later on, the agape degenerated into gross sexual orgies.

AGATHODEMON In Greek, this name means a beneficent demon or spirit that followed a person throughout his life.

AGENT In parapsychology, a person whose mental states are to be apprehended by the recipient.

AGE OF ALCHEMY Although alchemy became known in Europe as late as the eighth century A.D., through the writings of the Arab philosopher and Hermetic Geber, it had been practiced long before, in both Egypt and China.

8

AGES, ASTROLOGICAL Anciently, a period of some 2,000 years during which the point of the Spring Equinox recedes through one sign of the Zodiac of Constellations. Since the constellations have no precise boundaries, the points of beginning and ending are mere approximations. However, it is absurd to date the beginning of the precessional cycle, of presumably 25,800 years, from the particular time in history when it was decided no longer to treat the Equinox as a moving point, but instead to freeze it at no degrees Aries. It is probable that midway between the Equinoctial points are the Earth's Nodes, where the plane of its orbit intersects that of the Sun, at an inclination of approximately 50 degrees; but since the Equinoctial point is now considered as a fixed point and the motion takes place only within its frame of reference, it appears that a study of the circle which the celestial pole describes around the pole of the Ecliptic will be required in order to determine when it passes an East point, to mark the time of beginning of the first of twelve astrological ages of 2150 years each, into which the precessional cycle is subdivided. On this manner of reckoning, the Earth might now be in the Capricorn Age, as well as any other. Historical records show the Equinox as having once begun in Taurus, at which time Taurus was regarded as the first sign of the Zodiac.

AGES OF CIVILIZATION In mysticism, after the Great Flood submerged the continent of Atlantis, seven cycles of civilization followed. They are known as the epochs of the Ancient Indian, the Persian, Egyptian, Greco-Roman, Anglo-Saxon or Sardis, Philadelphia, Laodicea.
Each epoch constitutes a progression of the human soul, wherein operate the soul-body, the life-body, the physical-body.
Each civilization lasts one twelfth of the Platonic year, that is, 2160 years.

9

In the first post-Atlantean age, the physical world was an illusion and of a transitory character. People then were concerned primarily with the spiritual world.

The Persian period dated from 5000 B.C. to 3000 B.C. It was marked by the two principles of good and evil, Ahura Mazda and Ahriman respectively. There was a continuous conflict between the light and the darkness, light representing the good and virtuous and darkness symbolizing the forces of evil.

The span of 3000 B.C. to 747 B.C. belonged to the Egypto-Chaldean or Assyrian-Babylonian-Egyptian-Hebraic culture. This age was marked by the triad of Osiris, his consort Isis, and their son Horus. In this age too the mystery cults flourished in the Near East, in the Mesopotamian area, in the Mediterranean littoral, and in Egypt.

The next civilizations — the Greco-Roman and the Anglo-Saxon era — extend from 747 B.C. to 1413 A.D. Man has now become aware of himself and his physical environment.

The sixth civilization will be the ancient Persian era 'resurrected.' It will be called Philadelphia, and will be characterized by human love and spiritual interests.

The seventh civilization, termed Laodicea in the Apocalypse, will involve the concept of hope and the future life.

AGLA In Kabbalistic mysticism this expression is composed of the initials of four Hebraic words meaning Thou art powerful forever, O Lord. The term was used as a magic formula in medieval Germany. It was also used specifically to invoke demons.

AGLAOPHOTIS An herb growing in the deserts of Arabia and used by sorcerers to evoke demons.

AGNISHMATTAS In Occultism, one who has been 'sweetened by fire.' The term refers to a class of Pitris, or solar

10

ancestors. They are the counterparts of our lunar ancestors, the Barhishads.

AGORAPHOBIA   Fear of unenclosed spaces. This fear is usually indicative of a Mercury-Saturn aspect.

AGRIPPA VON NETTESHEIM (1486-1535)   Henry Cornelius Agrippa von Nettesheim has a prominent place in the sphere of occultism. He was a physician, soldier, and magician. He was on friendly terms with most of the scholars of his time. His personal life was a series of honors followed by misfortune, wealth and poverty. He gained military and diplomatic experience in his travels in Europe. Once he held court positions, but he fell into disfavor. On one occasion the debts he incurred brought him imprisonment in Brussels. While in Italy he delivered lectures on the mystic Hermes Trismegistus.
Agrippa's principal work is The Occult Philosophy. It is a defense of magic. He attempts to make a synthesis of the natural sciences and occult arts. He stresses however the significance of religion. But to him religion meant an amalgam of Christian elements, Neoplatonic theories, and Kabbalistic mysticism.

AHANKARA   In Occultism, the compound Sanskrit word denotes the egoistical principle in man. It springs from the false notion that the self is different from the Universal One-Self.

AIN SOPH   In Kabbalistic mysticism, this expression denotes the Limitless, Nameless Deity.

AIR SIGNS   The mental or intellectual signs, in astrology. They are: Gemini, Libra, Aquarius. Collectively, these signs are called the Air Asterism.

AKASA   In Pythagorean thought, the fifth element. It is a celestial ether or astral light that occupies all space. In

11

certain Buddhist teachings, it is the cosmic spirit-substance, the vast reservoir of Being.

AKAWAIO Carib-speaking peoples whose indigenous system of beliefs has been used with elements of Christianity to produce the Hallelujah religion.

AKKUM This expression is formed from the initials of the Hebrew words Ovede Kokhavim u-Mazzalot: those who worship stars and planets. The reference is to the non-Jews, the pagans.

AKSAKOF, ALEXANDER (1832-1903) A Swedenborg enthusiast and the pioneer spiritualist of Russia. He translated Swedenborg's works into Russian and wrote several important books, including Animismus und Spiritismus, and Spiritualism and Science.

AKWA A word used by the Akawaio to name the force which manifests itself as light and is symbolized by the sun. In the Hallelujah religion, it is identified with Heaven, the abode of God, and is sometimes translated as 'glory.'

AKWALU A word used by the Akawaio to express the concept of spirit, which is the life force in all creatures and nature spirits. The Hallelujah religion identifies it as spirit.

AKWALUPO A word used by the Akawaio to mean shade, shadow, or ghost spirit. It means 'without light or life' and refers to something which is past or dead. The concept of akwalupo is an important element of the Hallelujah religion.

ALAYA A Sanskrit word meaning 'the indissoluble.' In Occultism, the term signifies the universal soul. Mystically, the concept is identical with Akasa in its highest elements and with Mulaprakriti as 'Root-nature.'

ALBEDO This astrological term means whiteness. It is a measure of the reflecting power of a planet, in ratio to its absorptive capacity; expressed in a figure which represents the amount of light reflected from an unpolished surface in proportion to the total amount of light falling upon it. The albedo of the Moon and Mercury is 7; of Venus, 59; of the Earth, 44; of Mars, 15.

ALBERTUS MAGNUS (c. 1206 - 1280) Bishop of Ratisbon and philosopher with a European reputation, Albertus also probed into the occult sciences. He experimented with magic and produced remarkable phenomena. Among his writings is a survey of alchemy and its practice. He sees magic properties in plants, herbs, and stones in terms of healing and dreams. Many legends declared that he possessed the philosopher's stone, that he could change the seasons and atmospheric conditions, at will. In one of his experiments he succeeded in producing an android, an automaton of human shape that he endowed with speech.

ALBIGENSES A French religious sect that flourished in the twelfth century. A crusade against these heretics resulted in 1209 in the massacre of some 15,000 Albigensian adherents. A poem on the crusade, in some 9000 lines, was composed by a certain William of Tudela. The Albigenses believed that there is an eternal transmigration of souls. They rejected the creation and the sexual practices. They also refrained from meat, butter, cheese, milk. Their sole sustenance was based on vegetables and fish.

ALBIGERIUS An ancient Carthaginian seer. In a trance state he could make his soul leave his body and wander at will. His feats are mentioned by St. Augustine, the Church Father.

ALBUMAZAR An Asiatic astrologer who flourished in the ninth century A.D. He was the author of many astrological treatises that exerted a great influence in the Middle Ages.

ALCHEMY The art of alchemy, in its experimental sense, was a forerunner of modern chemistry. Alchemy was based partly on mysticism and partly on experimentation. It aimed primarily at the transmutation of base metals. Developing in the second century A.D., it reached its height in the Middle Ages. A dramatic presentation of the practice of alchemy is contained in Ben Jonson's play The Alchemist.

ALCHEMY, ASPECTS OF There were three branches of alchemy, each subject to occult interpretations. These aspects were: cosmic, human, and terrestrial.

ALCHINDUS An Arabian sage who wrote a work entitled The Theory of the Magic Arts. He lived in the eleventh century.

ALCUIN (735 ? - 804) English scholar and Churchman. He was attached to the court of Charlemagne. He was reputed to have been a student of astrology.

ALEMAN, JOHANNES Italian converted Jew who lived in the fifteenth century. As a Kabbalist, he taught Pico della Mirandola the esoteric doctrines of the Kabbalah.

ALEUROMANCY This is a phase of divination by means of flour. Messages, enclosed in balls of dough, are regarded as prophetic of future events. The practice is still in vogue among the Chinese.

ALEXANDER OF ABONUTEICHOS A Paphlagonian who belongs in the second century A.D. He claimed that he had a manifestation of the god Asclepius in the form of a serpent. With the help of this serpent, Alexander made oracular pronouncements and performed mystery rites. A contemporary writer, the noted satirist Lucian, depicted him as an impostor. But Alexander's cult survived after his death.

ALFARABI (d. 934) A Turkish adept who is reputed to have acquired proficiency in seventy languages and to have accepted the patronage of the Sultan of Syria. He wrote many works on various subjects.

ALFRIDARYA A science that conceives all planets as influencing man. It is also assumed that each planet controls a certain number of years in a person's life. This science is somewhat akin to astrology.

ALGOBULIA A Greek expression that denotes a human desire to suffer pain. The more common equivalent is masochism.

ALKABETZ, SOLOMON A Kabbalist who belongs in the sixteenth century. He lived in the Kabbalistic center of Safed, in Palestine.

ALKAHEST An Arabic term used in alchemy. It is the Universal Solvent. In mysticism it denotes the higher, spiritual Self.

ALKINDI, ABU YUSUF An Arab Neoplatonic philosopher. He flourished in the ninth century. Among his notable writings were treatises on medicine, astronomy, and astrology.

ALMAGEST The title of a treatise on astronomy by Ptolemy. The Almagest was also used in astrological studies.

15

ALMANAC A book or table containing a calendar of days, weeks, and months, to which are added astronomical or other data. Its use dates back to the Alexandrian Greeks. The Roman almanac, the fasti, listed the days on which business could be transacted. The earliest almanac of which there is a record is that of Solomon Jarchus, 1150 A.D.

ALMUTEN In astrology, the planet of chief influence in a Nativity by virtue of essential and accidental dignities. This term, of Arabian origin, is infrequently used in modern astrology.

ALOMANCY A method of divination by means of salt.

ALPHA AND OMEGA The first and the last letters of the Greek alphabet. In a religious and mystic context, they symbolize infinity and the Power of God. He is the beginning and the end of all things.

ALPHABETIC VALUES The numeric values of the letters of the English alphabet are found by arranging them in rows under the numbers from one to nine:

1	2	3	4	5	6	7	8	9
A	B	C	D	E	F	G	H	I
J	K	L	M	N	O	P	Q	R
S	T	U	V	W	X	Y	Z	

The values of the different numbers are added to determine the numeric value of a person's name. Vowel vibration is determined by adding the values of the vowels and reducing them to a primary number. The 'personality number' is found by adding consonantal values.

ALPHITOMANCY This is a branch of divination by means of wheaten or barley cakes. These were used in a kind of trial by ordeal. A person accused of a crime was

16

presumed, if guilty, to be incapable of swallowing such cakes and was consequently condemned.

ALROY, DAVID   A Bagdadi magician and false prophet who belongs in the twelfth century. He was reputed to have performed many miracles. He was put to death by his father-in-law. His adherents, however, remained faithful to his memory.

ALRUNES   Female sorceresses capable of assuming many different shapes. They are supposed to be able to predict the future, and they are still consulted by some Norwegians.

ALTITUDE   In astrology, elevation above the horizon, measured by the arc of a vertical circle. A planet is at meridian altitude when it is at the Midheaven, the cusp of the Tenth House.

ALVEYDRE, SAINT YVES D'   A modern occulist, Saint Yves d'Alveydre tried to establish interrelationships between letters, colors, and the planets.

AMBIENT   This term means: encircling. In modern astrology, it is applied to the Earth's surrounding magnetic field.

AMDUSCIAS   In medieval demonology, a grand duke of Hell who commands twenty-nine legions. He reveals himself in the shape of a man when called forth, but he normally has the shape of a unicorn.

AMENTI   The Egyptian Underworld through which the dead traveled. The Book of the Dead contained many 'words of power' to assist the traveler. By knowing their names, he could compel the supernatural beings to do his will.

AMERICAN INDIANS   Among the American Indians the belief was prevalent that supernatural beings, in the form of

17

nature spirits, populated the universe. These spirits, however, were innocuous and did not intrude on human affairs. Bush spirits, on the other hand, were regarded as potentially malefic, especially in the nocturnal hours.

AMERICAN SOCIETY FOR PSYCHICAL RESEARCH This Society, with headquarters in New York and a branch in California, was founded in 1885 and reorganized in 1904. The purpose and the scope of the Society is to investigate claims of telepathic clairvoyance, precognition, retrocognition, veridical hallucinations and dreams, psychometry, dowsing, and other forms of paranormal cognition; also claims of paranormal physical phenomena such as telekinesis, materialization, levitation, and poltergeists. The Society also studies writing, trance speech, hypnotism, alterations of personality, and other subconscious processes in so far as they may be related to paranormal processes; in short, all types of phenomena called parapsychological, psychic, or paranormal.

AMPHISBAENA Like many of the fanciful, imaginative creatures conceived by the medieval mind in the Physiologus and the Bestiaries, the amphisbaena was a fabulous creature. It was known also in Greek antiquity. Its name stems from the belief that it had two heads, one at each end, thus making possible both a forward and a backward movement.

AMULETS This word stems from an Arabic root meaning 'to carry.' An amulet is something carried or worn upon the person. Some are inscribed with magic formulas while others are free of any writing. The amulet is worn as a protection against magic phenomena, the evil eye, sickness, loss of property, and similar calamities.
The inscribed formula may be in the nature of a geometric design, drawn on clay, metal, deerskin, or parchment. The

18

object itself may be an Abraxas gem, the tail of a fox, a figurine, a lizard, a mandrake, a chameleon, or colored threads, a ring, a finger-nail, a key, or a knot. A frequent type of formula is a magic square so arranged that the sum of the numbers in each row, taken perpendicularly, horizontally, and diagonally, is identical.

An amulet or talisman against nightmares, incubi, or succubi was an image of a scorpion whose body was covered with a mystic inscription. Another amulet used in banishing nightmares consisted of anagrams or secret symbols written on pieces of paper, crushed into a ball, and swallowed.

In Hebraic tradition, a kamea was an amulet consisting of an inscribed parchment, called Pitka, or a small bunch of plants. An effective charm against sorcery was three grains of madder. The snout of a wolf, fixed on a door, served an apotropaic purpose.

Certain talismans, again, were efficacious on specific days of the week, and the efficacy was determined by astrological computation.

Amulets have special effectiveness in association with burial-grounds and crossroads. Thus a bone or a plant or herb found in such a spot had a particular potency.

Belief in the efficacy of amulets has survived in many European countries, particularly in Greece and Italy, to this day. Variant expressions for amulets are: phylacterion, periamma, periapton, amuletum, fascinum, bulla adligatura.

ANACHITIS A stone used in divination for the purpose of conjuring water spirits.

ANAHITA In Iranian mythology, this divinity was equated with Ishtar and, astrologically, presided over the planet Venus.

ANALOGETICISTS The mystic followers of the philosopher Ammonius Saccas, who flourished in the 3rd century A.D.

They interpreted myths and legends by analogy. In this respect their interpretations were akin to the mystical Kabbalistic writings.

ANANISAPTA A Kabbalistic term. It was written on parchment as an apotropaic talisman against disease.

ANARETA This term is of Greek etymology, meaning: destroyer. In astrology, it is the planet which kills, for it applies to a planet that unfavorably aspects the hyleg.

ANARETIC POINT Also Anaretic Place. In astrology, the degree occupied by the Anareta.

ANATMA In yoga, this term denotes the not-self, the entire subjective and objective manifested cosmos. It is used in opposition to the higher self and exercises itself until the consciousness is released from error.

ANATHEMA In the Eastern Orthodox Church, to make anathema signifies to hand over to evil. The expression literally means to curse, and is used to excommunicate persons guilty of heresy or immorality.

ANATOMICAL SIGNS In astrology, the signs are associated with different parts of the human anatomy, as follows:
Aries: head
Taurus: neck
Gemini: arms
Cancer: chest
Leo: back and heart
Virgo: abdomen
Libra: loins, kidney
Scorpio: organs of generation
Sagittarius: thighs
Capricorn: knees
Aquarius: legs
Pisces: feet

ANAXIMANDER (c. 610 — 546 B.C.) Greek philosopher. He invented the sun-dial. He is believed also to have discovered the obliquity of the ecliptic. He conceived the origin of all things to be the Infinite, which he regarded as the Divine.

ANAXIMENES Greek philosopher who flourished c. 546 B.C. He maintained that all things arise from air, which, when rarified, becomes fire: when condensed, it becomes progressively wind, cloud, water, earth, stone. He is the first to conceive the cosmos as governed by physical laws.

ANCHOR The anchor was an early Christian symbol. It represented hope and salvation.

ANCIENT ASTROLOGY In Iranian mythology, the supreme, benefic spirit, Ahura Mazda, was equated, astrologically, with the deity who ruled the heavens.

ANCIENT PORTENTS In antiquity, weather phenomena and all kinds of sounds were regarded as occult forebodings, usually malefic, but not invariably so.

ANCIENTS In occultism, the Ancients is a designation of the seven creative rays whose source was Chaos.

ANDRAS In medieval demonology, the Grand Marquis of Hell. He commands thirty legions. He appears to have the body of an angel and the head of an owl. He rides a black wolf and carries a pointed saber.

ANDROGYNE The alchemists' famous 'union of opposites' was symbolized by the androgyne (or the hermaphrodite) which watched over the beginning and end of every process involving initiation and magic.

ANGAKOK An Eskimo shaman or member of a priesthood. He has exclusive power to communicate with the supernatural world.

ANGELA DE FOLIGNO (1250 - 1300) An Italian mystic. She asserted that knowledge and fear of divine justice lead to the revelation of Love.

ANGELIC ASTROLOGY In astrology, certain planets are associated with angels: for example — Sun, with Michael. Moon, with Gabriel. Mercury, with Raphael. Venus, with Arnad. Mars, with Samael. Jupiter, with Zadkiel. Saturn, with Cassiel. Uranus, with Arvath.

ANGELS In Catholicism, these are pure spirits without bodies: created before man. They are classified into nine choirs: Seraphim, cherubim, thrones, dominations, virtues, powers, principalities, archangels, angels.

ANGLE Any of the four cardinal points in a Figure, or map, of the heavens; variously referring to the Zenith, or South Vertical, the Nadir, or North Vertical, and the East and West horizons: the cusps of the Tenth, Fourth, First and Seventh Houses, or the Medium Coeli, Imum Coeli, Oriens (Ascendant) and Occidens (Descendant) of a Solar or of any Celestial Figure.

ANGULAR In astrology, the reference is to a planet in an angle or in an angular House.

ANGULAR VELOCITY In astrology, the angle through which a planet sweeps in a unit of time. Technically, the daily motion of a planet, expressed in degrees and minutes of arc, is its Angular Velocity.

ANGURVADEL In Icelandic legend, this was a sword that possessed magic properties.

ANIMA MUNDI   This Latin expression means The Soul of the World. Ancient philosophers conceived that a soul or spirit pervaded the entire cosmos.

ANIMAL MAGNETISM   A term given by Anton Mesmer to hypnotism. It implies a responsive influence existing between the heavenly bodies, the earth, and animated beings. Mesmer himself wrote:

> The human body has a property which renders it susceptible of the influence of the heavenly bodies, and of the reciprocal action of those which environ it. It manifests its analogy with the magnet, and this has decided me to adopt the term of animal magnetism.

ANIMALS, DREAMS OF   The ancient Roman encyclopedist Pliny the Elder, in his monumental Historia Naturalis, asserted that viviparous animals were subject to dreams, just like human beings.

ANIMATION   From the most ancient times in the East magicians were credited with the power to turn inanimate objects into living creatures, or to change living beings into objects.

ANIMISM   This term denotes a belief in spirits or powers. Animism was a prevalent belief in Roman antiquity. Functional spirits were assumed to guard or control special activities, from sowing and reaping to life and death. The term, derived from *anima*, 'soul,' was used by Sir Edward Tylor, author of *Primitive Culture* (1871) to explain his theory of the origin of religion.

ANOLIST   Anciently a diviner who conjured demons at an altar.

ANOMALY   In astrology, the angular distance of a planet from its perihelion or aphelion.

ANPSI   A term used in parapsychology to denote 'animal psi,' or the ability of an animal to communicate with the environment.

ANSUPEROMIN   A sorcerer who belongs in the reign of Henry IV of France. He was reputed to have participated in Sabbat assemblies.

ANTASKARANA   In Occultism, this is the bridge between the higher Manas and the Lower Manas, or between the spiritual ego and the personal soul.

ANTHESTERIA   An ancient Greek festival in Attica, at which the dead received special attention and services from the living relatives.

ANTHROPOMANCY   An ancient method of divination by observation of the entrails of a sacrificial person.

ANTHROPOSOPHY   An esoteric spiritual science, conceived by Adolf Steiner (1861-1925). It postulates the need for a spiritual science to bring man into harmony with his environment and with the universe itself. It has followers and exponents in many countries, and has set up Rudolf Steiner Schools.

ANTIPATHIES   In astrology, the unaccountable aversions and antagonisms people feel toward each other when positions in their Nativities are in conflict.

ANTIPATHY   In astrology, disharmony of two bodies, usually planets, which rule or are exalted in opposite Signs. For example: Saturn ruling Capricorn has an antipathy for the Moon ruling Cancer.

ANTISCION   In Tranian astrology, this term denotes the reflex position of a planet's birth position, in that degree on the opposite side of the Cancer-Capricorn axis, of which either no degrees Cancer or no degrees Capricorn is the Midpoint.

ANTISEDENTIA   In astrology, this is an older term describing retrograde motion.

ANTS   In ancient prognostications, ants were often used in divination.

ANUBIS   In the initiation mysteries practiced by the Egyptians, Anubis, represented as a jackal, was raised to the rank of 'Superior of Mysteries.'

ANUPAPADAKA   A Sanskrit term meaning 'one who does not fall as others do.' In Buddhism, the term is applied to Dhyana-Buddhas, a class of celestial beings who issue from the bosom of Mahat and are therefore the source of emanation of the Hierarchy of Buddhas. The term is also a mystic statement of the doctrine of the Inner God.

APAP   In mysticism, Apap symbolizes the serpent of evil, as described in the Egyptian Book of the Dead.

APHETA   In astrology, the prorogator. The planet or place that exercises an influence over the life and death of the native.

APHORISM   In astrology, this term refers to considerations involved in the summing-up or synthesis of the various testimonies in the Figure.

APION   An Alexandrian Greek who flourished in the first century A.D. He was reported to have conjured Homer's spirit, to ascertain the epic poet's parentage and birthplace.

APOCALYPTIC MYSTICISM   In apocalyptic literature, including passages in certain books of the Books — Isaiah,

Ezekiel, Amos, Zephaniah — and in the Apocalypse of St. John, mystical elements involve explanations of meteorological and astronomical phenomena.

APOCRYPHA This term, of Greek origin, means hidden or secret things. Certain books not included in the canon of the Old Testament or the New Testament are regarded as apocryphal. They were considered as recording imaginary events and miracles. Among such books are The Dream of Moses, The Testament of the Twelve Patriarchs, The Protoevangelium.

APOLLONIUS OF TYANA One of the most famous magicians of ancient Greece, Apollonius of Tyana was said to be the son of Proteus, the sea god. In search of occult knowledge and experience, he traveled widely, as far as India. He lectured on arcane subjects, relating his personal encounters with strange creatures, vampires and demons. His reputation as the possessor of supernatural powers became so widespread that in Asia Minor temples were dedicated to him as a supreme thaumaturgist. In Rome, he was brought to trial for practicing divination. He had seen, by clairvoyance, the death of the Emperor Domitian. During the Middle Ages his renown became legendary, while he himself attained the distinction of the Archmagician.

APOSTOLIC CIRCLE A group of spiritualists who claimed to communicate with biblical figures through the mediumship of Mrs. Benedict during the middle of the nineteenth century. The sect published a periodical, Disclosures from the Interior and Superior Care for Mortals, and established a temporary center at Mountain Cove, Virginia.

APOTROPAIC CHARMS All kinds of amulets or periapts, trinkets and charms have been and still are in use as protective agents against sinister, malefic forces or spirits. A rabbit's foot is sometimes used as a love charm. Fern seed, gathered on the Eve of St. John's Day, is reputedly effective for the same purpose. Hemp seed scattered in a churchyard: double walnuts: potatoes, beads, leeks, pieces of coal. All these objects are regarded as having beneficent properties. In another direction, amulets are used by witches and sorcerers to destroy cattle, to injure enemies, to bring destruction.

APPARITIONS IN WAR During World War I there were reports of troops who saw 'angels' during the retreat of Mons, also Bowmen, who were popularly presumed to be the spirits of old medieval archers who had fought on the Continent.

APPLICATION In astrology, this term refers to a body in motion toward a point whence it will aspect another body.

APPLIED NUMEROLOGY Apart from the mystic significance of numbers in esoteric works such as the Kabbalistic writings, numerology, in a popular sense, is used in practical application. It claims to disclose hidden talents in a person, to predict coming events, to attain a well-balanced attitude to living. In this pragmatic sense, applied astrology combines with numerology to form a synthesis of calculations on life cycles and their impact on the ordinary man.

APPORTS In spiritualism, apports are objects that become manifest and materialize with the aid of a medium.

APPULSE In astrology, the approach of one orbital body toward another.

APSIS In astrology, the points of greatest and least distance of a heavenly body from its centre of attraction.

APULEIUS A Roman philosopher and novelist who flourished in the second century A.D. Apuleius was accused of securing a wife by magic practice. In his defense he delivered a speech, still extant, in which he discussed the range and characteristics of magic. The speech includes a great amount of material on occult and supernatural techniques.
Apuleius himself had been initiated in the mystery cult of Isis.

AQUARIUS In astrology, the Water-carrier. The eleventh, southern sign of the zodiac. Mystically, Aquarius is associated with the Great Flood. Kabbalistically, this sign stands for the legs of the archetypal man and the locomotive functions of the human organism.

ARABIAN POINTS Also Arabian parts. In astrology, Fortuna, or the Part of Fortune, is best known. Instead of revolving the Figure, the Arabs gave rules whereby planetary House positions could be inserted in a Figure based on a birth-moment.

ARAMAIC In Hebraic mysticism and Kabbalistic literature, Aramaic is the language in which the treatise called the Zohar, the Book of Splendor, was composed. It was published toward the end of the thirteenth century by Moses ben Shemtov de Leon, of Castile.

ARARITHA In Hebraic Kabbalistic mysticism this is a seven-letter word, of magic significance, that denotes the number 813.

ARATHON In works on magic, Arathon is listed as one of the seven Olympian Spirits. He is the celestial spirit of Saturn.

ARBATEL A manual of magic, published in the latter part of the sixteenth century and dealing with the functions and nature of the spirits that pervade the cosmos.

28

ARC   In astrology, a portion or segment of a curved line, such as a circle or ellipse. Hence the orbital distance separating two bodies, or between two points.

ARCANUM, THE GREAT   This is the Great Secret that was the essence of the alchemical art. The secret, it is asserted, was not the transmutation of metals. It was actually the transformation of man's character to a higher plane.

ARCHANGEL CALENDAR   A medieval publication by Johannes Trithemius (1462-1516), abbot and occultist, and Agrippa of Nettesheim, also an occultist. The theme of the work involves the tradition that every 354 years, 4 months, and 4 days a change occurs in the guiding Power that gives history its impulse.

ARCHOBIOSIS   This Greek term denotes the primal beginning of life.

ARC OF VISION   In astrology, the least distance from the Sun at which a planet is visible when the Sun is below the horizon.

ARDAT-LILE   In Semitic legend, a female demon who copulated with human males.

ARHAT   In Buddhism, a person who has attained understanding of the beyond. He can thus perfect himself and be released

from five subjective 'fetters' which bind him. These fetters are: desire for life in form, desire for formless life, spiritual pride, self-love, the last vestiges of ignorance or error.

ARIES   In astrology, the Ram. The first, northern sign of the zodiac. In Egyptian religion, the deity Amon-Ra was represented with ram's horns.

In occultism, in its symbolical aspect, the sign represents the Sacrifice. The Ram also symbolizes the spring or the beginning of the new year. Kabbalistically, the sign represents the head of the grand man of the cosmos.

ARISTOTLE AND AFTER-LIFE Aristotle rejected the concept of survival after death except in the case of the intellectual part of the three-fold soul of man. Survival, to Aristotle, excluded sensibility.

ARITHOMANCY A form of divination by observing numbers.

ARKITES Priests who attended the Ark of Isis or the Hindu Argua. There were seven such dedicated priests.

ARMILLARY SPHERE In astrology, a skeleton sphere suggested by concentric rings of the celestial circles of the equator and the ecliptic revolving within a horizon and meridian divided into degrees of longitude and latitude. It was invented by Eratosthenes who by this means computed the size of the earth, and inclination of the ecliptic to the equator; also the latitude of the city of Alexandria. The armillary sphere is often used as a decoration. There is a specimen cast in bronze and supported on the shoulders of Atlas, at Rockefeller Plaza in New York.

ARNHEM LAND The aborigines now living in Arnhem Land in Australia decorate their huts with paintings depicting spirits from the land of Geimbo. Fishing scenes are sacred to them since the spirits of ancestors are supposed to send them materials by sea.

ARNOLD OF VILLANOVA He was a physician who belonged in the thirteenth century. He traveled in Europe and Africa, displaying interest in the interpretation of dreams, alchemy, and similar occult areas. He was reputed to have made transmutations of metals. Even as a physician he relied to a great extent on Kabbalistic symbols, occult invocations, and herbal concoctions of magic import. There was also a belief that he could communicate with the Satanic agencies.

ARNUPHIS An Egyptian sorcerer who belongs in the second century A.D. In a military campaign in which the Emperor Marcus Aurelius was engaged Arnuphis saved the Roman army by inducing a downpour of rain.

ARPHAXAT An ancient Persian sorcerer. He met his death by a thunderbolt.

ARTEMIDORUS A Greek writer of Ephesus, who belongs in the late second century A.D. He traveled widely for the purpose of collecting, classifying, and interpreting dreams. He is the author of a treatise on this subject, entitled Oneirocritica, which is extant. He also produced a work on palmistry, under the name of Cheiroscopica.

ARTEPHIUS He was a twelfth century mystic, a Hermetic. There was a legend that he had lived for more than a thousand years, by means of demoniac aid. He is the author of The Art of Prolonging Life, written allegedly at the age of 1025. In Chinese, there are similar beliefs regarding longevity, associated largely with the rejuvenating efficacy of the herb known as ginseng.

ASAT A Sanskrit word designating the unreal or manifested universe. Its opposite is Sat. In a more mystical sense, the word designates the unmanifested nature of Parabraham.

ASCENDANT In astrology, the ascendant is the rising degree of the ecliptic.

ASCENDING   In astrology, this term refers to any planet on the eastward side of the line between the cusps of the Fourth and Tenth Houses, which by the diurnal motion of the Earth is rising in the heavens.

ASCENDING ARC   In theosophical Occultism, the term signifies the passage of life-waves through the chain of any celestial body. The earth and every other celestial body make up limited series or groups of globes, each existing on a different cosmic plane in a rising series.

ASCENSION   In astrology, the vertical rising of a planet above the Ecliptic, equator, or horizon.

ASCENSIONAL DIFFERENCE   In astrology, the difference between the Right Ascension of any body and its Oblique Ascension.

ASCENSION, SIGNS OF LONG   In astrology, these signs are: Cancer, Leo, Virgo, Libra, Scorpio, Sagittarius.

ASCENSION, SIGNS OF SHORT   In astrology, these signs are: Capricorn to Gemini inclusive.

ASCETICS   These were men who, for religious reasons, practiced self-denial, austerities, and similar self-imposed hardships. In the Eastern Orthodox Church the vigils, prayers, and fasting are ascetic practices.

ASCH METZAREPH   A Hebraic expression meaning The Cleansing Fire. It is the title of a Kabbalistic work dealing with alchemy.

ASCLEPIUS   A treatise purporting to describe the religion of ancient Egypt and to record the magic rites used by the Egyptians to draw the cosmic powers into their statues.

The work probably dates from the second or third century A.D. and contains few genuine Egyptian elements.

ASPECTARIAN In astrology, a chronological roster of all aspects during a particular period.

ASPECTS In astrology, the aspects of the planets in relation to each other. These aspects determine the significance, whether favorable or not, of the planet. The more important aspects are:

Trine, marked Δ when two planets are four signs apart.
Sextile, marked ＊ when two planets are two signs apart.
Quintile, when two planets are 72° apart.
These three aspects are favorable.
Conjunction ♂ when two planets or stars are of the same sign. This aspect may be favorable or unfavorable.
Opposition ♂ when two planets are six signs apart.
Quartile ☐ when two planets are three signs apart.
Semi-quartile ½☐ when two planets are 45° apart.
These last three aspects are unfavorable.

ASPORTS The disappearance of objects from a room in which a seance is held. Objects are said to pass through barriers and reappear in another setting. The process is the reverse of apport phenomena.

ASSAPUT In ancient Chaldean divination, Assaput was a prophetic sound pregnant with prediction. Insects, natural phenomena such as rain and thunder were similarly used to interpret coming events. Among the Romans, practices of the same type were in force.

ASSASSINS A secret Persian movement founded in the eleventh century A.D. The members were addicts of hashish, which induced visions. The founder was Hassan Sabah, and the English designation of Assassin is a corruption of his name.

ASTARA FOUNDATION A world-wide organization, with headquarters in California. Its purpose is avowedly to guide members toward a fuller life. It embraces the problem of death, the afterlife, and possible communication with the dead. Its tenets are drawn from the sacred writings of the major faiths and from ancient mystery cults.

ASTAROTH In medieval demonology, a powerful grand duke in Hell. He knows both the past and the future, freely answers questions about occult subjects, rides a dragon, and holds a viper in his left hand. He is cited as one of the seven princes of Hell who visited Faust.

ASTERISM In astrology, a constellation. Sometimes misleadingly applied to a zodiacal sign. But asterism may be applied to the three signs of the same element.

ASTEROIDS In astrology, the asteroids Ceres, Juno, Pallas, Vesta are of dubious influence.

ASTHAR VIDYA The oldest Hindu treatise on magic, some fragments of which are still extant.

ASTRAL BODY In occultism, this is a replica of the physical, corporeal body, but more subtle and tenuous. It penetrates every nerve, fibre and cell of the physical organism and is constantly in a supersensitive state of oscillation and pulsation. The psychic faculty within the astral body is impressionable to extrasensory vibrations. The astrological concept is that of a magnetic field wherein the individual does most of his thinking, and from which he draws impressions by way of interpreting changes in the field due to cosmic radiation.

34

ASTRAL LIGHT In occultism this is an invisible etheric aura that encircles the universe.

ASTRAL PROJECTION In occultism, the partial or complete separation of the astral body from the physical body, and visiting another locality. This occurs in sleep — though, as a general rule, one does not recall the experience on waking. The adept can command his astral body to go any place he desires in order to make observations and investigations and to acquire essential information.

ASTRAL VISIONS Many astral visions have been chronicled in comparatively recent times: three suns in 1942; a rainstorm of crosses in 1503 and of blood in 1551; and an army in the sky, a rain of fish, and huge balls traveling toward the sun, all in the sixteenth century. More recently, 'flying saucers' have captured the headlines.

ASTROLATERS In mysticism, this term is applied to those who worship the stars.

ASTROLATRY This term denotes the worship of the stars. In antiquity, particularly in the Middle East, among the Chaldeans, astrolatry was a regular practice.

ASTROLOGICAL ANATOMY In astrology, the Sun operates through the anterior pituitary gland. The Moon is the substance of the body. Mercury is associated with the thyroid gland. Venus, with the thymus gland. Mars, with the cortex. Jupiter, with the posterior pituitary gland. Saturn affects the medullary portion of the adrenal gland. Uranus, the parathyroid gland. Neptune, the pineal gland. Pluto, the pancreas.

ASTROLOGICAL COLORS In astrology, the colors of the spectrum are associated with specific planets.

The Sun — orange, gold, yellow.
The Moon — white, pearl, opal, iridescent hues.
Mercury — slate color.
Venus — sky blue, pale green.
Mars — red, carmine.
Jupiter — purple, deep blue.
Uranus — streaked mixtures.
Neptune — lavender, sea-green.
Pluto — luminous pigments.

ASTROLOGICAL DAYS In astrology, certain planets are considered to have added strength or to exercise rulership, on certain days of the week.

ASTROLOGICAL FLAVORS In astrology, planets are associated with certain flavors.
The Sun — sweet, pungent.
The Moon — odorless.
Mercury — astringent.
Venus — warm, sweet.
Mars — astringent, pungent.
Jupiter — fragrant.
Saturn — cold, sour.
Uranus — cold, astringent.
Neptune — seductive.
Pluto — aromatic.

ASTROLOGICAL FORMS In astrology, certain shapes and forms are associated with specific planets:
The Sun — circles, curves.
Moon — crooked lines.
Mercury — short lines.
Venus — curves.
Mars — angles, straight lines.
Jupiter — curves.
Saturn — short lines.

36

Uranus — broken lines.
Neptune — curves.
Pluto — straight lines, sharp angles.

ASTROLOGICAL JEWELS In astrology, certain planets are associated with particular jewels and precious stones.
Sun — diamond, ruby, carbuncle.
Moon — pearl, opal, moonstone.
Mercury — quicksilver.
Venus — emerald.
Mars — bloodstone, flint.
Jupiter — amethyst, turquoise.
Saturn — garnet, all black stones.
Uranus — chalcedony, lapis lazuli.
Neptune — coral, ivory.
Pluto — beryl, jade.

ASTROLOGICAL METALS In astrology, certain planets are associated with particular metals.
Sun — gold.
Moon — silver.
Mercury — quicksilver.
Venus — copper.
Mars — iron.
Jupiter — tin.
Saturn — lead.
Uranus — radium.
Neptune — lithium, platinum.
Pluto — tungsten, plutonium.

ASTROLOGICAL PATHOLOGY In astrology, certain ailments are associated with planetary influences.
Sun — ailments of heart and spine, fevers, spleen.
Moon — endocrine imbalance, catarrhal infections.
Mercury — nervous disorders.
Venus — blood impurities.

Mars — infectious diseases.

Jupiter — maladies resulting from surfeit.

Saturn — skin diseases, rheumatism, melancholia.

Uranus — inflammations.

Neptune — glandular imbalance.

Pluto — acidosis, arthritic conditions.

ASTROLOGICAL VEGETATION In astrology, herbs are classified according to planetary influences:

Sun: almond, celandine, juniper, rue, saffron.

Moon: chickweed, hyssop, purslain, moonwart.

Mercury: calamint, endive, horehound, marjoram, pellitory, valerian.

Venus: artichoke, foxglove, ferns, sorrel, spearmint.

Mars: aloes, capers, coriander, crowfoot, gentian, ginger, honeysuckle, peppers.

Jupiter: aniseed, balm, myrrh, wort, lime, linden, nutmeg, jessamine.

Saturn: aconite, fumitory, ivy, medlar, moss, sloes, senna.

No additions to these ancient classifications have been made with regard to Uranus, Neptune, Pluto.

ASTROLOGY AMONG THE NATIONS In the course of the centuries astrologers have made predictions in regard to military campaigns, invasions, sudden death of emperors and kings, disastrous floods, famine, disease. All such phenomena were reputedly the result of planetary positions and unfavorable celestial conditions.

ASTROLOGY AND DOMESTICITY Astrology offers advice, by consultation of the stars, of dejections and exaltations, conjunctions and oppositions, on when and whom to marry, on the propitious time for any undertaking, on favorable days for certain household operations, and on a large number of small daily domestic activities.

ASTROLOGY AND THE BODY Astrologically, the twelve zodiacal signs exert influence on various parts of the human body. The head is the province of Aries. Capricorn governs knees. Pisces affects the feet.

ASTROLOGY, ATTITUDE TO In Catholicism, predicting the future by the position or course of the stars, with reference to natural phenomena such as drought, storms, and so on is regarded as lawful. With reference to foreknowledge of human actions, astrology is regarded as heretical.

ASTROLOGY, BRANCHES OF There are distinct branches of astrology: natal or genethliacal, dealing with the birth Figure. Horary: a Figure cast for the birth-moment of an idea or an event.
Electional: choosing the propitious moment for an undertaking.
Mundane or Judicial: referring to the influence of the planets on populations or countries or cities.
Medical: application of astrology to health.
Meteorological: application of astrology to weather conditions.
Agricultural: application of astrology to planting and harvesting of crops.

ASTROLOGY, INFLUENCE OF Astrology has currently reached such a point of widespread popularity that a New York department store advertises stationery imprinted with zodiacal notes. In other directions too names are borrowed from the zodiac. For instance, a company takes the name of the Gemini X-ray Chemical Corporation. Drinking glasses are decorated with the signs. Ladies' handbags are embroidered with Virgo and Scorpio and Libra. A watch is advertised as a Zodiac Spacetronic Watch. Cocktails are named for Taurus, etc. Other signs of the zodiac appear in commerce and industry, as follows: Sagittarius Productions,

Capricorn Designs, Aries Bake Shops, Aries Document-
aries, Taurus Press, Libra Studios, Leo Dresses, Pisces
Antiques, Virgo Fashions. In a wider sense, college students
and others all over the country are probing into astrological
phenomena, sorcery, witchcraft, spiritualism, mystery
cults.

ASTROLOGY IN ROME   The first Roman Emperor, Augustus,
banished astrologers from Rome, but they were recalled by
later Emperors. Tiberius, Augustus' immediate successor,
had himself a knowledge of astrology. He had studied the
art under Thrasyllus. The latter was a noted astrologer of
Alexandria.

ASTROMANCY   A system of divination by observation of the
stars. The practice of astromancy had to do with the popular
concept of astrology and fortunetelling. Modern scientific
astrology rejects this view.

ASTRONOMOS   In Egyptian mysticism, this Greek expression
denotes an initiate who has reached the seventh stage in
the mysteries.

ASWATTHA   A Sanskrit word signifying the mystical Tree of
Knowledge, represented as growing in a reversed position,
with the roots extending upward and the branches downward. The roots of the Tree of Knowledge, or the Tree
of Cosmical Life and Being, typify the invisible world of
spirit, while the branches typify the visible cosmical world.

ATEN   In astrology, the solar disc, or the light that proceeds
from the sun.

ATHANOR   In alchemy, this was the furnace where the transmutation of base metal into gold was performed. In an
occult sense, athanor is the astral fluid.

ATHAZER   In astrology, an ancient term applied to the Moon when in conjunction with the Sun or separated from it by an arc of twelve degrees, 45 degrees, 90 degrees, 150 degrees, 160 degrees, or 180 degrees.

ATHOS   Mt. Athos is the core of Eastern Orthodox monasticism. It is 6000 feet high, in a peninsula jutting into the north Aegean Sea. Organized by St. Athanasius late in the fourth century, the monastic life gradually became an independent republic consisting of twenty monasteries. Nowadays the jurisdiction of the monasteries belongs to the Patriarch of Constantinople. Seventeen of the monasteries are Greek, one is Serbian, one Bulgarian, and one Russian. Eleven monasteries are coenobitic, that is, the monks live together communally. Nine are idiorhythmic, that is, the monks perform their monastic duties individually, not as a community. No females, not even female animals, are permitted on Mt. Athos.

ATLANTIS   The island or, as some say, the continent of Atlantis, situated in the Western Sea or in the Mediterranean, was, according to ancient tradition, submerged in proto-historical times by a Great Flood or an earthquake. Atlantis is mentioned by the Greek philosopher Plato, who describes its high cultural attainments. The question of the actual existence of Atlantis has long been a matter of dispute. Quite recently, however, an American explorer has published an account of his investigations. These are supported by diagrams, photographs, calculations and other evidences that, in the author's view, tend to give credence to the factual reality of Atlantis.
The title of the book is Voyage to Atlantis: the oceanographer's name is James W. Mavor, Jr., and the publishers are G.P. Putnam's Sons.

ATMAN   In yoga, the true self, in contrast with the false self of individuality, which every man assumes that he is. In

41

Vedantic philosophy, the ever-present universal spirit, free from mind or matter, the Supreme Soul. In occultism, the essential and radical faculty which gives man consciousness of Selfhood.

ATOM   In theosophical occultism, the ultimates of nature are atoms, material primates which can be divided into composite parts, and monads or indivisible primates.

ATTITUDE TO SUPERNATURAL   The attitude toward the supernatural among the Kwakiuth of the Nòrthwest American coast is a desire to abuse, shame, or kill the supernatural beings. There is no sense of awe.

AUGURELLI, AURELIUS   An Italian alchemist who flourished in the sixteenth century.

AUGUST ORDER OF LIGHT   An Oriental occult society that set up its quarters in England in the nineteenth century.

A-U-M   These mystical letters symbolize Brahma the Father, Vishnu the Son, and Siva the Holy Spirit. The letters reflect man's descent from the Spiritual World and his ascent to the Eternal World. This concept belongs in Hindu mysticism. One of the most holy words in Brahmanical literature, Aum or Om, is a syllable of invocation as well as of benediction and affirmation. The word should be uttered only under the most solemn circumstances and, according to many Hindus, in the intimacy of one's 'inner closet.' The word is also used reverently in many of the youth communes that have sprung up recently in the United States.

AURA   In mysticism, an invisible psychic essence that emanates from animate beings or objects.

AURICEGG   A term used in esoteric philosophy to denote the seat of all the monadic, spiritual, vital, etc. faculties of man. It is the source of the human aura and of everything else in the human septiform constitution. It endures eternally, throughout both the pralayas and the manvantaras.

AUROBINDO SRI (1872 - 1950)   The Indian seer and patriot renounced politics in 1910 to devote his life to discovering how the universe might be made divine. Sri Aurobindo founded an ashram which is distinguished by having no creed or ritual except the practice of meditation. He has been acclaimed as the hierophant of the new age, that of the God-man — the gnostic being who excels man in things of the spirit.

AUSTROMANCY   A form of divination by observation of the winds.

AUTOMATIC WRITING   Writing words without awareness. Automatic writing can be employed with many patients to help them write out conflicts, fears, anxieties.

AUTOMATISM   Human activity that is performed without any conscious awareness. This includes complex actions ranging from automatic writing or drawing to sleep-walking.

AVALOKITESVARA   In esoteric philosophy, a Sanskrit word designating the Higher Self, a divine, active ray of the Divine Monad.

AVASTHAS   In yoga, the three states of consciousness:
  (a) the waking state, when there is awareness of objects of the external world.

(b) the dream state, where there are only subjective or mental images of things, without rational control over them.

(c) the deep sleep state, when nothing, either subjective or objective, is seen: only a condition of utter rest which, on waking, is remembered.

AVATARA A person whose soul or mind is specially formed by descending into humanity from the spiritual regions beyond human life. The belief is that avataras occur in world history when the cyclic course of events requires a change. This change the avatara is instrumental in producing.

AVENAR A Jewish astrologer who flourished in the fifteenth century. He computed the advent of a Hebraic Messiah.

AVESHA In yoga, this term denotes entering the body of another person. A disciple, for instance, may step aside, while the master uses his body. Again, avesha may be akin to mediumship, when the disciple is aware of what happens and participates in an occurrence without interfering with its operation. Also, when a yogi, in extreme old age, needs a new body, the yogi, dying in his own body, may enter that of a child or a person recently deceased. The dead child then revives, but it has now experienced changes in character and ability which may perplex the parents.

AVICENNA (980 - 1037) An Arab philosopher who wrote on medieval philosophy and also produced important alchemical treatises. There was a tradition that the spirits were under his control.

AVIDYA A Sanskrit word denoting ignorance or absence of knowledge. In esoteric philosophy, the term denotes lack of knowledge of Reality, resulting from Illusion or Maya.

AVITCHI A Sanskrit term meaning uninterrupted hell. This concept is maintained by theosophy.

AVYAKTA This term in yoga denotes what is not manifested. In Nature, things are seen by us one at a time, for man is incapable of dealing with more than a small part of Nature at a time. Hence by the restrictions in life one learns to live: by the restrictions of being we gain power to be: by the restrictions of knowing we acquire power to know. [By exercise within these limitations we expand our consciousness and will develop correspondingly.]

AXIAL ROTATION In astrology, the diurnal motion of the Earth around its axis; or a similar motion by any other celestial body.

AXIS, INCLINATION OF In astrology, there is an inclination of the axis in relation to the plane of the orbit.

AYIN HA-RA A Hebraic expression that denotes the Evil Eye. Since Talmudic times, in order to avert any mishap or misfortune caused by the Evil Eye, the practice has prevailed of using amulets, sacred herbs and similar apotropaic means to counteract any malefic effects.

AYMAN, JACQUES A seventeenth century dowser who was able to uncover crimes and find the guilty perpetrators by means of his divining rod.

AZAZEL A Hebraic term whose meaning is not known. In Talmudic writings, the expression denotes the mountain on which a scapegoat was sent to carry off people's sin into the wilderness on the Day of Atonement.

AZILUTH In Hebraic Kabbalistic mysticism, the world of emanations. It is the prototype of all other worlds.

AZIMENE   In astrology, this term refers to a planet posited in certain weak or lame degrees or arcs which, if ascending at birth, were regarded as making the native blind or lame, or otherwise afflicted.

AZIMUTH   In astrology, a point of the horizon and a circle extending to it from the zenith; or an arc of the horizon measured clockwise between the south-point of the horizon and a vertical circle passing through the centre of any object.

AZRIEL   (1160 - 1238)   A Spanish - Jewish Kabbalist. Author of works on Kabbalistic mysticism.

B

BA In Egyptian tradition, the Ba is the outer manifestation of the soul.

BAAL SHEM TOV This Hebraic expression means Master of the Good Name. It is applied to Rabbi Israel ben Eliezer (1700 - 1760), who founded Chassidism, Pietism. This is a mystic Judaic system based on Kabbalistic principles.

BAARAS A mysterious plant called by the Arabs The Golden Plant. It was used by alchemists in their experiments in the transmutation of metals.

BABA The name by which Sathyanarayana Raju, the Indian mystic who claims to be the reincarnation of Krishna, is known by thousands of his followers.

BABYLONIAN TRINITY In ancient Babylonian religious belief, there was the concept of a divine trinity. It consisted of Anu, the celestial deity; Enlil, the earth god; Enk, god of the waters.

BACIS In Greek antiquity, a seer of Boeotia, he is mentioned by the Roman orator and statesman Cicero. Persons who had mantic inclinations often assumed the generic name of Bacis.

BACON, ROGER (1214 - 1294) The Franciscan monk tried to base 'natural magic,' astrology, and alchemy on the experimental method.

BACOTI Among the Tonkinese, this name is applied to sorcerers and diviners.

BAHAI A Persian mystic cult that originated in the nineteenth century. The founder was a mystic who called himself Bab, the Gate. Bahai postulates the need for a unified faith for a unified humanity.

BAHIR A Hebrew term meaning luminous. The Book Bahir is a source book on the mystic Judaic Kabbalah. The Book Bahir and the Zohar, the Book of Splendor, together constitute the two most important works in the mystic Kabbalah. It belongs in the 12/13th century.

BAHYA IBN PAKUDA A Jewish judge in the rabbinical court at Saragossa. He belongs in the eleventh century. In his book The Duties of the Heart he regarded the soul elevated toward God and liberated from the shackles of earthly existence as evidence of purification, and he maintained that the ultimate goal of man was communion with God.

BAILEY, CHARLES A famous apport medium of Melbourne. He began his mediumship in 1889 and was for many years the private medium of Thomas Welton Stanford, who collected apport materials now preserved at Leland Stanford University. Bailey was repeatedly charged with fraud.

BALZAC, HONORE DE (1799 - 1850) The great French novelist was also the author of a Rosicrucian drama entitled Seraphita.

BAMBOO BOOKS These are Chinese chronicles of prehistoric events.

BANSHEE A being that is popularly assumed to be supernatural. Traditionally, among the Irish, a banshee utters lamentations under the window of a house where a person is on the point of death.

BAPHOMET The deity of practitioners of witchcraft and the goat-idol of the Templars. The name is supposed to be compounded of three words meaning 'the father of the temple of universal peace among men.' Baphomet has also been identified as a pantheistic and magical representation of the Absolute.

BARADUC, HYPPOLITE A noted French psychical researcher who claimed to have proved by photographic means that something misty leaves the body at the moment of death. He described his experiments in several books, among them The Human Soul, published in Paris in 1913.

BARBANELL, MAURICE A well-known spiritualistic investigator who for some thirty-seven years has had visual evidence of certain psychic phenomena and manifestations that led him to conclude that such manifestations were caused by non-corporeal beings no longer living.

BARDO THODOL The original title of the Tibetan Book of the Dead.

BARNAUD, NICHOLAS A physician who belongs in the sixteenth century. He is the author of a number of treatises on alchemy.

BARON SAMEDI In Voodoo cults, the Baron Samedi is the Master of the Cemeteries. He is invoked during black magic ceremonies. The Baron Samedi Cross plays a part in funeral rites.

BARREN SIGNS In astrology, these signs are: Gemini, Leo, Virgo. The Moon in Sagittarius and Aquarius is also said to signify a tendency toward barrenness.

BARRETT, FRANCIS Professor of Chemistry in London. He also lectured on the Kabbala and on magic. In addition, he gave private instruction in the occult arts. In 1891 he published The Magus, in which he describes, with illustrations, the characteristics of demons, conjurations, spells, necromancy.

BARRETT, SIR WILLIAM FLETCHER (1845 - 1926) A physicist and early psychic researcher who had a leading role in founding the Society for Psychical Research in Great Britain and the American Society for Psychical Research. His many published works include Death-Bed Visions, written in 1926. He believed in the existence of a spiritual world, survival after death, and the possibility of communicating with the departed.

BARRIOS, DANIEL LEVI (MIGUEL) De (1626 - 1701) A Marrano, that is, a cryptic Jew, who was born in Spain and died in Amsterdam. He ultimately became a mystic. For a time he was a follower of the false Messiah Shabbatai Zevi.

BASIC TECHNIQUE (BT) The system used to test clairvoyance. Each card is laid aside by the experimenter when called by the subject. After the run has been completed, the responses are verified.

BASILEA, SOLOMON ABIAD (1680 - 1743) A Jewish Kabbalist of Mantua, in Italy. He was also a Biblical commentator.

BASILEUS A Greek term meaning king. In the Eleusinian mystery cult he was the chief who supervised the mystic performances.

BASILIDEANS A Gnostic sect based on a doctrine similar to that of the Ophites. It was founded by Basilides of Alexandria, who claimed to have been instructed by Glaucus, Peter's disciple.

BASILISK A fabulous creature that had the head of a snake, and a three-pointed tail. Its glance was fatal. In medieval folklore, it acted as a guardian of treasure.

BAT In Chinese occultism the bat symbolizes happiness.

BAT KOL A Hebrew expression that means Daughter of a Voice. The phrase refers to a reverberating prophetic utterance from heaven. The angel Gabriel was generally credited with these pronouncements. In legal matters, these statements were not regarded as decisive.

BATU In Egyptian mythology, he is the primordial man, the counterpart of the Biblical Adam, or the Kabbalistic Adam Kadmon.

BAZARD, SAINT-AMAND (1791 - 1832) In 1820 he founded a French esoteric society entitled Amis de la Vérité — Friends of the Truth.

BEANS In Egyptian tradition, beans were regarded as possessing magic properties. Black beans were presented as an offering to the gods of the Lower Regions.

BECHOROT A Talmudic treatise that deals with the first-born in man and animals.

BEHOLDING SIGNS In astrology, signs which have the same declination, that is, which are at equal distance from the

Tropics, as Aries and Virgo, Taurus and Leo, Gemini and Cancer, Libra and Pisces, Scorpio and Aquarius, Sagittarius and Capricorn. Because such pairs of signs were either both Northern, or both Southern, they were regarded by Ptolemy as of 'equal power.' This consideration, however, applied only when two such signs were joined by a body in each, mutually configurated.

BELEPHANTES According to the Greek historian Diodorus Siculus, Belephantes was a Chaldean astrologer. He rightly predicted that Alexander the Great's entry into Babylon would be fatal to the Emperor.

BELIEFS OF OCCULTISTS Among the major tenets of contemporary occultism are: that man is evolving to higher degrees of spiritual life; that the entire cosmos is governed by a hierarchy of Intelligences; that the cosmos is constituted totally of energy.

BELIN, ALBERT A Benedictine monk who flourished in the seventeenth century. Author of treatises in alchemy, astral figures, talismans.

BELL One way of establishing communication with the other world is described in an eighteenth-century book on magic: get a bell made from lead, tin, iron, copper, quicksilver, silver and gold; write on the bell the words Adonai, Jesus, Tetrogrammaton; place it for seven days in the middle of a ditch in a graveyard.

BELPHEGOR In medieval demonology, an archdemon credited with ingenious discoveries and inventions.

BELTANE In Celtic mythology this was the name of the first day in the month of May. It was the occasion of a special festival which probably had its origin in the festivals dedicated to the goddess of fertility in ancient Egypt.

BENARES In yoga, the holy Hindu city of Benares is represented by a spot between the two eyebrows. This is considered the occult psychic centre.

BENEDICT, MRS. The official medium of the Apostolic Circle, known simply as Mrs. Benedict, was associated with the Katie Fox Circle in Auburn, New York.

BENEFIC ASPECTS In astrology, planetary relations or familiarities which permit the unobstructed release of cosmic energy. The so-called benefics arc: Venus, Jupiter, and possibly the Sun.

BENJEES A people in India, reputed to practice devil worship.

BERBIGUIER A French peasant who belongs in the mid-eighteenth century. He had visions depicting Christ's Heavenly Throne. He was haunted by spirits and declared that windows opened of their own accord, that Satanic hands tore at his vitals.

BEREAN SOCIETY An English society that flourished in the nineteenth century. It studied theoretical occultism.

BERIGARD OF PISA A seventeenth century French alchemist who lived in Italy. At Pisa he held the Chair of Natural Philosophy.

BERNHEIM, HIPPOLYTE M. (1840 - 1919) French psycho-therapist. He studied and experimented with the phenomena of hypnotism.

BEROSUS A Babylonian priest of Bel, who belongs in the third century B.C. He is the author of a history of Babylon from the origins to the death of Alexander the Great. He also established a college for the study of astrology, on the Greek island of Cos.

BERSERKER In Norse history, they were the bear-skin warriors who were attached to the Byzantine court. Virtually they were wolf-men.

BERTHOLD A Crusader who in the thirteenth century reputedly founded the Order of Carmelites. He was a hermit in Calabria who, after seeing Elias in a vision, returned to Mt. Carmel.

BESANT, ANNIE (1847 - 1933) English theosophist who became a follower of Madame Blavatsky. She proposed a protégé of hers, Jiddu Krishnamurti, as a Messiah.

BESIEGED In astrology, a benefic planet situated between two malefics, within orbs of each, is said to be besieged and therefore unfortunately placed. Some astrologers restrict the application of the term to a Significator when between and within orbs of two benefics. In earlier times, the expression referred to a planet situated between any two planets. In was then considered that a planet between Venus and Jupiter was favorably besieged. But if the planet was between Mars and Saturn it was in an extremely unfavorable position.

BESTIAL SIGNS In astrology, the signs which have been symbolized by animals: Aries, Taurus, Scorpio, part of Sagittarius, Capricorn, Pisces.

BETH EHOLIM A Hebraic expression meaning House of God. It is the title of a mystic Kabbalistic treatise concerning angels, demons, and souls.

BETHOR The angel of Jupiter, known in occultism as one of the seven stewards of heaven. His day is Monday.

BEYOND The term The Beyond denotes in mysticism the state beyond the field of manifestation.

BEYREVRA A Hindu demon, master of souls that roam through space.

BHAGAVAD GITA The Bhagavad Gita is an Indian scriptural text consisting of eighteen chapters, each dealing with a particular aspect of human life and with the method of becoming the whole man. The central themes are brotherhood and the progress of man toward divinity. In the text, Shri Krishna, a spiritual teacher, is presented as instructing in the art of spiritual living.

BHAVA In yoga, an external or manifest state of being. Among human beings, there are three states:
  (a) the bound state, relating to those who live on a material, sensual plane.
  (b) the strong group, who have ambition and purpose.
  (c) the divine estate, relating to those who are thoughtful in action, peaceable, considerate, interested in spiritual purposes.

BHUTAS In Oriental mysticism, these are astral entities of deceased human beings. They are equated with ghosts or spirits.

BIBLICAL NUMEROLOGY Numbers used in the Bible all have a special mystical significance and purpose. Occult and apocalyptic and cosmic undertones and allusions are present, for instance, in the number 3. The number 4 too and multiples of 4 recur frequently in significant contexts. 9 is the symbol of man. 12 is associated with the signs of the zodiac, the tribes of Israel, and the 12 apostles. The Holy City had 12 gates. 7 generally symbolizes a completed circle. There are 7 virtues, 7 trumpet blasts, 7 vials of wrath.

BIBLICAL SUPERNATURALISM In Biblical times all types of witchcraft, divination, oracles, magic phenomena were in operation. In most cases such practices were derived from Babylonian and Egyptian sources. The Bible considers a sorcerer evil: he was publicly stoned to death.
Moses possessed a wand that produced water from rocks, and he could turn the wand into a serpent. The witch of Endor could exorcise spirits. Miriam was healed of leprosy by incantations. The High Priest of the Israelites wore, as part of his ceremonial equipment, the Urim and Thummim, two objects that had an oracular function.
In Isaiah there are references to sorcerers, enchantments, astrologers, and prognostications. King Manasseh 'used enchantments and dealt with familiar spirits and wizards.' While Paul was at Philippi 'a certain damsel possessed with a spirit of divination met us.'
In Acts 19.13 there is mention of strolling exorcists.

BICORPOREAL This term refers, in astrology, to double-bodied zodiacal signs: Gemini, Sagittarius, Pisces. Ptolemy denoted by this term the mutable or deductive signs. To Ptolemy, Virgo also was bicorporeal.

BIJA (VIJA) A Sanskrit word signifying seed of life-germ. It is used in esoteric philosophy to designate the root source and vehicle of the mystic impulse to seek self-expression at the appropriate time after a pralaya or during manvantara.

BILOCATION In mysticism, the presence of the same individual in more than one place at the same time. There are records

56

of saints who achieved bilocation. St. Philip Neri and St. Catherine of Ricci visited each other without leaving their respectives homes in Rome and Prato.

BIRDS　Birds of every kind are mystically equated with spiritual elements.

BIRD'S NEST　In Kabbalistic mysticism this is the celestial region from which at the end of time the Messiah will come.

BIRTH AND DEATH　In Kabbalistic mysticism, birth implies the descent of the soul, while death refers to the ascent of the soul to heaven. This concept coincides to a remarkable degree with Neoplatonic theory.

BISHOP, BRIDGET　The first woman tried for witchcraft in the colony of Massachusetts. She was convicted, in 1692, and hanged. It is quite likely that she and several other black servants implicated in the Salem affair were actually practicing voodoo.

BITTER SIGNS　In astrology, this expression refers to the Fire Signs: Aries, Leo, Sagittarius. They were regarded as hot, fiery and bitter.

BLACK CAT　A black cat was frequently associated with the occult practices of witches. Ben Jonson, in the Masque of Queens, writes in this connection:
"I from the jaws of a gardener's bitch
Did snatch these bones, and then leaped the ditch,
Yet I went back to the house again,
Killed the black cat, and here's the brain."

BLACK DOVES　In Egyptian religion, this term denotes the priestesses of the goddess Isis.

BLACK GLANCE In the occult arts, this expression denotes the Evil Eye.

In some parts of Italy and in Sicily the Evil Eye is called Jettatura.

BLACK HEN According to 'The Black Hen,' a key book of magic in the Christian West, a magician could summon the devil and receive any reward desired by cutting in two a black hen which had never laid an egg. The act had to be accomplished at a crossroads, at the stroke of midnight, as the magician murmured the words 'Eloim, Essaim, frigativi et appellavi,' then, clutching a branch of cypress, turned to the East and uttered the great call for the devil to come.

BLACK MASSES During the Middle Ages black masses were celebrated in honor of the devil during the witches' sabbaths. Derived from Gnostic masses of an earlier era, black masses were said in the open air. The back of a naked woman served as the altar. When black masses became indoor entertainments, frequently patronized by the nobility, the stomach was used instead. Black masses are still popular in many regions of the world.

BLAKE, WILLIAM (1767 - 1827) English poet and artist. A visionary, he rejected materialism and interpreted normal occurrences as apocalyptic visions, in which another, a spiritual world, subsisted along with the physical world.

BLAVATSKY, HELENA PETROVNA (1831 - 1891) Russian theosophist; co-founded the Theosophical Society. She is the author of mystical works, among them Isis Unveiled and The Secret Doctrine. The latter borrows largely from the mystical contents of the Kabbalistic writings.

BOAT OF THE SUN   In Egyptian religion, this was the sacred boat called Sektet, the boat of the setting sun. It was steered by the souls of the dead.

BODHI   In Buddhism, this term denotes a proper understanding of the nature of the Beyond.

BODHISATTVA   In Buddhism, one who in one or more future incarnations will become a Buddha. In esoteric teachings, one whose ego is fully conscious of its inner divinity and becomes clothed with the Buddhic ray. Such a man is the representative on earth of a Celestial Buddha, or an incarnation of his own Divine Monad.

BODIN, JEAN (1530?-1596)   The author of one of the earliest essays on the philosophy of history was also a student of demonology. His Démonomanie des sorciers (1580) is a defense of witchcraft. It demonstrates that spirits have communication with mankind, explains diabolic prophecy, and sets forth the characteristics of sorcerers.

BOEHME, JACOB (1575 - 1624)   A German cobbler. A visionary with philosophical inclinations. He interpreted Biblical contexts mystically, and meditated deeply over the question of evil and suffering. 'There is no difference,' he wrote, 'between eternal life, re-integration and the discovery of the philosophers' stone.' He taught that 'everything derives from eternity and everything must return to it.'

BOETHUSIANS   A Sadducee sect in opposition to the Pharisees. The basis of the conflict was the validity of the Hebraic Oral Law and the problem of life after death. The sect disappeared in 66 A.D., during the revolt against Rome.

BOHM, HANS   A German wandering preacher who attracted followers by playing on drum and flute. He proclaimed that the Virgin Mary had appeared to him. He was condemned to the stake in 1477.

BOLINGBROKE, ROGER   Bolingbroke was an English wizard who flourished in the fifteenth century. He was notoriously reputed to be a necromancer, skilled also in astrology and the black arts. In the reign of King Henry VI of England he was hanged for using witchcraft in an attempt to kill the monarch.

BONATTI, GUIDO   An Italian astrologer and adept in the Black Arts, who flourished in the thirteenth century. He wrote prolifically on these subjects. He was reputed to have made an apothecary wealthy by fashioning a wax figure of a ship and endowing it with magic properties.
Like Michael Scot the occultist, he was consigned to Hell by Dante.

BONIFACE VIII, POPE (1235?-1303)   This Pope was reputed to have been interested in occultism. He is consigned to the Inferno by Dante.

BONNEVAULT, MATURIN DE   A French sorcerer who belongs in the seventeenth century. Father of Pierre Bonnevault.

BONNEVAULT, PIERRE   A French sorcerer who belongs in the seventeenth century.

BOOK OF BALLYMOTE   An Irish book dating in the fourteenth century. It contains instructions in enchantments and other magic procedures.

BOOK OF CHANGES A Chinese compilation of divinatory interpretations. The collection was formed at different times, being completed in the third century B.C.

BOOK OF CONTEMPLATION This is the title of a mystical Kabbalistic treatise, attributed to a certain Chamai Gaon. The text was published in Germany in the nineteenth century.

BOOK OF FORMATION In Hebrew, this is the Sefer Yezirah. It is a treatise of great antiquity. In its six chapters, by means of mystical numerical calculations based on the values of letters of the alphabet, it expounds the creation of the world. A legend declares that by studying the text several Kabbalistic occultists were able to create a calf, deer, and fawns.

BOOK OF THE MEASURING ROD The title of a mystic Kabbalistic treatise dating in the fourteenth century. Its contents are traditionally ascribed to the revelations of the Prophet Elijah.

BOOK OF THE SECRET A Persian treatise that describes visions and the method of producing them.

BOOK OF WONDER The title of a mystic Kabbalistic treatise dating in the fourteenth century. Its contents are traditionally ascribed to the revelations of the Prophet Elijah.

BOSTON SOCIETY FOR PSYCHIC RESEARCH The Boston society was founded in 1925 by Walter Franklin Prince, who had served previously as research officer of the American Society for Psychical Research. The Boston society published bulletins and books on subjects of interest to its members.

BOTANOMANCY A form of divination by observation of certain herbs.

BOURIGNON, ANTOINETTE (1616-1680) A famous visionary whose numerous works argued against any external form of worship and in favor of mystical perfection.

BOZANO, ERNESTO (1862-1945) The dean of Italian psychical researchers wrote numerous books and articles, collected a unique library on psychic and spiritualistic phenomena, and concluded after many years of research that the survival of the spirit is beyond question.

BRAGADINI, MARCO ANTONIO An Italian Rosicrucian who was also an occultist and alchemist. He was executed in 1595 for transmuting base metal into gold.

BRAHMA In Hinduism, the universal soul. Its counterpart is the individual soul, or atman.

BRAHMANASPATI In Hindu astrology, this term denotes the planet Jupiter. In Vedic mythology it is known as Brihaspati, signifying the power of prayer.

BRAHMASRAMA In Occultism, a compound term used to signify an initiation room where the neophyte is struggling to attain union with the inner god.

BRAIDISM A theory of hypnotism postulated by James Braid, a British physician who belongs in the nineteenth century. Braidism asserts that hypnosis represents bodily consequences of suggestion under conditions of trance.

BRANT, SEBASTIAN Brant flourished in the sixteenth century. He is the author of The Ship of Fools, in which he attacks alchemists.

BREATHING   Much importance is attached to proper breathing in yoga. Swedenborg was convinced that his powers were linked with a system of breathing. Trance seances begin with a change in respiratory rhythm. According to Hindu teachings, breathing exercises have a major role in levitation.

BRITISH NATIONAL ASSOCIATION OF SPIRITUALISTS The first meeting of the association was held on April 16, 1874. The name was changed in 1882 to The Central Association of Spiritualism, which published three successive organs: W. H. Harrison's Spiritualista (1879-1881), The Spiritual Notes, and Light (from 1882 onward). The association was founded largely through the efforts of Dawson Rogers. It was reorganized in 1884 as The London Spiritualist Alliance.

BROTHERHOOD OF LUXOR   An ancient esoteric society, associated with Lukshur in Baluchistan.

BROTHERHOOD OF THE TROWEL   A secret society that flourished in Italy in the fifteenth century.

BROTHERHOOD OF THE WHITE TEMPLE   An esoteric sect associated with a mystical Church and College of the Brotherhood, situated in the Rocky Mountains.

BROTHERS OF MERCY   A religious sect that was founded around 1540.

BROTHERS OF THE SHADOW   In the occult arts this expression refers to the adherents of the Left-hand Path. They were the adepts in Black Magic. This is particularly the case in Tibet, where sorcerers are known as Dugpas, wearers of the Red Cap.

BRUHESEN, PETER VAN A Dutch physician and astrologer. He flourished in the sixteenth century. Author of an astrological almanac.

BRUXA In Portugal the bruxa, the witch or sorceress, is far from extinct. In isolated country districts she still plies her occult trade, particularly the concoction of love philtres. In 1968 a bruxa was brought to trial in Lisbon. She was an illiterate peasant, age fifty-four. There was, however, not enough evidence to convict her of the illegal practice of medical treatments.

In Oporto another bruxa, known to have performed wonders, was brought to trial on a charge of extortion. But her refutation was that she had heavy expenditures in her efforts to drive out the evil spirits that assailed her client.

BT In parapsychology, these letters are the initials of Basic Technique. This is the clairvoyance technique in which cards are laid aside by the experimenter as they are called by the subject.

BUBER, MARTIN (1878-1965) One of the leading exponents of Chassidic religious mystical philosophy. Buber was a student also of the mystic religions of China and India and medieval Christianity. He maintained that the Judaic experience of divine immanence, as expressed by the Talmud, has a unique importance for all peoples. He also maintained the mystical concept of Man's communion with God. Religious redemption is his central theme.

BUCHAN, JOHN (1875-1940) Scottish statesman and novelist. In his autobiography he refers to his previous state of incarnation.

BUCHANAN, J. RHODES (1814-1899) A pioneer in psychometric research, the American scientist claimed the discovery of phrenomesmerism. He believed that all substances threw off an emanation perceptible to mediums, that 'the past is entombed in the present,' and that he had received a communication from St. John.

BUDDHA   The word is the past participle of a Sanskrit root meaning 'to awaken' or to 'perceive.' It designates a person who has awakened from the living death of ordinary mortals and become one with the Paramatman, the Self of Selves. In esoteric teachings, a Buddha is one whose higher principle has learned everything that can be learned in this manvantara and has reached Nirvana.

BUDDHAS OF COMPASSION   In their various degrees of evolution, the Buddhas of Compassion constitute a sublime hierarchy reaching from the Silent Watcher on earth downward. Having raised themselves from humanity to quasi-divinity, they renounce their right to cosmic peace in order that they may let the light of the inner god manifest itself in man.

BUDDHIST MYSTICAL SCHOOL   To the adherents of this type of mysticism the universe consists of six elements, its activity consists of the three mysteries of action, speech, and thought.

BUDDHIST NUMBERS   The ethical teachings of Buddha are called the Tripitaka, The Tree Baskets. The Four Noble Truths are the Buddhist principles that offer surcease from the misery of physical existence.

BULL   In antiquity and in the ancient mystery cults, the bull represented the potency of the male principle culminating in divinity.

BULL, TITUS   The New York physician published in 1932, under the title Analysis of Unusual Experiences in Healing Relative to Diseased Minds and Results of Materialism Foreshadowed, a remarkable summary of his treatment of many cases of obsession. He endorses the spiritualistic methods of treating the disorder.

BURMESE   Among the Burmese, exorcism, divination, astrology and the occult arts in general are commonly practiced.

BURMESE SOUL   In Burmese thought the soul of a person is independent of his body. It has the faculty of leaving the body and returning to it. This is a Tibetan concept also.

BUTTERFLY   In antiquity, the butterfly represented the human soul.

BYTHOS   A Greek term meaning depth. In the mystic system of Gnosticism it denotes chaos, that is, spatial depth before the fact of creation.

C

CAACRINOLAAS In medieval demonology, a powerful demon who is the Grand President of Hell.

CADENT In astrology, cadent houses are those which fall away from the angles: the third, sixth, ninth, and twelfth houses. Cadent planets are those which occupy cadent houses and whose influence is thereby weakened.

CAGLIOSTRO, COUNT (1745-1795) An Italian alchemist, Hermetic, and magician, whose original name was Giuseppe Balsamo. In Sicily he committed a number of crimes, fled across Europe, studying alchemy and sorcery. He acquired a fortune by selling love potions, magic elixirs. His last years were spent in imprisonment, in the fortress of San Leo.
His achievements included the manufacture of a diamond, by alchemical means. He also conjured a dead woman. He was the founder of an occult society called The Egyptian Lodge.

CAHAGNET, ALPHONSE A nineteenth century French artisan. He recorded the words spoken in trance by somnambulists and published three books on his investigations. He also communicated his findings to the Vatican.
Cahagnet is the author of The Celestial Telegraph.

CALCULATION OF THE CUSPS In astrology, the best known systems for calculating the cusps of the intermediate Houses are as follows:

67

Campanus: The vertical circle from the zenith to the east and west points of the horizon is trisected. Through these points are drawn the House circles, from the north and south points of the horizon. The house cusps are the points at which the ecliptic at that moment intersects the horizon.

Regiomontanus: The celestial circle is trisected, instead of the prime vertical, and great circles extend from north and south points of the horizon to the points of trisection. The house cusps are at the points at which the ecliptic intersects the horizon. At the equator the two systems give the same cusps, the disparity increasing as one approaches the earth's poles.

Horizontal: Starting with great circles at the meridian and ante-meridian, the horizon and the prime vertical, add other great circles from zenith to nadir which trisect each quadrant of the horizon. The cusps will then be the points at which on a given moment the ecliptic intersects the vertical circles.

Placidus: The diurnal motion of the earth causes a celestial object to intersect the cusp of the twelfth House, after a sidereal-time interval equal to one-third of its semi-diurnal arc: to intersect the cusp of the eleventh House after a sidereal-time interval equal to two-thirds of its semi-diurnal arc: and to culminate at the meridian after an interval of sidereal time that corresponds to the semi-diurnal arc. The semi-arc from the meridian that intersects the eastern horizon gives the Ascendant: and the second and third House cusps are similarly extended below the horizon. The Placidian cusps are now in almost universal use.

CALENDAR A system of reckoning and recording the time when events occur. Time is reckoned by the Earth's rotation on its axis with reference to the Sun, a day: by the Moon's revolution around the Earth, a month: by the Earth's revolution around the Sun, a year.

The Mohammedan calendar is strictly a lunar calendar, the year consisting of twelve lunar months.

The Egyptian calendar divided the year into twelve months of thirty days each, with five supplementary days following each twelfth month.

The Hindu calendar is one of the early lunisolar calendars. The year is divided into twelve months, with an intercalated month bearing the same name, inserted after every month in which there are two lunations, which is about every three years.

The Chinese calendar begins with the first new Moon after the Sun enters Aquarius. It consists of twelve months, with an intercalary month every thirty months, each month being divided into thirds.

The Jewish calendar is a lunisolar calendar, which reckons from 3761 B.C., the traditional year of the Creation.

In Anglo-Saxon England the year began on December 25th, until William the Conqueror ordered it to begin on January 1st, the day of his coronation.

CALI In medieval demonology, the queen of demons. Human victims were sacrificed to her.

CALL In parapsychology, the subject's guess, or cognitive response, in trying to identify the target in an ESP test.

CALMECAC In ancient Mexico this was an institution where the occult arts were studied.

CALMET, DOM AUGUSTIN (1672 - 1757) A Benedictine monk and Bible exegete, also an occultist. Author of a work on angels, apparitions, demons, spirits, vampires.

CALUMARATH (KAID-MORDS) The name given by the Persians to the first man, who lived a thousand years and reigned one hundred and sixty.

69

CALUNDRONIUS A stone endowed with magic properties. It can be used for apotropaic purposes against demons and enchantments and spells.

CAMBODIAN SORCERY Two kinds of sorcerers operate in Cambodia: soothsayers, ap thmop, who forecast future events, and sorcerers who are also medicine men, kru. The latter are also exorcists.

CAMBODIAN SPIRITS It is a Cambodian belief that a ghost arises from a decomposing corpse.

CAMBRIEL, FRANCOIS Author of a French treatise on alchemy, published in 1943 under the title of Cours de Philosophie hermétique.

CAMPANELLA, TOMASO (1560 - c. 1639) Italian occultist. He wrote treatises on alchemy, magic arts, and astrology. He had been a Dominican friar. After being imprisoned on charges of heresy, he turned to the occult arts.

CAMP MEETINGS Assemblies of spiritualists have been held since 1873 in such places as Lake Pleasant, Massachusetts, and Lily Dale, New York.

CANCER In astrology, the Crab. The fourth, northern sign of the zodiac. In the mystery cult of Orpheus, it is the entrance of the soul into incarnation. In occultism, this sign stands for tenacity to life. Kabbalistically, it signifies the vital organs of the grand old man of the skies and therefore the life forces.

CANDLEMAS The feast celebrated on February 2 in memory of the Purification of the Virgin in the Christian version of the first of the pagan 'sabbaths.'

CANDLES Candles made of human fat are used in black magic to discover hidden treasure. Demonographers state that witches approach the devil bearing candles.

CANNABIS INDICA Indian hemp: a drug that was used for centuries as an aphrodisiac. This plant grows in Central and Western Asia and the Western Himalaya, in India, Africa, and North America. The resin extracted from the plant is called *cannabinon*, from which cannabinol stems, a red oily substance found in the flowering tops of the female plant. Extracted from the plant in pure form, it is known in India as *charas*.
Charas is smoked and eaten. Powdered and sifted form of this resinous substance is *hashish*.
Another, weaker form is known as *bhang*, which is used as a drink. In Mexico, it is known as *marihuana*. Another form is *ganja*, made from the cut crop of the female plant: it is used for smoking.
Cannabis Indica produces some 150 different preparations of the drug. For some 5000 years this hemp plant has been known and used from China to Egypt, and is now so used in the cities of the world.
In the second millennium B.C. the Chinese were already acquainted with the properties of the hemp plant. In 800 B.C. it was introduced into India, and from that time on it has been cultivated extensively and continuously. In the seventh century B.C. the Assyrians began to use the drug for its narcotic powers. In the second century A.D. the ancient Chinese physician Hua Tu administered a narcotic draught to his patients before an operation. The drug was known as *Ma Fu Shuan*. It was also used

71

by Dioscorides, the Greek army physician, in the first century A.D., to relieve cases of earache.

CANONIZATION   In the Eastern Orthodox Church there are two principal requirements for canonization. These are a virtuous life and the saint's intercession in the performance of miracles. When the repute of the saint has become established, the Church authorities investigate his life and the authenticity of the miracles.

CAPNOMANCY   A method of divination by observation of the fumes rising from poppies thrown on live coals.

CAPRICORN   In astrology, the Goat. The tenth, southern sign of the zodiac. It represents the dual movement of life plunging into the depths and reaching toward the heights. Esoterically, it is viewed as the scapegoat of the Israelites. Kabbalistically, this sign stands for the knees of the grand old man of the heavens and is the emblem of material servitude.

CARDAN, JEROME (1501-1576)   Italian mathematician, Kabbalist, and astrologer. In one of his works, De Subtilitate, he discusses demons, charms, and philtres. He also wrote a treatise on astrology and the casting of horoscopes, with historical examples.

CARDINAL SIGNS   In astrology, these signs are Aries, Cancer, Libra, Capricorn, whose cusps coincide with the cardinal points of the compass. Aries is East: Cancer, North: Libra, West: Capricorn, South.

CARIBBEAN TRIBES   Among these tribes, even after their disintegration as the result of the Spanish Conquest, the belief persisted in the supernatural, in spirits and malefic powers and in the status of the shaman or medicine man

72

as an aide between human beings and the supernatural. This attitude continued long after the advent of Christianity.

CARPOCRATIANS A Gnostic sect founded in the second century A.D. by Carpocrates of Alexandria. Its ritual included secret symbols, signs, and cryptic expressions. The sect disappeared in the sixth century.

CARRINGTON, HEREWARD (1881 - 1959) The English spiritualist has written many books on psychic phenomena. He founded the American Psychical Institute and Laboratory in 1921. After investigating Mrs. Eileen Garrett at the Institute, he concluded that there are indeed mental entities that exist apart from the conscious or unconscious mind of the medium.

CARTOMANCY A method of telling a person's fortune by interpretation of a pack of playing cards.

CASSIEL In the 'Book of Spirits' Cassiel is identified as the chief of the spirits.

CAT The cat has been called 'the first pet of civilization.' It has always been associated with occultism. Of all animals, the cat alone looks a person straight in the eye. It is believed that the glance of a cat can inspire terror. Such a fear of cats is called ailurophobia. Hitler had such a fear. Napoleon too feared the approach of the cat. Joseph Bonaparte, King of Naples, once collapsed in a friend's house because he had sensed the presence of a cat, although no such cat was visible. But a search produced a kitten hiding in a sideboard. At the sight of a cat Henry III fainted. Buffon, the famous French naturalist, dreaded the animal. Oliver Goldsmith, the English novelist and poet, and James Boswell, the biographer of Dr. Samuel Johnson, were similarly scared of cats. But Albert Einstein the mathematician was quite fond of them. Lafcadio Hearn had a strange affection for them, and wrote of them with sensitivity. The French novelist, Pierre Loti, had visiting cards printed for his own pets. In ancient India the cat was sacred. Reference is often made in Sanskrit literature to the influence on man exerted by the cat. In ancient Britain, sacred rites were held in honor of the animal. In Wales, Hywel Ddda, a Welsh prince, enacted a law, in the tenth century, for the protection of cats.

Among the Egyptians, the cat was raised to divinity. The Egyptian word for tomcat is kut, while a tabby is called kutta. As a deity, the cat was 'The Sayer of Great Words'. Killing a cat was punishable by death. In Lower Egypt, the city of Bubastis was dedicated to feline worship. The feeding of these sacred animals was itself a high privilege. The cat fed on catfish. Every year, some 700,000 pilgrims journeyed to Bubastis to the cat festival, held in May. There was music, and wine ran copiously. The temples were packed with penitents making vows to the cat divinities. Cat amulets were on sale in public places: figurines of cats in amethyst, calcite, and red cornelian.

Among cat goddesses, the most important was Ubasti. She was represented in bronze as a cat-headed woman. Prayers and sacrifices were part of the ritual of feline worship. After death, cats were embalmed and shipped to Bubastis for burial.

When the Egyptian cat cult died out, cat influence spread to Europe. Cat Clans sprang up in Celtic and Teutonic regions. In the first century B.C. the cat motif was dominant. Roman legionary soldiers bore a cat sign on their shields. The crest of the Germanic tribe of Catti was a brindled cat. The Cattani of Scotland likewise had a cat on their crest.

The last remaining Cat Clan is still in existence, in the Scottish Highlands, where the Clan Chattan, a federation of clans originally formed to settle disputes among member clans, holds sway. Several of these clans bear on their crest the motto: Touch not the cat bot — that is, without a glove. Popularly, the members of the Clan Chattan are known as the People of the Cat.

In Scandinavia Freya is the cat-goddess. She is depicted as drawn in a chariot by two cats. Girls contrived to wed on Freya's Day, Friday. If the day was sunny, it was said that the bride had fed the cat well.

In Europe in the Middle Ages, cats, preferably black, were associated with nocturnal magic rites. Along with witches, cats were tortured as purveyors of evil. Cats were even believed capable of speaking the language of their mistresses. An eighteenth century witch, Moll White, had a cat which was believed to have talked in English. Business men used to select the cat as a symbol of efficiency.

In medieval times a movable penthouse used in siege works was called a cat. A cat-o-nine tails was a thong for punishing criminals. Cat's eyes in human beings are considered exotic and magnetic. An old Massachusetts law warns owners of cats not to keep the animal out doors at night, under penalty of a stiff fine.

CATACLYSMIC PLANET In astrology, this expression refers to Uranus, which combines both the magnetic and the electric elements, producing sudden affects.

CATHERINE DE MEDICI (1519 - 1589) Queen of France. She was skilled in astrology.

CATOPTROMANCY A method of divination by means of a magic mirror. This technique was known by the ancients. It is mentioned by Apuleius the Roman philosopher and novelist, Pausanias the Greek traveler, and St. Augustine the Church Father.

CAT-WITCH In Finnish mythology, there is a tale of an old witch who, after death, turns into a cat.

CAYCE, EDGAR As a boy in Hopkinsville, Kentucky, he was boxed on the ear by his father. Since that time, when in difficulties, he went to sleep: next morning the situation was remedied. He put a book under his pillow: next morning, he knew the book by heart. In sickness, he would induce a trance state, and heard a voice saying: Yes, we can see the body. Again and again he helped others in difficulties. He had no medical knowledge but in his trance he prescribed medical procedures which were invariably successful. In each case, he heard the voice: Yes, we can see the body.

Cayce's 'miracles' received national attention. Letters and requests for help came from all directions. On the point of death, he suddenly, contrary to medical diagnosis, regained consciousness. In a trance, he announced the name of a murderess, giving the caliber and number of the pistol used, together with other details.

His diagnoses always confused and often refuted physicians. Cayce was investigated by medical men and psychologists. At Virginia Beach, a hospital was opened for Cayce's treatments. It closed in 1929. Cayce died in 1945. There is still no rational conclusive explanation of his unquestioned powers.

CAYM In medieval demonology, a grand master of Hell. He reveals himself as a blackbird or as a man carrying a tapered saber. He appeared to Martin Luther. He commands thirty legions.

CAZIMI In astrology, this Arabian term refers to the centre of the solar disc.

CAZOTTE, JACQUES A French occultist and seer. He was executed during the French Revolution. In 1788 he announced the deaths of many leading figures of the Revolution, including that of Condorcet. He foretold the details of his own death on the scaffold.

CECCO D'ASCOLI Noted Italian astrologer. He flourished in the thirteenth century. He was burned at the stake by the Inquisition.

CELLINI, BENVENUTO (1500 - 1571) An Italian artist, goldsmith, and sculptor. In his autobiography he describes a conjuration of spirits of demoniac character. The manifestation occurred in the Roman Forum, at night. The phenomenon was the work of a friend, a priest who was also an occultist.

CELTIC AMULETS Among the ancient Celts amulets and coral and phallic figures were in force as apotropaic agents.

CENSORINUS A Roman scholar who flourished in the third century A.D. He is the author of a treatise dealing in part with the influence of the planets on human life.

CEROMANCY A form of divination by dropping melted wax into water and observing the results.

CHABAD A word formed from the Hebrew initials of terms used in Kabbalistic writings. These terms, in English, are: wisdom, reason, intuition.

CHAINS OF ST. PETER Two chains were preserved: one that bound Peter in Jerusalem, the other in Rome. When, around 439 A.D., the Empress Eudoxia brought the chain from Jerusalem to Rome, and placed it near the Roman chain, the two chains joined miraculously. The Feast of St. Peter ad vincula commemorates the incident.

CHAKRAS In Oriental mysticism the seven chakras are the organs of the astral body. Chakras are usually called Lotus flowers. The word itself signifies wheel, but esoteric speculation has resulted in extensions of the original meaning. A Chakra now means a period during which the wheel of time turns once, or certain centers of the body which collect streams of pranic energy.

CHALDEANS The Chaldean priests and astrologers were repeatedly banished from Rome and Italy under the first emperors.

CH'AN In the Ch'an sect of Buddhism the devotees practice vegetarianism.

CHANCE In parapsychology, the complex of undefined causal factors irrelevant to the purpose at hand.

CHAPPAN DEO A Hindu expression meaning Fifty-six. Chappan Deo is a Hindu god who represents the largest number of places to which a lost wife or child may have strayed.

CHARING CROSS SPIRITUAL CIRCLE The first spiritualistic association in London was superseded in 1857 by the London Spiritualistic Union.

CHARNOCK, THOMAS An English alchemist, who flourished in the sixteenth century.

CHASTE The Chaste were an ancient Hebraic esoteric sect who were concerned with the mysticism of letters.

CHAYOTH   A Hebrew expression which, in Hebraic mysticism, refers to holy living creatures who are of animal form.

CHAZARS   A Tartar tribe in the Crimea who became converts to Judaism under their king Bulan around 750 A.D. They were conquered by Christian Russians in the eleventh century.

CHEMICAL WEDDING OF CHRISTIAN ROSENKREUTZ A Rosicrucian work, published in 1469, by Johannes Valentinus Andreas. It is an account of a man's pilgrimage in terms of alchemy and the spiritual teaching of Rosicrucianism. Symbolically, it represents man's power to transcend the physical world.

CHERUB   Plural: Cherubim. A Hebrew expression meaning a winged celestial being, part human and part animal. They served as the chariot of the Almighty and as guardian angels. Figures of cherubim decorated the doors and walls of the Temple of Solomon. Two cherubim, made of olive wood and covered with gold, were set up in the inner Sanctuary of the Temple, their overarching wings touching each other in the middle of the chamber beneath which rested the Ark. The Ark itself had two cherubim of gold set up, facing each other, at the two ends of the Ark-cover, their wings spread out. Between these two cherubim the Deity revealed himself and communicated his commands. Yahweh is therefore referred to as He Who is Enthroned upon the Cherubim. There were no cherubim in the Second Temple. In the vision of Ezekiel the Divine Throne rested on the wings of four cherubim, each of which had faces — those of a man, a lion, an ox, and an eagle — and each had four wings, under which were the hands of a man. The soles of their feet were calves' soles. Each cherub had a wheel at its side which moved with the cherub, and both cherub and wheel were full of eyes.

Cherubim were also the guardian spirits of the Tree of Life. In the angelic hierarchy, the cherubim came to be variously placed in the scale, but their function remained primarily that of guardian angels. Winged guardians of similar forms are found in Babylonian, Assyrian, Hittite, and Egyptian mythology, and representations of them appear on sculpture and monuments. It has been suggested that the cherubim were the personifications of clouds, winds, or storms.

CHEU KYONGS In Tibetan mysticism, Cheu Kyongs denotes 'protector of religion.' This is a group of beings of diabolical origin, rendered submissive by a magician. These beings protect priests from hostile assaults.

CHHAYA In esoteric philosophy, this Sanskrit word signifies the astral image of a person.

CHILD FROM THE EGG In the mystic sect of the Gnostics, this expression denotes the creator of the universe.

CHILD PRODIGIES In the course of history, children have shown unique mathematical capacities, without having any training or even ability to read or write. Among such prodigies are: André Ampère, the French scientist, Truman Safford, American mathematician, George Bidder, who belongs in the nineteenth century, and Zerah Colburn, a nineteenth century American professor of languages.

CHILDREN OF THE FIRE MIST In theosophical mysticism, these are messengers sent from the planet Venus to guide the evolutionary process on earth.

CHILIASM The doctrine of the millennium, the year 1000. In the Middle Ages there was a widespread belief throughout Europe that the end of the world would occur in the year 1000.

CHIN (LING - CHIN) A plant, also called 'magic-fungus,' used by the hsien of ancient China. The hsien believed that certain roots and herbs, when eaten, would cure disease, rejuvenate the body, and prolong life. Chief among such plants was the chin, believed to contain vitalizing agents of marvellous efficacy.

CHINESE ASTROLOGY In Chinese astrology, Taurus is the White Tiger: Leo, the Red Bird: Scorpio, the Black Dragon: Aquarius, the Black Warrior.

CHINESE ELEMENTS In Chinese cosmological thought, there are eight elements or trigrams. These are: heaven and earth, mountain, thunder, water, wind, fire, moving water.

CHINESE HEAVEN Among the Chinese a circular figure, with a hole in the centre, represents heaven. The hole is the way to transcend the earth.

CHINESE POLTERGEISTS Jesuit missionaries who worked in the Chinese field in the eighteenth century produced accounts of the activities of poltergeists.

CHIROGNOMY The art of determining traits of character by the study of the hand. The future is linked with the left hand. The closed hand symbolizes avarice; the double sun line, instability; the line of Saturn stopping in the center, prudence, etc.

CHIROMANCY Palmistry, or divination by examination of the hand, is based on the Kabbalah. The more specialized art of describing traits of character by the study of the hand is sometimes called chirognomy.

CHOD   In Tibetan yoga, this term refers to an ascetic exercise in which the subject is delivered, in an allegorical sense, to demons.

CHOU KUNG   The authorship of the *Hsiao-T'ze* was traditionally attributed to Chou Kung, son of King Wen, author of the *T'uan.* The *Hsiao-T'ze* and T'uan became the basis of occultism as set forth in the I Ching.

CHRESTOS   In pagan occultism, this term was applied to a disciple undergoing initiation. As a hierophant, he was 'anointed' or rubbed with oil.

CHRISTIAN KABBALISTS   Although the Kabbalistic writings were exclusively of Hebraic import, many non-Jewish scholars studied the mystic treatises and became Kabbalists themselves. Pico della Mirandola translated Kabbalistic works into Latin. Johann Reuchlin was the author of Kabbalistic theses: De verbo mirifico — On the Mirific Word, and De arte kabbalistica — On the Kabbalistic art. Paracelsus, the greatest physician of medieval Europe, was also a student of the Kabbalah.

CHRISTIAN SCIENCE   A religious system based on the sayings and acts of Christ. The sect was founded by Mary Baker Eddy. She evolved her system after reading Christ's healing performances in the New Testament. The Church of Christian Science was founded in 1879. The essence of the doctrine is contained in Mary Eddy's Science and Health. The core of the system is that illness is nonexistent and that to maintain health one should rely solely on God.

CHRONOCRATORS   In astrology, this term denotes Markers of Time. To the ancient, the longest orbits within the solar system were of Jupiter, twelve years, and Saturn, thirty years. The conjunction of Jupiter and Saturn brought periods of great global upheaval. Jupiter and Saturn were known as the chronocrators.

CHURCHES OF GOD Religious bodies that have various headquarters in the United States. The Scriptures are the basic authority, and the members are also Trinitarians.

CHURCH OF RELIGIOUS SCIENCE A system founded by Ernest Holmes in California, with branches in Canada, Europe, the Orient. It has its ministers, both men and women, healing services, and therapy by prayer.

CHURCH OF SATAN A church founded in San Francisco in 1966 by Anton Szandor La Vey. The high priest claims that his church has seven thousand members who are pleasure-seeking individuals who want to throw off the stifling factors of denials and other hypocrisies.

CHWEZI A pantheon of mythical hero-gods forming the basis of divination cults among the Nyoro people of Uganda. They are believed to have ruled the country for some time before disappearing as mysteriously as they had appeared. These spirits are identified with the well-being of the various clans of the Nyoro.

CINGALESE ASTROLOGY In Ceylon astrologers are considering to what extent astrological operations and calculations will be modified by the prospective landing on the moon. The question is of wide interest as the people of Ceylon are deeply involved in astrological prognostications and on the impacts of celestial phenomena. But in a general sense it is assumed that astrological influences affect earth-born man solely, and that the newer concepts of the moon's future relationships with the earth will not impinge on normal astrological traditions.

CINNABAR Red sulphide of mercury, from which quicksilver is obtained. Long before the theory of transmutation of metals led to the beginnings of alchemy, primitive *hsien* consumed cinnabar in an attempt to achieve immortality.

CIRCLE Symbolically, the circle represents Eternity. When the circle is represented thus $\odot$, it symbolizes the emergence of spiritual power. It also represents the concept of perfection. In Chinese thought, a black circle denotes the active male principle.

In astrology, the circle is the complete circle of the zodiac, or 360 degrees of sixty minutes each. To the ancient Chaldeans, the horizon was regarded as a complete circle: also the Zodiac.

CIRCLES OF POSITION In astrology, circles intersecting the horizon and meridian and passing through a star. The position of a star is expressed thereby: but the term is now obsolete.

CIRCULATIONS OF THE COSMOS This term is used in esoteric philosophy to mean the network of the paths followed by pilgrim-monads as they move from sphere to sphere.

CITY OF NINE GATES In yoga mysticism this expression refers to the nine orifices in the human body.

CITY OF WILLOWS The abode of the gods, reached after a long and difficult journey by initiates into the Hung or Triad Society.

CLAIRAUDIENCE A faculty for hearing sounds and words that are not normally heard by others at the same time. Many medieval saints were reputed to have spiritual clairaudience. Joan of Arc, who heard 'voices,' is another instance.

CLAIRVOYANCE The power of discerning things not present to the senses. The spiritual faculty is supposed to enable a person to see objects and persons across great distances. Emanuel Swedenborg, among many others, is supposed to have had such power. He claimed to have direct intercourse with the spiritual world after his spiritual senses were opened, in 1745.

CLEMENT OF ALEXANDRIA (c. 150-215 A.D.) Greek philosopher and theologian. He was a pagan converted to Christianity. There was a tradition that he had been initiated into the Eleusinian mystery cult.

CLERICAL EXORCISM In a recent issue of the London Sunday Times it was reported that Christopher Neil Smith, Vicar of St. Saviour's, in Hampstead, London, practices exorcism and is kept busy all the year round. His exorcism, directed ·to casting out evil spirits, consists of the laying on of hands. His sensitive hands can feel the presence of an evil spirit when he receives a sharp kind of electric shock. As the evil force leaves the victim, the pain vanishes.
The vicar has been practicing exorcism for some five years, but he was in training, under another priest, for twenty years. In all there are not more than twelve exorcists throughout Britain.

CLIMACTERICAL CONJUNCTION In astrology, this expression refers to certain Jupiter-Saturn conjunctions.

CLIMACTERICAL PERIODS In astrology, every seventh and ninth year in a Nativity supposedly brought about through the influence of the Moon in its position in the Radix.

CLOUDS The Pueblo Indians practiced a polytheistic and animistic religion. The main aim of their religion was to maintain harmony in society and assure fertility of crops. Since rain, the symbol of fertility, came from the clouds, the latter were identified with certain deities. Clouds were also identified with the souls of the dead.

CONTROL The term is used by spiritualists to denote the spirit that exerts control over the psychic life of a medium.

COFFIN RITE The last initiatory rite in the Egyptian and Greek mystery cults.

COLD PLANETS In astrology, this expression refers to the Moon and to Saturn.

COLLANGES, GABRIEL DE A noted French astrologer and Kabbalist who flourished in the sixteenth century.

COLLECTION OF LIGHT In astrology, when a planet is in aspect to two other bodies which are not within orbs of each other, a collection of light results through the action of the intermediary planet.

COLLYRIDIANS A Gnostic sect that flourished during the early Christian centuries.

COMBE, GEORGE (1788 - 1858) was a Scottish lawyer who migrated to the U.S.A. He promoted the study of phrenology. He was a follower of the phrenologist Spurzheim. Combe was the founder, in 1820, of the Phrenological Society. He also established the Phrenological Journal, in 1823. A brother, Andrew Combe (1797-1847), was also a phrenologist as well as a physiologist. At one time he was physician to Queen Victoria.

COMBUST In astrology, this term refers to the position of a planet that moves more than five degrees in the direction of the sun.

COMMANDING SIGNS In astrology, these signs are Aries, Taurus, Gemini, Cancer, Leo, Virgo, because they were considered more powerful by virtue of their nearness to the zenith.

COMMON SIGNS In astrology, this expression refers to the signs of the mutable quadruplicity: Gemini, Virgo, Sagittarius, Pisces. They are said to be flexible but vacillating.

COMMUNAL LIFE OF THE DEAD In the Greek epic poems of Homer the dead dwell together in a subterranean abode, where Hades and his consort Persephone rule over them. In this region both the good and the evil spirits of the dead live an equally grim existence. The needs of the dead are negative: hence they are not feared by the living.

COMPLETE MAN The complete man, corporeal, spiritual, and of divine origin, is represented by the zodiacal sign of Sagittarius.

CONFIGURATION In astrology, three or more planets in a birth map, that are joined together by aspects, whereby any stimulation will result in the combined action of all the planets which enter into the configuration.
Configuration also refers to a similar combination of mutual aspects between transitory planets.

CONJUNCTION An astrological term. When two planets are in the same degree of a zodiacal sign, the position is called conjunction. It may signify a favorable or unfavorable outcome.

CONSTANTIUS Under the Christian Roman emperor Constantius II (317-361), it was officially forbidden to observe the rising or setting of the sun and the stars.

CONTACT In astrology, this term is usually applied to an aspect from a directed planet to a sensitive degree created by a planet at birth. In a general sense the expression implies the energy discharge which occurs when an aspect becomes operative.

CONTEMPORARY WITCHCRAFT Angoon, on Admiralty Island off the coast of Alaska, has a population of a few whites and some four hundred Tlingit Indians. In 1957 the death of a Tlingit Indian child was the occasion for a sequence of magic rites. Cats and dogs were burnt in sacrificial ceremonies, while two young Indian girls, 'mediums for the witches,' were beaten with 'devil clubs' — bundles of thorns. Several villagers too were denounced to the United States authorities for practicing witchcraft.

CONTRA ASTROLOGOS This Latin expression means An Attack against Astrologers. It is the title of a treatise by the Italian philosopher and mystic Pico della Mirandola (1463 - 1494).

CONTRA ANTISCIONS In astrology, these are the same degrees of declination held by stars and planets tenanting opposite signs.

CONVERSE DIRECTIONS In astrology, those directions that are computed opposite to the order of the zodiacal signs.

COOVER, JOHN Dr. John Coover in the early decades of this century conducted telepathic tests at Stanford University. His elaborate experiments and his detailed findings led him to conclude that telepathy did not then have validity.

CORDOVEIRO, MOSES An eminent Kabbalist who flourished in the sixteenth century. He is associated with the Kabbalistic centre of Safed, in Palestine. It has been suggested that Spinoza the philosopher may have been influenced by Cordoveiro.

CORELLI, MARIE (1855 - 1924) The English novelist Marie Corelli was the author of a number of mystic novels dealing with psychic and occult themes. Among these works are:
The Secret Power. The story of the Masters of the World, a new age, and a new race.
The Sorrows of Satan.
Adath: a story of reincarnation.
The Soul of Lilith.

CORPSE In antiquity, particularly in the pagan cults of the Akkadians, Babylonians, Hittites, and Sumarians and in general among the peoples of the Mesopotamian region, a corpse had to be given due burial according to prescribed traditional rites. Otherwise, the corpse would return to earth with evil intent upon the living.

CORPUS HERMETICUM An important collection of philosophical writings cast in a pseudo-Egyptian framework and dating from no earlier than the second century A.D. It contains a mixture of Platonic, Stoic, Judaic, and Persian influences. It deals with the creation of the world, the ascent of the soul to the divine regions, regenerative processes through which the soul frees itself from the material world, etc.

CO-SIGNIFICATOR   In astrology, this term applies to planets and signs having a wind of rotary signification. Thus Aries is a co-significator of all Ascendants, because though it is not a sign ascending it is the first sign of the zodiac, as the Ascendant is the First House in the world.

COSMIC CONSCIOUSNESS   A phenomenon discussed at length by Richard M. Bucke (1837 - 1902) in his book, Cosmic Consciousness: A study of the Evolution of the Human Mind. Consciousness of the order of the universe, described by Walt Whitman as 'ineffable light. . . lighting the very light beyond all signs, descriptions, languages,' appears in exceptional males between the ages of thirty and forty. Cases cited by Bucke include Buddha, Jesus, Plotinus, Dante, Boehme, Balzac, and Whitman. The man who experiences sudden awareness of the meaning of life in the cosmos loses all fear of death as he sees that life is eternal, the soul is immortal, and the whole universe is grounded on love.

This is one of the tenets of Rosicrucianism, which is, according to its announcements, the application of simple, natural laws. It offers to expound the method of indulging in the privacy of one's own home in the mysteries of life as known to the ancients: how to throw off the shackles of the body, how man's mind may be attuned to the Infinite Wisdom, how to experience cosmic consciousness. This is achieved through momentary flights of the soul, resulting in man becoming one with the universe.

COSMIC CROSS   In astrology, two planets in opposition, each squared by a third planet, resulting in a T-square or T-cross. A fourth planet, opposing the third and squaring the first two, forms a Grand Cross. The T-square is a dynamic influence. The Grand Cross tends to diffusion.

COSMIC RHYTHM   The entire cosmic system is founded, in a mystic sense, on rhythm in animate and inanimate nature and in the human sphere in relation to the cosmic scheme. To the Greeks, the visible cosmos was only a manifestation of the spiritual background. The Ego, the soul, and the other members of a human being all have a distinctive rhythm, largely in harmony with the moon. Sickness, according to Greek medical practice in antiquity, was connected with certain rhythmic cycles. Hippocrates the physician stressed the significance of such rhythms relating to the course and duration and climax of a disease.

COSMOLARGY   A new secret system whose headquarters are in Peru, South America. The purpose of the system seems to be to generate a new kind of spiritual body that will be helpful to the physical counterpart.

COSMOS (KOSMOS)   The Greek word *kosmos* ('order') is used esoterically to signify the indwelling Boundless Life that expresses itself in myriad forms responsible for the infinite variety and unity in diversity of the world around us.

COSMOS   In Theosophical teachings, the cosmos means the invisible worlds, planes, and spheres inhabited by countless vitalized or animate beings.

COSTA BEN LUCA   An astrologer who flourished in the ninth century A.D. He wrote on occult themes. During the Middle Ages his influence was marked.

COUNCILLOR GODS   In astrology, this expression was applied by the Chaldeans, to the three bright stars in a constellation, which served to mark the position of the ruling planet of that sign, when in the sign. The expression is not in use nowadays because of the Precession and the availability of the modern Ephemerides.

COUNT OF SAINT-GERMAIN Neither the date nor place of birth of the Count of Saint-Germain is known. He claimed to have lived for two thousand years, to have talked with the Queen of Sheba, and to have discovered the elixir of life. He was in the service of Frederick the Great.

COURT DE GEBELIN, ANTOINE A French scholar who belongs in the eighteenth century. He wrote on the Tarot and its allegorical significance. Author of The Primitive World.

COVEN In modern witchcraft, a coven generally consists of six males, six females, and a high priest or priestess.

CRESCAS, HASDAI (1340-1401) Jewish philosopher. Born in Barcelona, where he was later fined and imprisoned. Authority on Judaic law and ritual tradition. He maintained that 'there are no other worlds' than the one system in which the earth is situated. He instructed thinkers such as Nicholas Cusanus, Giordano Bruno, Marsilio Ficino, Pico della Mirandola. Spinoza too was unquestionably indebted to Crescas for his concept of the universe.

CRESCENT The crescent, in medieval thought, was regarded as a symbol of Paradise.

CRITICAL DAYS In astrology, days which coincide with the formation, by the Moon, directional or transitory, of each successive semi-square or 45 degree aspect, to its position at birth: or at the commencement of any illness, operation, or event under Horary consideration. By noting the position of the Moon at successive crises, aspects thereto will indicate the prognosis. Favorable crises occur at the sextiles of the Moon to its radical place: but the ephemeral aspects it forms while in these positions determine the manner in which the crises will pass and the eventual outcome.

CRITOMANCY   A method of divination by observation of the paste of cakes and the barley flour sprinkled over a sacrificial victim.

CROISET, GERARD   A noted Dutch clairvoyant. He is called the Seer of Holland, and has achieved remarkable results in finding missing persons and in solving crimes by means of his clairvoyant and telepathic powers.

CROOKES, SIR WILLIAM (1832-1919)   English physicist and prolific inventor of scientific apparatus. He also engaged in psychical research.

CROSS   In legend and in religious mysticism, the cross assumes many forms, sometimes highly decorative, but always associated with four directions. It represents life, or activity, or fate.

CROWLEY, ALEISTER (1875-1947)   Crowley was a British Satanist who established a mystic cult based on occultism. In London he founded a Satanic temple, and also in Italy. Editor of an occult periodical, he also produced expositions on magic themes. At his death, a ritual of black magic was performed over his grave by his adherents.

CRYONIZATION   A method of freezing a corpse. The purpose is to maintain the body in that frozen state until a remedy is discovered for the disease that caused death. Then the corpse will be thawed out and, it is assumed, revert to its normal life. Professor Robert Ettinger is a researcher in this new biological field. The Cryonics Society of America, dedicated to the experiment, has branches in California, New York, and elsewhere.

CRYPT ESTHESIA In paranormal psychology, a term used by Professor Charles Robert Richet, the French physiologist and investigator of psychical phenomena. The expression denotes the acquisition of knowledge through abnormal channels, such as clairvoyance and telepathy.

CULMINATION In astrology, when a planet reaches the point of midheaven, this is called the culmination.

CULMINATOR In astrology, a swift-moving planet which in transit reaches a critical position, by conjunction or aspect, and thereby precipitates the externalization of a simultaneous state of displaced equilibrium caused by a lingering aspect from a slow-moving planet.

CUMONT, FRANZ (1868-1947) Belgian scholar. Historian of ancient pagan religions. One of his major works is a study of astrology in ancient Egypt, entitled L'Egypte des Astrologues, published in 1937.

CURRENT LITERATURE The tremendous current interest in psychic, supernatural, and occult phenomena is widespread and continuous, at all levels of society and sophistication. Popular novels, films, monthly magazines and newspapers produce a constant stream of occult episodes, Satanic encounters, first-hand accounts of presumably inexplicable situations involving spirits, witchcraft, and occult practices in their widest applications. The mystery of the flying saucers has created an intense concern about outer space possibilities. Dark beliefs that have haunted men for centuries have sprung into new life. There is a passionate

94

eagerness to discover and test whatever phenomena have been hidden in the heavens, under the dark spaces of the earth, in traditional legends of remote ethnic communities. The scientific mind has in these latter years begun to take a determined and serious interest in all such phenomena. The urgency to probe is desperate. The desire for assurance in what has been for centuries mere untested beliefs and attitudes based on hearsay and unverified records has created a vast almost universal challenge. The secrets of the earth, invisible as well as material, are subject to prolonged and minute investigations. Man is thus continuously questing and what he has already accomplished in this respect is merely a fore-runner of his advancing pilgrimage.

CUSP   In astrology, the imaginary line which separates a sign from adjoining signs, a House from its adjoining Houses. It is also an indeterminate arc, small in size, contiguous to the boundary-line between adjacent signs and Houses, wherein there is uncertainty regarding the planet's location at a particular moment, and ambiguity regarding the planet's influence in a borderline relationship. A birth planet is stronger when it is on the cusp than when it is in the last degrees of a House. The angular cusps are unquestionably the sharpest.

CUTHA TABLET   A Babylonian record associated with the city of Cutha. It contains an account of Creation.

CYCLES   One branch of theosophical study concerns the Law of Cycles, or Nature's repetitive operations. These cyclic operations — the succession of the seasons, the motions of the planets, etc. — are treated as manifestations of profound karmic causes.

CYCLIC RHYTHM   Every eighteen years, seven months and a few days, it is believed mystically, there occurs a particular relationship between a person's soul and the supersensible world. The first cycle occurs at the age of 18-19: then follow these cycles — 37-38; 55-56; 74-75.

CYNOCEPHALIA According to Pliny the Elder, the Roman encyclopedist who flourished in the first century A.D., a certain herb called cynocephalia, which means dog-head, was a protective agent against evil enchantments and poisons. If the herb, however, was plucked out of the ground, instant death followed.

D

DABAR In Hebrew, this term means the Word. In Kabbalistic mysticism, it is equated with the Greek Logos.

DACTYLOMANCY A method of divination by means of various arrangements and positions of finger rings.

DACTYLS Magicians, exorcists, and soothsayers who are supposed to have come from Phrygia and to have discovered the notes of the musical scale.

DAGGATUM These are Moroccan nomads of Jewish origin. They live among the Touareg, but do not assimilate with them.

DAIVIPRAKRITI A Sanskrit word meaning divine matter or substance. In Oriental occultism, it is the first veil of the Logos, or matter in its first and second stages of evolution from above.

DAVA In the Tibetan astrological system, this term denotes the Moon.

DAVIS, ANDREW JACKSON (1826-1910) The trance utterances of Andrew Jackson Davis were transcribed and published under the title The Principles of Nature, Her Divine Revelations, and a Voice of Mankind. Published in 1847, the book went through thirty-four editions in less than thirty years. It sets forth a mystical philosophy, discusses the Bible and Christ, and advocates a system of socialism. Davis believed that he was controlled by Swedenborg, whose views permeate the book. Later he was able to recall his trance utterances and to write books in his own hand.

DAY OF YAHWEH A day popularly anticipated, between the time of King Solomon and Amos, when Yahweh would bring unprecedented prosperity, intervene to eliminate foreign enemies, and reestablish his nation on a scale surpassing King Solomon's reign.
Amos and his successors reversed this interpretation. Yahweh would come, but to punish his sinful nation by immediate military conquest.
In post-exilic times the Day of Yahweh referred to the Day of Judgment.

DAY TRIPLICITY In astrology, it was considered that in the daytime some planets are stronger when posited in signs of a certain element: i.e., Saturn in an air-sign, the Sun in a fire-sign, Mars in a water-sign, Venus in an earth-sign.

DEAD SEA In Biblical tradition, this is the sea that was created by the flooding of Sodom and Gomorrah. To the Arabs, it is known as the sea of Lot.

DEATH In the Story of San Michele, Dr. A. Munthe asserted that hypnotism in the case of a dying person exerted a soothing influence.

DEATH BY SORCERY In many parts of the world individuals are said to have died by exorcism and the casting of spells. Standing aloof from others in his community, the doomed individual finds that everyone else accepts his impending departure. Sacred rites are performed to hasten his journey to the land of the dead. Banished, obsessed, and terrified, the victim of the sorcerer's art accepts his fate.

DECAN In astrology, ten degrees of each zodiacal sign are dedicated to a planet which assumes influence when it passes through this ten-degree space. This ten-degree space is called a decan. There are thirty-six degrees at ten degrees. In these the planets, except the Sun and the Moon, alternate.

DECILE In astrology, an aspect formed when planets are thirty-six degrees apart. It has a slightly benefic influence.

DECUMBITURE In astrology, this term denotes: lying down. A horary figure erected for the moment when a person is taken ill, wherefrom to judge the possible nature, prognosis and duration of the illness.

DEDUCTIVE TYPE In astrology, this expression refers to a certain quality or habit of mind that characterizes those born when the Sun was in a Mutable sign: Gemini, Virgo, Sagittarius, or Pisces.

DEE, JOHN Dr. John Dee (1527-1608) was an English mathematician who traveled to Europe to study astrology, alchemy, and other occult phases. He was imprisoned on charges of practicing enchantments against Queen Mary of England. Later, he was pardoned and sent on government service: during this time he collaborated with a certain Edward Kelley, reputed to be an occultist. Dr. Dee was the author of a Liber Mysteriorum, The Book of Mysteries. He was credited with communication with the dead by means of crystallomancy.

DEGREE RISING In astrology, the degree of the zodiacal sign posited on the Ascendant, or cusp of the First House at birth, and generally considered the most important in the Nativity. The rising degree is based on the exact moment of birth, or of the event for which the Figure is cast, and the correct geographical latitude and longitude. If either factor is unknown the Figure is usually cast for sunrise, which places the Sun's degree upon the horizon, resulting in a Solar Figure. As it is based only on the earth's apparent motion around the Sun, some astrologers term it a Heliard Figure.

DEGREES In astrology, the celestial globe is marked by 360 degrees and each of the twelve signs of the zodiac is consequently thirty degrees.

DEHA In Hindu mysticism, this term denotes the body. Man has three bodies: the dense body, the subtle body, and and a causal body.

DEIKNYMENA This expression, that stems from the Eleusinian mystery cult, refers to esoteric truths taught by demonstration in the secret ceremonies.

DEJA ENTENDU A French expression meaning already heard. This term refers to the feeling that sounds or voices have been heard in the past, despite the impossibility.

DEJA VU A French expression meaning already seen. This term refers to the feeling that a person, place, or object has been seen in the past, despite its impossibility.

DEJECTION A term used in astrology to denote the position of greatest weakness of the Sun and the Moon and the other planets.

DEMIURGOS A Greek Platonic expression used by Philo Judaeus, the Hellenistic-Jewish philosopher, for the Creator.

DEMONOLOGY That branch of learning dealing with malevolent spirits. The Greek term *daimon* meant genius or spirit, but the word demon today means a wicked spirit. According to Michael Psellus, demons are grouped in six great classes: (1) demons of fire; (2) demons of the air; (3) earth demons; (4) those inhabiting the waters of the earth; (5) subterranean demons who cause earthquakes and volcanic eruptions; and (6) shadows.

DEMON PREACHER In Scottish history there is a reference to a certain Dr. John Fian, a notable sorcerer. In a church at North Berwick he was credited with repeatedly preaching to a number of notorious witches. Brought to trial and convicted of consorting with Satan, he was burned at the stake in Edinburgh, in 1591.

DEPRESSION In astrology, the distance of a celestial body below the horizon: its horizontal distance north.

DESCENT INTO HADES In legends and myths of many nations, both human beings and divinities are able to descend into the Lower Regions, the home of the dead. Such myths were prevalent among the Babylonians, the Egyptians, Greeks, and Romans. The purpose of such descents was varied. Sometimes the living wished to ask a favor from the dead, or to visit deceased relatives, or to control or conciliate the spirits of the Underworld.
In medieval religious literature, in miracle plays and in art, the Descent into Hell became a popular theme.

D'ESPERANCE, ELIZABETH (1855-1919) A medium whose experiences are recounted in William Oxley's Angelic Revelations and in her own Shadow Land. The strangest phenomenon of her mediumship relates to dematerialization. The lower part of her body is supposed to have dematerialized.

DETRIMENT In astrology, the placement of a planet in the opposite sign from that of which it is said to be the Ruler. Frequently the term is applied to Debility by sign position, which includes the opposite sign to that which it is in its Exaltation, as well as to those of which it is Ruler.

DEUTEROSCOPY A technical term for what is popularly called second-sight.

DEVA A Sanskrit word, related etymologically to the English word deity. In Hinduism and Buddhism, the word signifies a divine being. In Zoroastrianism, it means a maleficent supernatural being. In esoteric Oriental teachings, Devas are the unselfconscious sparks of Divinity that penetrate matter in order to bring about selfconsciousness of inherent Divinity.

DEVACHAN A Sanskrit word used in Oriental mysticism to designate the state between earth lives into which the human monad enters after the physical body dies. In this divine region the monad rests in bliss.

DEVI The mother goddess worshipped by the Shaktas as the personification of the female creative principle of the universe.

DEVIL In the Tarot pack of cards, the Devil is the fifteenth mystery. In its form, this card combines the four primal elements of fire, air, water, earth.

DEWI SRI The rice goddess to whom the Balinese make offerings to insure a good harvest.

DEXTER In astrology, this term is applied to an aspect which is computed backward, against the order of the signs;

in which the aspected body is elevated above the aspecting body.

DHARANA A Sanskrit word denoting a state in the practice of Yoga. In this state the mind is firmly fixed upon the object of investigation.

DHARMA In Hindu mythology, a sage whose numerous progeny personify virtues and religious rites. Dharma is worshipped as the supreme God in Bengal. In Hinduism and Buddhism, dharma means religious law, duty, or social function. Hindus who derive their faith from the Vedas and the Upanishads refer to it as *manava dharma* (religion of man), *dharma* (perennial religion), or *arsha dharma* (religion founded by the rishis).

DHARMAKAYA A Sanskrit term signifying the glorified spiritual body. In Hindu mysticism, a state of illuminated consciousness.

DHYANA A Sanskrit term signifying deep contemplation and complete detachment from the material world. In Buddhism, it is one of the six Paramitas of perfection.

DHYAN-CHOHANS In Oriental esoteric teachings, the Sanskrit word meaning 'Lords of Meditation' refers to Cosmic Spirits or Planetary Spirits, three classes of men who have achieved perfection during former manvantaras and guide the evolution of the earth in its present manvantara.

DIABOLIC ENCOUNTER John of Tynemouth, who belongs in the fourteenth century, describes how a saint was tempted by a fiend:
When St. Godric paused, weary from his labor, a stranger, standing by, observed him for a long while. Then he spoke thus: "Did the Fathers of old whom you believe you are imitating thus labor in the desert, wan and hungry? Look!

103

From morning to night you have scarcely dug five feet of soil, when you ought to show your devotion to the Lord by the amount of your labor."

Smilingly, the man of God answered him: "You, then, first show me an example of good work." For Godric thought that the man was righteous, sent by the Lord to teach him. And so, handing him the spade, he said: "The hour of my usual spell of prayer compels me to return to the oratory. I shall come back and listen to you and I will willingly hear what you are good enough to explain." The other quickly seized the spade and energetically began to turn the soil. When Godric came back he found that more work had been accomplished than he was wont to finish in eight days. Then the other man spoke thus: "You ought to have emulated the example of the Fathers, with much sweat and labor."

The holy man shuddered, for he realized that the man was not a real man. He was quite dark and hairy and very tall and for all his labor he showed not a single sign of sweat or effort.

Godric returned to his cell and, taking a book with him, he went back and said: "Tell me who you are and for what purpose you have come here."

The other replied: "Don't you see that I am a man like yourself?"

"If you are a man," said Godric, "tell me whether you believe in the Father, the Son, and the Holy Ghost, and adore along with me the Mother of my Lord."

The other man said: "Don't worry about my belief. Your question does not concern me."

And Godric, going up to him, took out the book containing pictures of the Savior and Holy Mary and St. John, and quickly thrusting it in the man's face, said: "Behold, if you believe in God, kiss these pictures devoutly."

Unable to cope with this, the man spat out a kind of spittle on the book and disappeared mockingly.

DIABOLIC HELP A medieval tale, one of the collection of miraculous incidents compiled by Caesar of Heisterbach in the thirteenth century, runs as follows:

There was a young scholar in the Church of St. Simeon, in the diocese of Treves. One day he was given a theme by his master. He was sitting sadly, unable to compose a poem on the given subject, when the devil appeared to him in the form of a man. The devil asked: "What is the trouble, boy?"

The boy replied: "I am afraid of my master, because I can't write my verses on the subject he gave me." "Do you want to do homage to me? I'll do your verses."

The boy did not realize the devil's evil intention and answered:

"Yes, master. I'm ready to do what you order me, provided I have the verses and won't get whipped."

He did not know who the man was. At once the devil dictated the lines. The boy did not see him any more.

When he gave the verses at the proper time to his master, the latter was amazed at their excellence.

"Tell me," he said, "who dictated these verses to you?" "I did them myself," the boy said. But the master insisted. Then the boy confessed everything.

The master said:

"My boy, that wicked man who dictated the verses was of course the devil. Do you repent for having paid homage to him?"

"Yes," said the boy.

"Then renounce the devil and all his works," ordered the master.

And the boy did so.

DIAKKA In occultism, this is a malefic spirit that is of low development. It passes through a process of higher evolution in the course of time.

DIBBUK In cabbalistic lore, the dibbuk is the spirit of the dead. It can enter the body of a living person.

DICE Among the multiple techniques of divination and fortune-telling, the throwing of dice is one of the most ancient devices, and was well known in antiquity, particularly among the Romans.

DICHOTOME In astrology, this expression of Greek origin, meaning cut in half, is applied to that phase of the lunar orb, or of an inferior planet, in which only half of its disc appears illuminated, that is, the First and Third Quarters, in which the body is assuming the shape of a half-moon, and in which the Moon is said to be oriental.

DIGNITIES AND DEBILITIES In astrology, conditions of placement wherein a planet's influence is strengthened are called Dignities; if weakened, they are called Debilities. These are of two kinds: essential and accidental.

DIONYSIUS THE AREOPAGITE Converted to Christianity by St. Paul. In the Theologia Mystica, possibly erroneously ascribed to Dionysius, there is an exposition of Christianity in relation to Neoplatonism.

DIRECTIONS (Also PROGRESSIONS) In astrology, these expressions refer to the changing influences resulting from the various moving bodies of the solar system as they affect the individual through the sensitive points produced by the impact of planetary rays during his first year of life. There are three basic systems of calculation: Transits, Primary Directions, Secondary Progressions.

DISC WORSHIP In antiquity, a form of sun-worship: prevalent in Mesopotamia, Egypt, and other regions, including Mexico.

DISEMBODIED STATE In yoga, when a person thinks of himself, there is a corresponding thought of oneself as embodied or objective. To be without such a thought is to be in a state of excorporeal reality. The reference is to the mind functioning apart from the body, in astral movement, for instance, and to the insight wherein the mind functions without thinking of itself.

DISPOSITOR In astrology, this term denotes the Ruler of the Sign on the cusp of a House, who is the dispositor of a planet posited in that House. When the dispositor of any planet taken as a significator is itself disposed of by the Ruler of the Ascendant, it is considered a strongly favorable indication.

DISSOCIATE SIGNS In astrology, these are adjacent signs and signs that are five signs apart: those which bear to each other a twelfth, second, sixth, or eighth House relationship.

DIVINATION Divination, the technique of presumably gaining knowledge of future or otherwise unknown events, was practiced from the earliest times on record, through the Biblical period down to the immediate present. Divination is prevalent in all countries, and at all intellectual levels. It assumed a great variety of forms. In the eleventh century B.C. in I Sam. 2.8.3. Saul prohibited divination by necromancy. All kinds of diviners, including interpreters of dreams, sorcerers, necromancers, were condemned by the major prophets.

DIVINE APPROACH In Hindu mysticism, there are four stages in the approach to the Deity: nearness, similarity, being with, conjunction.

DIVINE, FATHER An American Negro, whose original name was George Baker. He founded a Peace Mission movement. His followers accepted him as a personification of God.

His original 'Heaven' in Sayville, Long Island, was a communal dwelling established in 1919. His group expanded rapidly until his Kingdom of Peace included many 'Heavens' and owned property valued at $10 million. He did not allow his followers to smoke, drink liquor, or use cosmetics. He was born in Hutchinson's Island, Georgia, probably in 1877, and died in Philadelphia, Pennsylvania, in 1965.

DIVINE GUIDANCE   A popular magazine invites, in one of its advertisements, prospective clients, who require guidance, to consult the Goddess Athena.

DIVINE SOUL   In occult teachings, the divine soul clothes the divine ego, as the divine ego clothes the divine monad or Inner God.

DIVINING ROD   A branch or rod which is reputed to lead the possessor to an underground spot where water and minerals appear. The practice of using such a rod is termed dowsing. The dowser may use the rod to trace missing persons as well.

DIVISION OF THE WORLD   In antiquity, the world was divided in relation to the four celestial quarters. In the South was Babylonia: in the North, Assyria. The West was Persia; the East, Syria and Palestine.

DIXON, JEANE   A Washington real-estate broker who has gained great popularity as a seeress. According to her admirers, for more than a quarter of a century she has had an uncanny ability to predict events. 'The Gift of Prophecy,' which glosses over her false predictions and extols the accurate ones, has sold almost three million copies.

DJADID UL-ISLAM This Arabic expression means New Moslems. They are a small sect of crypto-Jews or Marranos. In 1738, in the town of Meshed in Persia, they were forced to accept Mohammedanism. Secretly, however, they continued to observe Jewish ritual.

DOBU In the South Sea island of Dobu the natives, in the 1930's, still used incantations to discover cases of theft and adultery, and also to induce sickness.

DOMAL DIGNITY In astrology, this term describes a planet when it tenants its own sign. A planet so placed was described in ancient astrology as 'domiciliated.'

DONMEH This expression means renegades. They were a Judeo-Moslem sect descended from the followers of the false Messiah Shabbatai Zevi.

DOPPELGANGER A German term meaning a double. In occultism, this was the astral body, like the Egyptian Ka.

DORYPHORY In astrology, this is a Ptolemaic term that describes a planet which serves as a sort of bodyguard to the Sun, rising shortly before it — either in the same or the contiguous sign. The doryphory of the Moon similarly rises after it.

DOUBLE The age-old belief in the existence of an etheric or astral counterpart of the physical body capable of independent movement in space is used to explain cases such as the following: Alphonse de Liguori was imprisoned in his cell at Arezzo for five days. During this period he supposedly was seen in Rome, at the bedside of the dying Pope. Similar experiences are recorded by Goethe, Shelley, Maupassant, and Swedenborg.

DOUBLE CUBE This is a figure whose length equals twice its breadth and height. King Solomon's Temple was traditionally regarded as having this form.

DOUBLE TRIANGLE In Pythagorean mathematical symbolism, the double triangle represented health.

DOWSING The practice of searching for underground metals and water supplies, even missing objects and persons, by means of a divining rod.
The practice has long historical traditions that go back to the Middle Ages. It is performed successfully too among primitive tribes. It has furthermore a roster of notable persons who have been dowsers, in France and Britain and in other countries. British Columbia, Canada, and the Government of India had official dowsers whose func· tion was to discover water supplies.
In 1933 the British Society of Dowsers was founded. It publishes literature and a periodical relating to all phases of the subject.
The rod used in dowsing may be of wood or metal, forked, straight, twisted. Sometimes even the hands of the dowser are sufficient to sense the presence of water. The rod has been called Jacob's Rod, a Magic Rod, a Divining Wonder.

DOYLE, SIR ARTHUR CONAN (1858-1930) The famed creator of Sherlock Holmes is known also as the 'St. Paul of Spiritualism.' After studying the subject for a third of a century, he published The New Revelation and allied himself with spiritualism.

DRAGON'S HEAD, DRAGON'S TAIL In astrology, these are points or nodes in which the ecliptic is intersected by the orbits of the planets. The Dragon's Tail is a point where a planet begins its northern latitude. The Dragon's Tail is a point where a planet begins its southern course.

DREAMS To the ancients, particularly the Greeks, dreams were a link between the actual immediate state and the future. Dreams were regarded as prognostications of coming events, and were so interpreted, especially by the Greek priest-physicians. Dreams were recorded in temples so that use might be made of them when identical dreams occurred. A famous dream book, which included interpretations, was produced by Artemidorus Daldianus, who belongs in the second century A.D.

In Biblical literature, dreams are tantamount to prognostications. References to such dreams occur in Genesis 20.3: Genesis 31.23: Genesis 37.5: Job 33.15: Numbers 12.6: I Kings 3.5.

The Greek historian Xenophon discusses dreams as a means of divination.

According to Sigmund Freud in his The Interpretation of Dreams, the dream is the fulfillment of a wish.

The supernatural character of dreams is suggested by J. W. Dunne's experiences. Dunne kept a careful record of his dreams and found that many of them anticipated future experiences.

DREAM WORK The manner in which dreams are formed as well as the elements contributing to their composition. Most prominent among these elements are: memories, emotions, and wishes.

DRUIDS The Druids were the ancient priests, teachers, and judges in Gaul. They practiced divination and other occult techniques.

The Druids appear in Julius Caesar's description of Gaul in his Commentaries on the Gallic War. In Celtic literature they are sorcerers, skilled in spell-binding, incantations, augury, dream interpretation. They could control the weather, induce storms, snow, mists. They were also capable of walking unharmed across burning beds of coal, and had communication with animal language. Their powers included the ability to change their own form and to enchant men into new forms. For the purpose of such transformations they used a wand of rowan, hawthorn, oak, or yew.

In the Hebridean Islands, off the West coast of Scotland, there are the reputed sites of Druid altars dedicated to human sacrifices.

DRUID STONES The two vertical stones of the Druid trilithons, covered by the horizontal stone, symbolize, in ancient Druid worship, two cosmic forces.

DRUSES A religious sect in Southern Syria. Their location is in the Haurian Hills and Mount Lebanon. They practice esoteric rites and call themselves the Disciples of Hamsa. Hamsa appeared to them as a prophet, a Messiah, in the ninth century.

DUMAH In Hebraic mysticism, this name refers to the angel involved in the silence of death.

DUMB SIGNS In astrology, mute signs: Cancer, Scorpio, Pisces. One of them on the Ascendant and Mercury afflicted, or Mercury aspected by a malefic posited in one of them is cited as the possible cause of speech impediment.

DU POTET, BARON JULES DENIS SENNEVOY A Frenchman who in the nineteenth century was one of the early investigators of spiritualism. He also related animal magnetism to the occult arts. He experimented with paranormal manifestations such as stigmata, trance-speaking, and clairvoyance.

DWELLER In occultism, this term denotes the astral counterpart of a dead person. The dweller is malefic in intent.

DYBBUK In Jewish folklore, this term denotes a wandering spirit or soul that enters a human body. It leaves the living body of the victim only when it is properly exorcised. Belief in the dybbuk became widespread in the sixteenth century. A particular legend is associated with a Jewish woman who had become possessed of a dybbuk. Following ancient ritual, devout men of the synagogue performed the dramatic exorcism. The phenomenon was in recent times presented on the stage. A. Anski's play achieved wide popularity.

DYSIS In astrological terminology, the dysis is the western angle or point of setting.

E

EAGLE In astrology, a small constellation located approximately Capricorn twenty-nine degrees. Sometimes called the Vulture.
Frequently associated with the sign Scorpio. By the Greeks and Persians, the Eagle was held sacred to the Sun and Jupiter.

EARTH AXIS In a popular magazine an advertisement announces a coming shift in the axis of the earth. This shift, it is predicted, will cause oceans to overrun and will be highly destructive to life.

EARTH-PLANET In mysticism, there are seven stages in the earth-planet. They are designated as follows:
the Polarian period,
the Hyperborean period,
Lemurian period,
Atlantean period,
the Seven Seals,
the Seven Trumpets.

EARTH SIGNS Those of the Earth Triplicity: Taurus, Virgo, Capricorn. The ancients symbolized these types by the Earth element, because of their predominant Earthiness or practicality.

EASTERN CHURCH The Eastern Orthodox Church has always practiced exorcism in the case of persons possessed by evil spirits. The practice of exorcism is still in operation.

ECKANKAR In a popular magazine Eckankar is advertised as an ancient science of Soul Travel. It offers instruction in out-of-the-body projection.

ECKHART, MEISTER (1260-1327) A German Dominican monk who was a mystic. He wrote on the nature of the soul. He is called the Father of German Mysticism.

ECLIPSE OF THALES May 28, 585 B.C. Predicted by Thales of Miletus. It stopped a battle in the war between the Medes and the Lydians. Among other historic eclipses were: eclipse which occurred at noon in the first year of the Peloponnesian War, when several stars became visible: traditional date — August 3, 432 B.C.: eclipse which occurred when Agathocles, King of Syracuse, was sailing with his fleet toward Africa, on August 15, 310 B.C. On the day of a solar eclipse, March 7, 51 B.C. Caesar crossed the Rubicon.

ECLIPTIC In astrology, the most significant part that gives the astrologer his answers to his calculations is the ecliptic or the Sun's trajectory. It rises in the East at the moment of birth or any undertaking which is subjected to the casting of a horoscope.

ECLIPTIC: VIA SOLIS, THE SUN'S PATH The Sun's apparent orbit or path around the Earth. Or the orbit of the Earth as viewed from the Sun. So named because it is along this path, at the points where it intersects the Equator, the eclipses occur.

ECTENIC FORCE A physical force postulated by Count Agenor de Gasparin to explain rapping and table-turning. It is supposed to emanate from a person and be subject to his will.

ECTOPLASM In spiritualism, this term denotes the proto-plasmic substance that is materialized from the body of a medium.

EDISON, THOMAS ALVA (1847-1931) In his Diary, Edison, the famous American inventor, makes a number of obser-vations on human conduct, ambitions, hopes, experiences. On the Life after Death, he writes:

The thing which first struck me was the absurdity of expecting "spirits" to waste their time operating such cumbrous, unscientific media as tables, chairs, and the ouija board with its letters. My convinced belief is merely that if ever the question of life after death, or pyschic phenomena generally, is to be solved, it will have to be put on a scientific basis, as chemistry is put, and withdrawn from the hands of the charlatan and the "medium."

My business has been, and is, to give the scientific inves-tigator — or, for that matter, the unscientific — an ap-paratus which, like the compass of the seaman, will put their investigations upon a scientific basis. This apparatus may perhaps most readily be described as a sort of valve. In exactly the same way as a megaphone increases many times the volume and carrying power of the human voice, so with my "valve," whatever original force is used upon it is increased enormously for purposes of registration of the phenomena behind it. It is exactly on the lines of the tiny valve which in a modern power-house can be operated by the finger of a man and so release a hundred thousand horse-power.

Now, I don't make any claims whatever to prove that the human personality survives what we call "death." All I claim is that any effort caught by my apparatus will be magnified many times, and it does not matter how slight is the effort, it will be sufficient to record whatever there is to be recorded.

Frankly, I do not accept the present theories about life and death. I believe, rightly or wrongly, that life is undestructible, it is true, and I also believe that there has always been a fixed quantity of life on this planet, and that this quantity can neither be increased nor decreased. But that does not mean that I believe the survival of personality has been proved — as yet. Perhaps it may be one day. Perhaps some apparatus upon the lines of my "valve" may prove it, but that day is not yet, nor have I as yet secured any results to definitely prove such survival.

What I believe is that our bodies are made up of myriads of units of life. Our body is not itself *the* unit of life or *a* unit of life. It is the tiny entities which may be the cells that are the units of life.

Everything that pertains to life is still living, and cannot be destroyed. Everything that pertains to life is still subject to the laws of animal life. We have myriads of cells, and it is the inhabitants in these cells, inhabitants which themselves are beyond the limits of the microscope, which vitalize and "run" our body.

To put it in another way, I believe that these life units of which I have spoken band themselves together in countless millions and billions in order to make a man. We have too facilely assumed that each one of us is himself a unit, just as we have assumed that the horse or dog is each a unit of life. This, I am convinced, is wrong thinking. The fact is that these "life-units" are too tiny to be seen even by the most high-powered microscope, and so we have assumed that the unit is the man which we can see, and have ignored the existence of the real life-units, which are those we cannot see.

There is nothing to prevent these entities from carrying on the varied work of the human body. I have had the calculations made, and the theory of the electron is, in my view, satisfactory, and makes it quite possible to have a highly organized and developed entity like the

118

human body made up of myriads of electrons, themselves invisible.

Further, I believe that these life-units themselves possess memory. If a man burns his hand, the skin will grow in exactly the same pattern again, and with the same lines as the hand originally had before the accident. Now, it would be quite impossible for those hundreds of fine lines to be meticulously reproduced if there were no memory for detail behind the rebuilding of them. The skin does not grow that way and in exactly the same pattern again "by chance." There is no chance.

But are all these life-units, or entities, possessed of the same memory, or are some, so to speak, the builders' labourers, and are others the units which direct those labourers?

It may be that the great mass of them are workers and a tiny minority directors of the work. That is not a matter about which we can speak with any certainty.

But what one can say with some assurance is that these entities cannot be destroyed, and that there is a fixed number of them. They may assemble and reassemble in a thousand different forms from a starfish to a man, but they are the same entities.

No man today can set the line as to where "life" begins and ends. Even in the formation of crystals we see a definite ordered plan at work. Certain solutions will always form a particular kind of crystal, without variation. It is not impossible that these life-entities are at work in the mineral and plant, as in what we call the "animal" world.

In connection with the problem of life after death, the thing that matters is what happens to what one may call the "master" entities — those that direct the others. Eighty-two remarkable operations on the brain have definitely proved that the seat of our personality lies in that part of the brain known as the fold of Broca. It is not unreasonable to suppose that these entities which direct reside within this fold.` The supreme problem is what becomes of these master entities after what we call death, when they leave the body.

The point is whether these directing entities remain together after the death of the body in which they have been residing, or whether they go about the universe after breaking up. If they break up and no longer remain as an ensemble, then it looks to me that our personality does not survive death; that is, we do not survive death as individuals.

If they do break up and do not remain together after the death of the body, then that would mean that the eternal life which so many of us earnestly desire would not be the eternal life and persistence of the individual, as individual, but would be an impersonal eternal life — for, whatever happens to the life-units, or whatever forms they may assume, it is at least assured that they themselves live forever.

I do hope myself that personality survives and that we persist. If we do persist upon the other side of the grave, then my apparatus, with its extraordinary delicacy, should one day give us the proof of that persistence, and so of our own eternal life.

Again, on spiritualism, he has these comments to offer:

A great deal is being written and said about spiritualism these days, but the methods and apparatus used are just a lot of unscientific nonsense. I don't say that all these so-called mediums are simply fakers scheming to fool the public and line their own pockets. Some of them may be sincere enough. They may really have gotten themselves into such a state of mind, that they imagine they are in communication with spirits.

I have a theory of my own which would explain scientifically the existence in us of what is termed our "subconscious minds." It is quite possible that those spiritualists who declare they receive communications from another world allow their subconscious minds to predominate over their ordinary, everyday minds, and permit themselves to become, in a sense, hypnotized into thinking that their imaginings are actualities, that what they imagine as occurring, while they are in this mental state, really *has* occurred.

But that we receive communications from another realm of life, or that we have — as yet — any means, or method, through which we could establish this communication, is quite another thing. Certain of the methods now in use are so crude, so childish, so unscientific, that it is amazing how so many rational human beings can take any stock in them. If we ever do succeed in establishing communication with personalities which have left this present life, it certainly won't be through any of the childish contraptions which seem so silly to the scientist.

I have been at work for some time building an apparatus to see if it is possible for personalities which have left this earth to communicate with us. If this is ever accomplished, it will be accomplished, not by any occult, mysterious, or weird means, such as are employed by so-called mediums, but by scientific methods. If what we call personality exists after death, and that personality is anxious to communicate with those of us who are still in the flesh on this earth, there are two or three kinds of apparatus which should make communication very easy. I am engaged in the construction of one such apparatus now, and I hope to be able to finish it before very many months pass.

If those who have left the form of life that we have on earth cannot use, cannot move, the apparatus that I am going to give them the opportunity of moving, then the chance of there being a hereafter of the kind we think about and imagine goes down.

On the other hand, it will, of course, cause a tremendous sensation if it is successful.

I am working on the theory that our personality exists after what we call life leaves our present material bodies. If our personality dies, what's the use of a hereafter? What would it amount to? It wouldn't mean anything to us as individuals. If there is a hereafter which is to do us any good, we want our personality to survive, don't we? If our personality survives, then it is strictly logical and scientific to assume that it retains memory, intellect, and other faculties and knowledge that we acquire on this earth. Therefore, if personality exists, after what we call death, it is reasonable to conclude that those who leave this earth would like to communicate with those they have left here. Accordingly, the thing to do is to furnish the best conceivable means to make it easy for them to open up communication with us, and then see what happens.

I am proceeding on the theory that in the very nature of things, the degree of material or physical power possessed by those in the next life must be extremely slight; and that, therefore, any instrument designed to be used to communicate with us must be super-delicate — as fine and responsive as human ingenuity can make it. For my part, I am inclined to believe that our personality hereafter will be able to affect matter. If this reasoning be correct, then, if we can evolve an instrument so delicate as to be affected, or moved, or manipulated — whichever term you want to use — by our personality as it survives in the next life, such an instrument, when made available, ought to record something.

I cannot believe for a moment that life in the first instance originated on this insignificant little ball which we call the earth — little, that is, in contrast with other bodies which inhabit space. The particles which combined to evolve living creatures on this planet of ours probably came from some other body elsewhere in the universe.

122

I don't believe for a moment that one life makes another life. Take our own bodies. I believe they are composed of myriads and myriads of infinitesimally small individuals, each in itself a unit of life, and that these units work in squads — or swarms, as I prefer to call them — and that these infinitesimally small units live forever. When we "die" these swarms of units, like a swarm of bees, so to speak, betake themselves elsewhere, and go on functioning in some other form or environment.

These life units are, of course, so infinitely small that probably a thousand of them aggregated together would not become visible under even the ultramicroscope, the most powerful magnifying instrument yet invented and constructed by man. These units, if they are as tiny as I believe them to be, would pass through a wall of stone or concrete almost as easily as they would pass through the air.

The more we learn the more we realize that there is life in things which we used to regard as inanimate, as lifeless. We now know that the difference between the lowest-known forms of animal life and trees or flowers or other plants is not so very great.

Small as these units of life are, they could still contain a sufficient number of ultimate particles of matter to form highly organized entities or individuals, with memory, certain varieties of skill, and other attributes of living entities. We, in our ignorance of all that pertains to life, have come to imagine that if certain things happen to a human being or an animal its whole life ceases. This notion has been repeatedly disproved in recent years. The probability is that among units of life there are certain swarms which do most of the thinking and directing for other swarms. In other words, there are probably bosses, or leaders, among them, just as among humans. This theory would account for the fact that certain men and women have greater intellectuality, greater abilities, greater powers than others. It would account, too, for differences in moral character. One individual may be composed of a larger percentage of the higher order of these units of life than others. The moving out of myriads of what we may call the lower type of units of life and the influx of myriads of units of a higher order would explain the change which often takes place in the personality and character of individuals in the course of their existence on this earth.

The doctors long ago told us that our whole bodies undergo complete transformation every seven years, that no particle that entered into the composition of our bodies at the beginning of one seven-year period remains in our bodies at the end of seven years later. This means that matter is discarded, new matter being replaced by the working life-units or individuals. This rough-and-ready way of describing the discarding of defective matter that is constantly going on in our make-up would not be inconsistent with the theory I have evolved.

A common saying is, "We are creatures of environment." This is true, at least up to a certain point. We have seen how environment has wrought changes upon animals, and even wiped out certain species altogether — as the discovery of numerous skeletons of mammoth animals of prehistoric days has proved. Units of life, it is perfectly reasonable to deduce, require certain environment to function in certain ways, and when environment undergoes complete change, they seek other habitats, other dwellings, so to speak, for the carrying on of their functions.

Numerous experiments conducted by medical scientists have revealed that the memory is located in a certain section of the human brain called the fold of Broca. Now, to return to what is called "life after death." If the units of life which compose an individual's memory hold together after that individual's "death," is it not within range of possibility, to say the least, that these memory swarms could retain the powers they formerly possessed, and thus retain what we call the individual's personality

124

after "dissolution" of the body? If so, then that individual's memory, or personality, ought to be able to function as before.

I am hopeful, therefore, that by providing the right kind of instrument, to be operated by this personality, we can receive intelligent messages from it in its changed habitation, or environment.

EDMONDS, JOHN WORTH (1816 - 1874) A distinguished jurist and influential American spiritualist who first became interested in the supernatural on learning of the Rochester knockings in January, 1851. He investigated the mysterious rapping sounds heard near Rochester by the Fox sisters, seeking to prove imposture. Convinced of the existence of supernatural forces, he announced his conversion to spiritualism in a public statement issued on August 1, 1853. He developed the gift of mediumship and received communications from Bacon, Swedenborg, and others. He was largely responsible for the growth and spread of spiritualism in America.

E D N In the Rosicrucian mystic system, these letters represent the Latin words: Ex Deo Nascimur — Out of God we are born.

EGBO An occult cult that was in operation in West Africa.

EGG In mystic religions and ancient cults, the egg represented the concept of immortality.

EGGREGORE A collective phenomenon. Occultists refer to the evocation of images such as flying saucers and the suns of Fatima as eggregori.

EGKOSMICI In Neoplatonic philosophy, this Greek expression refers to the intercosmic gods.

EGLINTON, WILLIAM (b. 1857) An English medium who was credited by spiritualists with producing direct spirit writing under absolute test conditions and with effecting the levitation of his body.

E G O In theosophical writings, the Latin word meaning 'I' is used to designate consciousness reflected back upon itself and thus enabled to recognize its own mayavi existence as a separate entity.

EGYPTIAN ASTROLOGY In ancient Egypt, Virgo, the zodiacal sign, represented the goddess Isis. It was also a hermaphroditic symbol.

EGYPTIAN CALENDAR In 4241 B.C. the Egyptian calendar was introduced. It consisted of twelve months of thirty days each, plus five feast days.

EGYPTIAN UNDERWORLD In the Egyptian Book of the Dead, a manual and guide for the spirits of the dead passing through the Lower Regions, there are reckoned to be 4,601,200 spirits who are concerned with the future life of a deceased person in the Lower Regions.

EIDOLON The Greek word meaning image is used in occultism to denote the astral image that coheres for a while in the astral realms following the physical death of a man. The eidolon fades out as the physical body disintegrates.

EIGHT In antiquity this number symbolized justice, as it is divided evenly into 4 and 4, then again into 2 and 2, then into 1 and 1. Among the ancient Hebrews eight was associated with purification after a state of uncleanness. This number is also ceremonially linked with festivals and special rituals.

EIGHTH HOUSE   In astrology, the Eighth House is the House of Death. It belongs to the sign of Scorpio.

EIGHTH SPHERE   In occultism, this expression denotes a sphere beyond the seven evolutionary stages. It is located mystically between the earth and the moon.

EIGHT TRIGRAMS (PAKUA)   The arrangements of divided and undivided lines forming the basis of the I Ching. These trigrams symbolize the eight fundamental elements of the universe and the attributes associated with them: Ch'ien is Heaven, father, strength; K'un is Earth, mother, docility; Chen is thunder, the eldest son, movement; Sun is wood and wind, the eldest daughter, penetration; K'an is water and the moon, the second son, danger; Li is fire and sun, the second daughter, brightness; Ken is the mountain, the youngest son, stand-still; Tui is the marsh, the youngest daughter, pleasure.

EIGHTY-ONE   This number, which represents nine multiplied by itself, is a significant number in Freemasonry.

EL   In the Kabbalistic numerological system called Gematria, this is the Hebraic appellation of God.

ELDED HA - DANI   A Jewish traveler who belongs in the ninth century. He wrote imaginative tales of the lost Ten Tribes living in Ethiopia and encircled by a fabled river called the Sambatyon.

ELEMENTALS   In occultism, these are beings below man and possess no physical bodies. There are four classes. Salamanders live in fire. Undines inhabit water. Gnomes dwell in the earth. The domain of sylphs is the air.

ELEMENTAL SPIRITS Belief in such beings goes back to early antiquity, to Assyrian incantations, to Egyptian rituals. One of the chapters in the Egyptian Book of the Dead is entitled: The Chapter of Knowing the Spirits of the West.

ELEMENTARIES In theosophical writings, these are the disembodied souls of the depraved. They have lost all hope of immortality.

ELEVEN In mystic numerology, this number represents imperfection.

ELEVENTH HOUSE In astrology, this term refers to loyalty, friends. It is governed by the sign of Aquarius.

ELLIOTSON, JOHN (1788-1868) An English physician who experimented with somnambulism and became the first major exponent of animal magnetism in London.

ELONGATION A common manifestation of the medium at a spiritualistic seance. The medium is supposed to stretch his body until his height is increased from a few inches to a foot. Home and other well known mediums have been credited with the ability to manifest elongation.

EMBOLISMIC MONTH In astrology, this denotes embolismic lunation. An intercalary month used in some ancient calendars, whereby to preserve a seasonal relationship between the lunar and solar calendar.

EMERALD TABLET An emerald tablet of magic significance. The ancient tradition was that it was found by Alexander the Great in the tomb of Hermes Trismegistus. There are extant Latin and Arabic versions of the original Phoenician contents of the tablet. The text is contained in the Leyden Papyrus.

EMOTIONS AND MUSIC   In antiquity there was a belief that various types of emotion were conditioned by the different musical scales or modes.

ENCAUSSE, GERARD   The author of several treatises on magic and the occult sciences (The Tarot of the Gypsies, Methodical Treaty of Occult Sciences, The Kabbala, The Knowledge of the Magi), Gerard Encausse is said to have predicted the failure of the German attack at Verdun in World War I. He founded a theosophical group known as Isis and is also known as Papus.

END OF DAYS   In Judaic tradition, this is the Day of Judgment, involving the Battle of Gog and Magog, the coming of the Messiah, resurrection, eternal peace.

ENERGUMEN   In Catholicism, this term applies to a person possessed by the devil.

ENGLEBRECHT, JOHN   A seventeenth-century seer whose ecstatic visions were published in Brunswick, Germany, in 1640. He foresaw the events unfolded by the French Revolution.

ENOCH   The seventh of the ten antediluvian patriarchs mentioned in Genesis. The Biblical record relates that he lived three hundred and sixty-five years. This record furnished the motif for two Jewish, post-Biblical, non-canonical, apocalyptic books. Both of them describe the travels of Enoch, under divine guidance, through the entire earth and the seven heavens. The divine revelation came to him regarding all the mysteries of heaven and earth. He in turn would reveal them to mankind. The older and larger book, usually designated I Enoch, was of composite authorship, written in Palestine, probably in Aramic, between the third and first century B.C. It is preserved complete in an Ethiopic translation only, though some fragments of the ancient Greek version likewise exist. II Enoch was probably written in Egypt, in Greek, during the first half century A.D. It has survived only in a Slavonic translation.

In occultism, Enoch is identical with the Egyptian Thoth, the Phoenician Cadmus, and the Greek Palamedes.

EN SOPH   In Kabbalistic writings the En Soph (literally, 'without end') is the Infinite One, or God.

EPACT   In astrology, this term, of Greek origin, is applied to a number that indicates the Moon's age on the first day of the year. As the common solar year is 365 days, and the lunar year 354 days, the difference of eleven indicates that if a new moon falls on January 1st in any year, it will be eleven days old on the first day of the next year, and twenty-two days old on the first of the third year. Hence the epacts of those years are numbers eleven and twenty-two.

EPHEMERAL MAP   In astrology, a map erected for the time of an event, to be judged by Horary Astrology.

EPHEMERIDES   In astrology, these are tables for finding the position of the sun, the moon, and the planets at a person's birth. These tables are used in casting horoscopes.

EPHEMERIS   Plural: Ephemerides. In astrology, an almanac listing the ephemeral or rapidly changing position which each of the solar system bodies will occupy on each day of the year: their longitude, latitude, declination, and similar astronomical phenomena. The astronomer's Ephemeris lists these positions in heliocentric terms: that of the astrologer, in geocentric terms. A set of Ephemerides which includes the year of the native's birth is essential in the erection of a horoscope. Ephemerides were first devised by astrologers to facilitate the erection of a horoscope. Finally, when they became in common use to navigators and astronomers, they were given official recognition and issued as the Nautical Almanac. The oldest almanac in the British Museum bears the date 131. It is said that Columbus navigated by the aid of an astrologer's Ephemeris.

EPHESIAN MYSTERIES In pagan mysticism, the teaching and guidance given in the temple of the goddess Diana in Ephesus. Instruction was offered to both men and women, who came from all regions of the ancient world. Ceremonies, rites, spiritual counsel constituted the core of the Mysteries.

EPHESUS A city on the West coast of Asia Minor. In antiquity, an important city, noted for its occult and mystic studies, particularly Gnosticism.

EPHOD Among the ancient Israelites, this was a garment worn by the High Priest. It was associated with the practice of divination.

EPWORTH Psychic disturbances, beginning with knockings, said to have occurred at Epworth Vicarage in 1716, in the home of Samuel Wesley, father of John Wesley.

EQUILATERAL TRIANGLE In Pythagorean mystical numerology, this figure symbolized the Supreme Being.

ERGAS, JOSEPH BEN IMMANUEL Born in Livorno in 1685: died in 1730. An Italian-Jewish Kabbalist. Author of a dialogue between a philosopher and a Kabbalist. He also wrote an introduction to the Kabbalah.

ESBAT A term that denotes the Sabbat, the assembly where witches foregathered to do homage to his Satanic Majesty.

131

ESKIMO FEAR   Eskimos of the far Northern regions have an extreme fear of the dead. Sickness, for instance, is regarded as the result of offending the Spirits.

ESKIMOS   Among the Eskimos, the angakok or shaman, the medicine man, performed the functions of tribal adviser, sorcerer, and prophet. With the help of spirits he foretold weather conditions, predicted future events. He could also fashion a figure of human form, composed of bones, fragments of corpses, and endow it with supernatural powers of levitation and malevolence.

In a general sense, the Eskimo believes that Nature is whimsical and unreliable and hence he accepts the concept of 'supernatural' phenomena more readily. Hence, too, mountains are endowed with evil intentions: a walrus may have sinister anti-human attitudes. Everything has a soul-spirit — the living form as well as any inanimate object.

ESKIMO SIN   To the Eskimo, sin is any offense directed against the supernatural.

ESKIMO SOULS   An Eskimo belief is that spirits or sorcerers cause disease. In the Polar regions and in Greenland and Canada, the belief is that sickness is caused by the loss of a man's soul. It is assumed to have been stolen or by torment extracted out of the patient. The shaman then proceeds on a spirit-flight to recover the soul.

ESKIMO VIEWS   Sickness, scarcity of food or any other occurrence interfering with daily life is, among the Eskimos, attributed to the machinations of evil beings or the spirits of the dead.

ESOTERIC DOCTRINE   Occultists claim to have preserved a body of mystical teachings which have been known and studied by highly evolved adepts in all ages. According to the occultists, the esoteric doctrine is the common property of mankind and is contained in its entirety in the aggregate of all the world's religions, but only partially in any one religion. The doctrine has been held from time immemorial by exalted seers and sages who promulgate parts of it to the world when the need arises. Its origins are found in the teachings of beings who incarnated in the Third Root-Race of the Fourth Round of the earth.

ESOTERIC FICTION Among imaginative works based on occult themes may be listed the following:

L. Adams Beck:	The House of Fulfilment.
Algernon Blackwood:	The Garden of Survival.
E. G. Bulwer-Lytton:	The Coming Race.
	Zanoni.
Rider Haggard:	She
	Ayesha
Lafcadio Hearn:	Karm
Arthur Machen:	Tales Strange and Supernatural.
Talbot Mundy:	Winds of the World.

ESP These letters represent extra-sensory perception. It belongs in parapsychology, a branch of systematic psychology. It involves sensitivity on the part of persons who are subject to clairvoyance and telepathy. In England, the U.S.A., Holland and in other countries there are research laboratories for testing persons claiming such psychic capacities. Duke University is particularly noted for its researches in this field, under the direction of Dr. Joseph Rhine, who has acquired an international reputation for his experimental work.

ESP investigates paranormal powers in a strictly controlled, scientific manner, and has invited the close interest of professional scientists, psychiatrists, and societies for psychical research.

ESP CARDS In parapsychology, cards, each bearing one of the following five symbols: star, circle, square, cross, and wavy lines.

ESSENES Members of an ancient Jewish mystic sect. They were active from the second century B.C. to the second century A.D. They lived in monastic seclusion. They were celibates and were reputed to follow mystic traditions and to possess a highly secretive esoteric literature. They believed in immortality but rejected resurrection. In 1947, at Qumran, the library of the Essenes was discovered.

ESSENES OF KOSMON A mystic sect, now no longer operative, that had its headquarters in Colorado.

ESSENTIAL DIGNITIES In astrology, a planet in a sign in which it is strengthened is in one of its Essential Dignities. The Essential Dignities are:

1. When a planet is in a sign of which it is the Ruler, when it is said to be in its own sign, or in its domal dignity. It is ambiguous to call this its House-position. If the sign which a planet rules is on the cusp of the House to which the planet is posited, the planet is the Lord of the House: but the strength as such depends on its Essential Dignity by virtue of its sign placement. Some astrologers consider that placement in any other sign of the same element as that of which it is the Ruler confers a degree of Dignity.

2. When it is posited in the sign in which it is said to be exalted, wherein its strength is augmented and its virtues magnified. A planet in its Exaltation is only slightly less favorably placed than when it is in its own sign.

3. According to ancient astrology, the placement of a planet in the same Triplicity as that of which it is the Ruler, in the same Term, or in the same Face, was considered to be Essential Dignities of varying degree.

ETHICAL CULTURE A system founded by Felix Adler in the late nineteenth century. The essence of the system is the emphasis laid on ethical conduct in all aspects of human relationships.

ETHIOPIAN BOOK OF ENOCH In this apocryphal book, seven angels are mentioned who keep watch in heaven. They are: Uriel, Raphael, Raguel, Michael, Zerachiel, Gebriel, Remiel.

EUDES DE L'ETOILE A Breton noble who belongs in the twelfth century. He proclaimed himself a prophet. His followers bore the names of their characteristics: Power, Judgment, Wisdom. He preached in famine-stricken areas and attracted numerous disciples. His influence was felt to be harmful and hence he was made prisoner. Brought before Pope Eugenius III, he declared himself to be the Judge of the Last Days of the world. His forked wand, he asserted, governed the course of fate. He died in prison: several of his followers were burned at the stake.

EURYNOME In medieval demonology, the prince of death. He has huge teeth, a hideous body covered with sores, and fox-skin clothing.

EUSEBIUS This Christian writer, who died in 309 A.D., declared that the origin of witchcraft lay with the evil angels who introduced the Black Arts among men.

EVEN NUMBERS In the symbolism of most cultures, even numbers are regarded as feminine. Plutarch assigned 'a certain receptive opening' to even numbers.

EVIL EYE In certain persons the glance of 'fiery and baleful eyes' was believed to have an evil potency. In ancient Assyria, the evil eye was exorcised by spells and incantations. Among the Romans the belief in the evil eye was widespread.

This belief is still current in many European countries, particularly in Italy. There it is called mal d'occhio. In Naples, it is known as jettatura. In Corsica, the peasants call it innochiatura.

In Iran, the spell cast by the evil eye is called nazar. In Scotland, cattle affected by the evil eye of a witch or sorceress were said to be 'overlooked' or 'struck.'

In Irish folklore, the evil eye is known as the eye of Balor. Irish who practiced this sinister performance were called eye-biting.

EVOLUTION   In theosophical teachings, evolution means that man contains everything contained in the cosmos of which he is an inseparable part, and that all the latent faculties and powers inherent in man are unfolded in a process manifested from eternity to eternity, in a beginningless and endless process. Evolution is one of the oldest concepts in ancient occultism, although the ancients preferred to use the word emanation. The heart of every organic entity is viewed theosophically as a divine monad which finds expression in successively improved forms as the ages pass.

EXALTATION   A term used in astrology to denote the position of greatest influence of the Sun and the Moon and the other planets.

EXISTENTIALISM   A philosophical system of recent origin in its contemporary impact. Jean-Paul Sartre, the French philosophical exponent, publicized it widely. Existentialism involves personal decision of the actor in a universe that has no ultimate direction. Existence is experienced and lived, but there is nothing beyond.

EXORCISM This term is used for the expulsion of demonic spirits from human beings or from places, or objects. Occult rites directed to this purpose include spells, incantations, conjurations, prayers. One method, used in the case of a Median princess possessed by the demon Asmodeus, was to mix incense with the heart and liver of fish and to set fire to the mixture, while the smoke fumes routed the demon.

In early Christian centuries, priests were the official exorcists, but later on learned laymen were permitted to practice.

The historian Josephus, in his Antiquities, relates how a certain Eleazar exorcised a demon in the presence of the Roman Emperor Vespasian.

The sacred books of the Hindus, the Vedas, contain magic prayers designed to exorcise evil spirits from the bodies of those so possessed.

The Dybbuk is a famous contemporary dramatization of a medieval case of possession and exorcism.

The medieval priest, following prescribed ritualistic ceremonies and formulaic utterances, calls upon the spirit by name. Threats too are used, also prayers and maledictions and magic expressions. In the Middle Ages anchorites, saintly men and others were frequently the victims of possession by demons. A large body of hagiographical material, in Latin, is extant, in which many cases of possession are cited and described in great detail. Caesar of Heisterbach, a Cistercian monk who belongs in the thirteenth century, produced a voluminous corpus, still extant, dealing with miraculous exorcisms. His collection, known as The Dialogue of Miracles, is full of accounts of many paranormal occurrences: visions, apparitions, diabolic interventions.

EXPOSE   Eileen J. Garrett is internationally noted for her psychic studies and her experiences with paranormal phenomena. In her book The Sense and Nonsense of Prophecy, she writes wittily and frankly about the professional fortune-tellers, crystal gazers, astrologers, numerologists, gypsy tea-readers, phrenologists, palmists, and cult leaders who inveigle a vast gullible public.

Yet there remains a residuum of psychic and paranormal phenomena that clamor for scientifically directed investigation. What Mrs. Garrett has done is to distinguish the humbug-dealers from the dedicated searchers for psychic truth.

EYEBESCHUTZ, JONATHAN   (1690 - 1764)   A Talmudic scholar who was born in Cracow and died in Altona. He was also a noted Kabbalist.

EYEWITNESS TO MAGIC   Ibn Khaldun, the Arab historian who belongs in the fourteenth century, describes the practices of the Nabatean sorcerers who inhabited the Lower Euphrates:

> We saw with our own eyes one of these individuals making the image of a person he wished to bewitch. The magician pronounces some words over the image, which is a real or symbolical representation of the person to be bewitched. Then he blows and emits from his mouth a little saliva and at the same time makes those organs vibrate which are used in the utterance of this malevolent formula. Next he holds over this symbolical image a cord which he has prepared, making a knot in it to signify that he made a pact with the demon who acted as his associate. A wicked spirit then comes forth from the operator's mouth covered with

saliva. Many evil spirits then descend, and the result is that the magician causes the victim to be attacked by the desired evil.

F

FABRE D'OLIVET, ANTOINE French occultist, contemporary of Napoleon. He attempted a revival of the Greek Pythagorean mystical system.

FACES In Kabbalistic mysticism, there are three faces, representing the corporal or animal aspect, the spiritual element, and the soul.

FAIRY TALES In the fairy tale, the supernatural is taken for granted. Animals speak. Humans change their form. Castles are erected in a trice. Forests disappear before the eyes. Inanimate objects move. In a very wide sense, the laws of nature as they are normally known are abrogated. Whatever is impossible in the world of reality becomes, in the legendary, traditional folktale, a readily accepted actuality.

FAKIR Broadly, a dervish, ascetic, or worker of miracles. Among claims made by Hindu fakirs is that of being able to walk over a bed of hot coals without suffering pain or burning.

FALK, HAYYIM SAMUEL JACOB (c. 1708 - 1782) A mystic Kabbalist who was born in Bavaria and died in London. He was known as the Baal Shem of London, that is, Master of the Name. He was, however, denounced as a follower of the false Messiah, Shabbatai Zevi.

FALK, CAIN CHENUL   A first century Kabbalist, reputed to have had communication with spirits.

FALSE MESSIAHS   Among false prophets in Judaic history, one of them, Theudas, belonged in the period when Judaea became a Roman province. In the eighth century a certain Serene appeared, proposing to banish the Moslems from Palestine. During the centuries, many other false Messiahs made their appearance: the Bagdadi David Alroy, David Reubeni, Shlomo Molcho: most notable of all, Shabbatai Zevi.

FAMA FRATERNITATIS   A document first published in 1614 and republished in seven editions within the next three years. It is the earliest extant work which mentions the Rosicrucian order. It tells of the long journeys of the reputed founder of the order, Christian Rosenkreuz, and of his return to Germany, where he imparted the wisdom he had collected to three chosen disciples.

FAMILIARITY   In astrology, a term used by Ptolemy to indicate an aspect or parallel between two bodies: or their mutual disposition, as when each is in the other's sign or house.

FAMILIARS   Spirits or supernatural attendants that protect and prompt magicians, sorcerers, or witches. Cornelius Agrippa had a black dog as his familiar. Paracelsus was said to carry his familiar in the hilt of his sword.

FANO, IMMANUEL (1548 - 1620)   An Italian - Jewish rabbi who was also a Kabbalist.

FATHERS OF CHARITY   A religious sect founded around 1540.

FEAR OF SICKNESS   Among Eskimos the incidence of sickness is attributed to the Spirits of the supernatural world. The remedy lies with the shaman or medicine man. He intercedes with the Spirits. He undertakes an astral, spirit-flight to recover the soul of the victim.

FEARERS OF SIN　The Fearers of Sin were an ancient Hebraic sect who practiced religious mysticism.

FELINE CORN　In folk legends and tradition, both ancient and modern, the cat is associated with harvesting. In Germany, for example, the peasant who cut the last corn was known as the tom-cat.

FELINE PRODUCTION　The ancient Egyptians placed great confidence in the living cat as a protective agent against supernatural malefic influences.

FELINE SYMBOL　In occultism, the cat is the symbol of the sun and the moon.

FEMININE SIGNS　In astrology, these are the even numbered signs: Taurus, Cancer, Virgo, Scorpio, Capricorn, Pisces.

FENGBUANG　In China, this bird corresponds to the phoenix. Mystically, it is the symbol of immortality.

FERHO　A Gnostic term denoting the greatest creative power. This term was in use among the Nazarene Gnostics.

FIARD, JEAN BAPTISTE (1736 - 1818)　A French cleric who published a pamphlet accusing occultists of collaborating with Satanic forces.

FIFTH HOUSE　In astrology, this term refers to the family and to occupations. It is governed by the sign of Leo.

FIGURE　An astrological or celestial figure, variously called Geniture, Map, Scheme, Chart, Theme, Mirror of Heaven,

Nativity, Horoscope, as cast, erected or drawn by modern astrologers. It consists of a circle of the heavens, representing the 360 degrees of the Earth's orbit, divided into twelve arcs — resembling a wheel of twelve spokes.

FINNS Among the Teutons, there was a belief that the Finns possessed uncanny powers and agents. A Teuton, suspected of communication with the Finnish masters of evil forces, was put to death.

FIRES At various times, and in different parts of the world, strange conflagrations have appeared: blazing space objects, fireballs, mountains in flames and similar igneous manifestations, without conclusive explanations. Various suggestions and conjectures, both in a material and a supernormal sense, have been advanced regarding such phenomena.

FIRE SIGNS In astrology, this expression is applied to the inspirational signs: Aries, Leo, Sagittarius.

FIRE-WALKING In India, Japan, Dutch Guiana and other Oriental countries ritual fire-walking forms part of mystic religious ceremonials. In the South Seas, too, there are regular rites involving walking barefooted over live coals and flaming fires. Monks, priests, villagers are credibly reputed by travelers and observers to have come unscathed from these performances. The practice was known as early as Roman antiquity. A tribe belonging to Sora, a Volscian town, performed this rite twice annually.

Authorities and eyewitnesses differ markedly concerning the alleged immunity from burns of participants in the ritual ceremony of fire walking, common to many peoples and prevalent in all ages. Hagiographic and mediumistic accounts of fire ordeals are found in Oliver Leroy's Les Hommes Salamandres, published in Paris in 1932.

144

FIRMICUS MATENUS, JULIUS A Roman writer who flourished in the fourth century A.D. He is the author of an astrological treatise in eight books.

FIRST CREATED In Hebraic mysticism, The First Created refers to the being who is intermediate between God and the rest of the cosmos.

FIRST HOUSE In astrology, this term refers to the house of life. It is governed by the sign of Aries.

FIRST POINT In astrology, this refers to zero degrees Aries. From this point longitude is reckoned along the ecliptic, and right ascension along the celestial equator.

FISH In ancient mystery cults fish were associated with divinity: for example, with Atargatis, the Syrian goddess who is equated with Astarte. She was represented as half woman, half fish.

FIVE In many mystic cults, the number five is associated with five virtues or five duties. In antiquity this number was linked with man. Man has five fingers on each hand. He has five outer senses. The five-pointed figure, the pentagram, is a symbol of the microcosm, in Hebraic mysticism. Five was regarded as a significant number with respect to the course of a developing disease. In Freemasonry too the number five is of import.

FLAGELLATION In antiquity, flagellation was a mystic initiation into secret cults. In this sense it was also prevalent in ancient Egypt and, as a religious discipline, throughout the Middle Ages. Flagellation became so widespread throughout Europe that the ecclesiastical authorities took action. In 1444 some hundred flagellants were condemned to the stake: others, in 1446.

FLAMEL NICOLAS (1330 - 1418)   Unlike most other alchemists, Nicolas Flamel died fabulously rich. He claimed to have discovered the secret of transmutation.

FLAMMARION, CAMILLE (1842 - 1925)   The famous French astronomer who originated the word psychic believed that unknown natural forces 'as real as the attraction of gravitation and as invisible as that' were responsible for levitation, telepathy, clairvoyance, and related phenomena.

FLAUROS   In medieval demonology, the grand general of Hell. He appears in the shape of a terrible leopard. He commands twenty legions.

FLEXED   In astrology, this is an alternate term for the mutable signs. This term is preferred by some modern astrologers.

FLUDD, ROBERT (1574 - 1637)   An English physician, mystic, alchemist, and Rosicrucian. He was the author of Rosicrucian Anatomy. He also wrote treatises in defense of the Black Arts.
One of Fludd's notions was that demons caused sickness, as he argued in his Integrum Morborum Mysterium, The Entire Mystery of Diseases.

FLYING SAUCERS   A recent phenomenon of flying saucers or discs, observed in space by many people in different places. Various conjectures have been made regarding the source and the purpose of the phenomenon. Attempts have been made to explain it from mathematical, physical, and spiritual viewpoints. A recent London report maintained that the unidentified flying saucers had a natural explanation.
The phenomenon is not altogether recent. These objects have been reported on and their appearance in various parts of the world has been discussed since 1860.

FODOR, NANDOR   Dr. Fodor is a distinguished psychoanalyst who has published a number of books dealing with psychic investigations and with his experiences in paranormal manifestations.

FOHAT   A mystical term used in Tibetan occultism to represent the primordial light. In theosophical teachings, it is the active potency of Sakti, the female reproductive power in nature. It is the essence of cosmic electricity. In the universe of manifestation it is a creative and destructive force. Esoterically, it is the universal propelling force.

FORCAS   In medieval demonology, the grand president of hell. He commands twenty-nine legions, appears in the shape of a strong white-haired man, and teaches many subjects, including logic and rhetoric.

FORCES   In yoga and occultism, there are four distinct types of Force:
a) the Forces of Nature, as heat, sound, electricity and other branches of physics.
b) the Forces of the vital air.
c) the Forces exerted by thought-form and emotion-form. On issuing from the creator such forms become independent entities.
d) Living entities such as human beings are also called Forces because by their own powers of thought and will they can introduce changes in the three other categories of Nature.

FORD, ARTHUR (b. 1896)   A Philadelphia medium, reputed to be the world's greatest clairvoyant. A televised seance with James A. Pike in which the medium allegedly made contact with the late Episcopal bishop's son, brought Ford into the national limelight. Ford helped to found Spiritual Frontiers Fellowship, an association that boasts member-

147

ship of more than five thousand leaders from every major faith.

FORKED OBJECTS   In occultism, these objects are reputed to be Satanic symbols, associated with the horns on the Goat-Fiend as manifested during the Witches' Sabbat.

FORMS OF DIVINATION   Among the branches of divination, whose purpose was to predict the future or to test the truth or falsity of a situation, were:

amniomancy: observation of the caul on a child's head at birth.

anthropomancy: consultation of the intestines of sacrificed children. The Emperor Julian the Apostate was believed to have practiced this method of divination.

apantomancy: observation of objects that appear haphazardly.

armomancy: observation of the shoulders of an animal that has been sacrificed for the purpose.

aspidomancy: divination by sitting on a shield, within a magic circle. The adept falls into a trance while pronouncing occult formulas and then utters prophetic revelations.

belomancy: divination by means of the flight of arrows.

bibliomancy: consultation of a passage or line in a book, selected at random.

botanomancy: divination by burning branches of brier and vervain, on which were inscribed questions to be answered.

catoptromancy: divination by means of a lens or magic mirror. The practice was in vogue in antiquity, and is mentioned by Apuleius, the Roman philosopher and novelist, Pausanias, the Greek traveler, and St. Augustine. This type of divination was also practiced by The Dyaks of Borneo and the Incas.

causimomancy: divination by fire. When an object cast into a fire did not burn, the omen was propitious.

chiromancy: evaluation of the lines of a person's hand with a view to interpreting character and fate: this is the practice of palmistry.

cubomancy: divination by thimbles. An ancient Greek technique, practiced by the Romans also, among them the Emperors Augustus and Tiberius.

daphnomancy: observation of the way in which a laurel branch burns and crackles in a fire.

empyromancy: observation of objects placed on a sacrificial fire.

gastromancy: divination by means of ventriloquism.

geloscopy: observation and interpretation of a person's laughter.

gyromancy: circumambulation of a chalked circle and observation of the position of the body in relation to the circle.

hepatoscopy: observation of a sheep's liver.

hippomancy: observation of a horse's pace.

ichthyomancy: inspection of the entrails of fish.

lampadomancy: divination by means of the flame of a lamp.

libanomancy: observation of the smoke of incense.

margaritomancy: divination by means of pearls.

metoposcopy: an occult procedure that evaluates a person's life and fate from the lines of the forehead.

oeonisticy: observation of the flight of birds.

ovomancy: divination by means of putting eggs on a fire and observing how they break.

sand: In Arab territories divination is practiced by drawing lines in sand and interpreting the resultant linear shapes.

xylomancy: observation of the position of twigs lying on the ground.

FORTIFIED   In astrology, this term denotes strongly placed: either elevated, in a congenial sign, or well-aspected.

FORTITUDE   In astrology, an ancient term indicating a quality or strength possessed by a planet when posited in its own sign or that of its exaltation.

FORTUNA, PARS FORTUNAE   In astrology, the Part of Fortune. One of the Arabian Points. A point that bears the same relation to the rising degree that the Moon bears to the Sun. It occupies the same house-position in a Figure based on a birth-moment, that the Moon tenants in a solar figure. Its symbol, a cross within a circle, $\oplus$, is utilized by astronomers to represent the earth. It is the ancient Chinese symbol Tien, a field: used by the Egyptians to signify territory. It is generally considered that the house position of Fortuna is an indication of the department of life that will most readily contribute to the financial welfare of the native.

FOUR AGES   In antiquity the cycle of humanity was divided into four stages. The Golden Age, the first one, was free from conflict and complexity. Next followed the Silver Age, then the Bronze Age, and finally the Iron Age.

FOUR BASIC TEMPERAMENTS   The four basic factors that condition the character of a person. In Aristotelian thought, the four temperaments are compared with the elements. The fiery temperament is choleric. The watery temperament is phlegmatic. The airy temperament is sanguine. The earthy temperament is melancholic. In Elizabethan literature these temperaments are called humors.

FOUR BEASTS   These four creatures, the lion, bull, eagle, and man himself, have been associated with the Evangelists.

The lion is the sign of St. Mark: the bull, of St. Luke: the eagle, of St. John: man, of St. Matthew.

FOUR DEGREES The four degrees of spiritual evolution refer to four types of men:
   a) the instinctive. The will is the motive factor.
   b) the emotional. They are conditioned by will and consciousness.
   c) the intellectual. They are conditioned by mental activity.
   d) the initiate. They rise above the self.

FOUR ELEMENTS In pre-Socratic philosophy, the four elements, the primal principles, are: fire, air, water, earth. They appear, in different combinations, in all matter. They also appear in the mystical interpretations of man in relation to the cosmos.

FOUR-FOOTED SIGNS In astrology, these are: Aries, Taurus, Leo, Sagittarius, Capricorn: sometimes termed 'animal signs.' One whose ascendant is posited in one of these signs was anciently presumed to possess some of the qualities of that particular animal: as bold as a lion, lustful as a goat, etc.

FOUR GODS Among the Hawaiians there is a belief in four great gods who have existed timelessly: these gods are Kane, Kanaloa, Lona, Ku.

FOURTH DIMENSION OF SPACE Spiritualists claim to find proof of the existence of a fourth dimension, in addition to length, breadth, and thickness, in the passage of matter through matter.

FOURTH HOUSE In astrology, this term refers to the house of children and of home. It is governed by the sign of Cancer.

FOUR WORLDS In Kabbalistic mysticism, there are four worlds. These are: Atziluth, which is the primal, archetypal form; the Briatic or creative world; Yetzirah, the formative world; Assiah, the world of shells, which is the material form.

FOX SISTERS Kate Fox (1841 - 1892), Margaret Fox (1838 - 1893), and Leah Fox played a dominant role in the movement of modern spiritualism. According to the testimony of their parents, Mr. and Mrs. John D. Fox, strange noises were heard by members of the family, then residing in Hydesville, beginning on December 11, 1847. On noting that when her father shook a window sash the noises seemed to reply, Kate began snapping her fingers to elicit responses from the unseen powers. The three sisters became professional mediums and attracted considerable attention to themselves and to the cause of spiritualism. Fraud was proven in several instances.

FRANCK, ADOLPHE (1809 - 1893) A French philosopher. Professor at the Sorbonne. Author of The Kabbalah; or the Religious Philosophy of the Hebrews.

FRANK, JACOB (1726 - 1791) A false Messiah. He gathered some of the followers of the false Messiah Shabbatai Zevi into a new Messianic movement. Ultimately Frank became a Catholic.

FRATRES LUCIS This Latin expression signifies The Brothers of Light. They constituted a secret sect that flourished in Italy in the first century.

FRAZER, SIR JAMES GEORGE (1854 - 1941) A Scottish anthropologist whose vast knowledge of primitive customs and traditions resulted in the publication of many works, including his masterpiece, *The Golden Bough*, first published in two-volumes (1890) and later enlarged into twelve (1911 - 1915). He was the first to apply the comparative method to the study of totemism and taboo. His studies are based on the 'psychic unity' of man throughout time.

FREEMASONRY An esoteric doctrine that reputedly dates back to the time of King Solomon's Temple. Some authorities associate it with the medieval guilds: others, with the Knights Templars.
It is founded on the idea of God as the Architect of the Cosmos. By means of symbolical language and secret initiatory rituals it posits a code of morality based on the brotherhood of man. In some respects, Freemasonry recalls the ancient mystery cults.

FRIENDS OF GOD They formed a mystical society that flourished in the fourteenth century in Germany.

FU-HI The I-Ching is attributed by the Chinese to Fu-Hi, a mythical sovereign who happened to see its mysterious outlines on a dragon which emerged from the Yellow River around 3000 B.C.

FU HSI (2953-2838 B.C.) The first of the Five Emperors of the legendary period of Chinese culture. He is said to have taught the people to hunt, fish, and tend flocks. From the markings on the shell of a tortoise, he is supposed to have constructed the eight diagrams on which is based the whole system of I Ching.

FUNERAL RITES From the very beginning belief in the supernatural seems to have been linked with funeral rites. Shells, carved objects, red ocher, and other evidence found at prehistoric burial sites all point to hope for survival beyond the tomb.

153

FUNG SHUI Foretelling events by analysis of figures or lines. It is a belief based on the contention that the linear shape and mass of the surrounding topography of a particular geographical area, together with the location, shape and size of dwelling, temples and other fixed objects, directly govern the prosperity or adversity experienced by the populace of that area; and that any changes in the skyline, or in the shape or position of the fixed objects, may influence the destiny of the area. The practitioner is known as *fung shui lo* (literally, "wind water man"), and *fung shui* is still seriously practiced in many parts of the Orient.

G

GABIROL, SOLOMON IBN (c.1021-c.1058)   Famous Spanish-Jewish philosopher and poet. In his major work, Fons Vitae, The Fountain of Life, a Neoplatonic treatise, he discusses form and matter, and establishes a hierarchy of all beings, a graduation which, on each level, shows a more perfect relation between form and matter.

GAFFARILLUS   A philosopher and alchemist who flourished in the seventeenth century.

GALACTIC CENTRE   In astrology, the gravitational centre around which the Sun revolves. Astrology has hypothetically placed this at zero degrees Capricorn, which is exactly confirmed by recently published results of calculations of spectroscopic radial velocity measurements as well as calculations by the parallax method of determining proper motion.

GALACTIC LATITUDE   In astrology, the angular distance of a celestial body from the median plane of the Milky Way.

GALL, FRANZ JOSEPH (1758-1828)   German physician. He founded the practice of phrenology. He examined the skulls of man and animals with a view to determine the relationship between mental capacities and the shape of the skull.

155

GANGA   The head or chief of the secret society known as the *Ndembo.*

GARDEN OF DELIGHT   In Hebraic mysticism, this expression denotes the occult arts. Akiba was the only one who entered this Garden and became an initiate.

GARLIC   Garlic has been used as a charm against the evil eye and attacks by vampires.

GATEKEEPERS   In Hebraic mysticism, when the soul returns in sequence to each of the seven heavens, there are gatekeepers who control admission for the initiated.

GATES   In Hebrew mysticism there are fifty gates to reason.

GAYATRI   A Sanskrit verse (*Rigveda* iii, 62, 10) repeated by orthodox Brahmans in the morning and in the evening. The words of the archaic hymn are: 'Tat savitur varenyam bhargo devasya dhimahi, dhiyo yo nah prachodayat.' Its esoteric meaning is said to be: 'Oh thou golden sun of most excellent splendor, illumine our hearts and fill our minds, so that we, recognizing our oneness with the Divinity which is the heart of the universe, may see the pathway before our feet, and tread it to those distant goals of perfection, stimulated by thine own radiant light.'

GEBER   An Arab of the ninth century who wrote on the occult arts.

GELUK-PA   This expression means The Path of Virtue. It is the name of a sect founded in Tibet in the eleventh century.

GEMATRIA   In Kabbalistic mysticism, a technique whereby the letters of words in Biblical contexts are interpreted in terms of their numerical value.

156

GEMINI   In astrology, the Twins. The third, northern sign of the zodiac. It is of dual significance, creative and destructive. In occultism it symbolizes the twin souls. Kabbalistically, the signs represent the arms and hands of the grand man of the universe, and accordingly the executive principle of humanity.

GENETHLIALOGY   In astrology, the branch that deals with the birth of individuals, whereby a judgment is formed of a person's characteristics from a map of the heavens cast for his given birth moment.

GENITURE   In astrology, a birth or genesis. This term is approximately synonymous with nativity, referring to the subject whose birth horoscope is under consideration. A reasonable discrimination would be to employ nativity with reference to the person, and geniture with reference to the configurations which show in his birth map. Ptolemy mentions a Lord of the Geniture in referring to the ruling planet in a given horoscope of birth.

GEOARC   In astrology, a term applied to one of the house divisions of a map erected for a given moment, when there is under consideration the effect upon an individual at a given point on the earth's periphery of his motion around the earth's centre, in the earth's daily rotation. The same subdivision of the same map is called a heliarc, when there is under consideration the effect based on the actual motions in orbit around the Sun, of all the planets — including the earth.

GEOMANCY   A form of divination by means of configurations of earth. In the Middle Ages geomancy was a popular form of numerology. Numbers were deduced from observation of the planets and stars.

GESP In parapsychology, these initials represent General Extrasensory Perception.

GHOSTLY CATS There are on record, in the Society for Psychical Research and elsewhere, accounts of cats who, after death, re-appeared in ghostly form.

GHOSTLY POWER Among the tribes of Tierra del Fuego and Eastern Brazil, the power of the shaman, the medicine man, was derived from the ghost of a corpse. This power was used by the shaman in divination, in forecasting weather conditions and the outcome of battle. He was the intermediary between the tribal community and the supernatural agencies that inhabited the cosmic spaces.

GHOSTS AND WAR The Dugum Dani are a tribe of neolithic warriors and farmers of the Grand Valley of Baliem, in the Central Highlands of Western New Guinea. They practice warfare as a sacred activity of their culture. The motive that lies behind this military ritual fought with spears and arrows is a sense of obligation. They maintain that the ghosts of the dead, if not avenged, will destroy their crops and cause sickness among the tribe. Any tribal group may raise the war cry, and the conflict itself lasts one day, but during the year the death toll on either side may be between ten and twenty killed.

GIB-CAT An Old English term for a tom-cat. The gib-cat, usually of a melancholy appearance, was associated with witchcraft. An old witch, says the Elizabethan dramatist John Marston, "is now turning into a gib-cat."

GICHTEL, J. G. In 1668 he founded a religious sect called Brothers of the Angelic Life.

GIFT OF TONGUES The power of speaking various languages or, when speaking one language, of being understood by people of another language. In Catholicism, this power was possessed by the apostles and other saints, among them St. Vincent Ferrer and St. Francis Xavier.

GILLES DE RAIS (1404-1440) A French nobleman who squandered a large fortune. In an attempt to recover his wealth, he devoted himself to sinister occult practices. He resorted to necromantic performances that involved in the course of his career the murder of children. He was put to death, having achieved, in a remarkably short life, the utmost infamy.

GIVER OF LIFE In astrology, the hyleg, or significator that holds the vital prerogative.

GLANYIL, JOSEPH (1636-1680) The English clergyman and philosopher who served as chaplain to Charles II defended the belief in the supernatural in Sorcerers and Sorcery (1666) and other works.

GLOBAL WHIRLWIND Popular magazines warn of a Coming Whirlwind that will sweep this earth. This coincides with the view that California is about to disappear into the sea.

GLOBE In occultism, every one of the physical globes scattered throughout space is accompanied by six invisible globes. Each visible globe and its six superior globes form a chain. The seven manifested globes are designated by the first seven letters of the alphabet. The lifewaves circle around them in seven great cycles, called Rounds. Each life-wave first enters and completes its life-cycle in A, then B, then C, and then D, the lowest of the manifested seven, which in our own planetary chain is the earth. A Globe-Round is the life-wave's penetration and emergence from any one of the seven globes. A Globe-

Round is accompanied by the birth of seven Root-Races, their efflorescence, and their passing away.

GLORIFICATION OF THE SUN Julian the Apostate, the pagan Roman emperor, glorified the sun as the supreme deity. This concept he derived from Zoroastrianism, in which Mithra is the Sun God.

GNOSIS This Greek term means knowledge. It is applied in particular to the secret knowledge of the ancient sect of Gnostics.

GOETIA A term, of Greek etymology, used in occultism. It denotes malefic, Black Magic.

GOG AND MAGOG These are enigmatic names that occur in Ezekiel's apocalyptic vision of the final assault of the armed forces of the North on the land of Israel prior to the inauguration of God's sovereignty. The historian Josephus identifies Gog and Magog with the Scythians, while the Sibylline Oracles place them in Ethiopia. In Hebraic literature they represent the rebel peoples who rise up against God.

GOLDEN LANE The Street of the Alchemists in Prague was a famous center of black magic, alchemy, and occultism in the sixteenth century. Paracelsus, Agrippa von Nettesheim, Trithemius, and many Kabbalists lived in Prague.

GOLDEN NUMBER Division of a proportion of a geometrical figure such that the smaller dimension is to the greater as the latter is to the whole. In the golden rectangle, for example, the width is to the length as the length is to the sum of the two dimensions. The Golden Number, with a value of 0.618, has been held to be a universal module and actually corresponds to a module of aesthetic

160

creations renowned for their harmony as well as to creations of nature (seashells, tree-branches, parts of the human body, etc.).

GOLEM A gigantic android, in Hebraic legend, endowed with life by magic means. A formula for the creation of such creatures was left by Eleazar of Worms in Germany. Many robots of this type appeared throughout the Middle Ages. In the sixteenth century Elijah of Chelm, a Kabbalist, produced an android that sprang into life on the incision of the divine tetragrammaton on the figure's forehead.

The most famous golem was created by Rabbi Judah Loew of Prague, late in the sixteenth century. The android served as a protection to the Jewish inhabitants of Prague. Every Sabbath Eve, to prevent desecration, the Rabbi removed the life-principle, which he had injected magically, from the robot's figure.

Monster robots have in recent years been the subject of popular literature and horror films.

GORGON In ancient mythology, a gorgon was one of three hideous sisters with serpentine locks and glaring eyes. Anything or anyone that met their glance was instantly turned to stone.

GOYA, FRANCISCO JOSE DE (1746-1828) Noted Spanish artist. Among his many excellent paintings of portraits and national scenes were many etchings dealing with violent, macabre Satanic themes.

GRADIAL TRANSIT, ARC OF In astrology, a term that indicates the arc a planet traverses from its birth position to its progressed position, when in any given year it is activated by a major transit through the arc.

GRAHAM, JAMES Dr. James Graham, who was virtually a follower of Cagliostro, founded in England a Temple of Health. He invented an elaborate bed that he considered conducive to erotic consummations. In his public lectures, he exhorted his audiences thus:

Suffer me to recommend my celestial, or medico, magnetico, musico, electrical bed which I have constructed, to improve, exalt, and invigorate the bodily, and, through them, the mental faculties of the human species.

The sublime, the magnificent, and, I may say, the super-celestial dome of the bed, which contains the odoriferous, balmy, and ethereal spices, odors, and essences, and which is the grand magazine or reservoir of those vivifying and invigorating influences which are exhaled and dispersed by the breathing of the music, and by the attenuating, repelling, and accelerating force of the electrical fire — is very curiously inlaid or wholly covered on the under side with brilliant plates of looking-glass, so disposed as to reflect the various attractive charms of the happy recumbent couple, in the most flattering, most agreeable, and most enchanting style.

Such is a slight and inadequate sketch of the grand celestial bed, which, fully impregnated with the balmy vivifying effluvia of restorative balsamic medicines and of soft, fragrant, oriental gums, balsams, and quintessence, and pervaded at the same time with full springing tides of the invigorating influences of music and magnets both real and artificial, gives such elastic vigor to the nerves, on the one hand, of the male, and on the other, such retentive firmness to the female that it is impossible, in the nature of things, but that strong, beautiful, brilliant, nay, double-distilled children, if I may use the expression, must infallibly be begotten.

GRANDIER Urbain Grandier was a priest of Loudun, in France. Accused of bewitching nuns of the local monastery, he was arrested on a charge of sorcery. He was tortured and burned alive in 1634. A pact that he reputedly made with Satan is preserved in the Bibliothèque Nationale in Paris.

GRAND TRINE   In astrology, two planets trine to each other, both of which are trined by a third planet.

GREAT YEAR   In astrology, this is a period of some 26,000 years divided into twelve parts corresponding to the twelve zodiacal signs.

GRIMOIRE   A textbook on black magic. Among the best known are the Grimorium Verum, the Grand Grimoire, and the Grimoire of Pope Honorius.

GRIS-GRIS   These are protective amulets worn by African tribesmen.

GROOTE, GERHARD   (1340-1384)   A Dutch professor of theology. In 1373 he founded in Holland the sect of Brothers of the Common Life. Members were both laity and monks. The purpose of the sect was to recover the sense of fraternal love.

GROSSETESTE, ROBERT   (1176-1253)   Bishop of Lincoln. Notable scholar and mathematician: studied at Oxford and Paris.
He participated in necromantic practices and was believed to have fashioned a head of bronze endowed with the faculty of prediction.

GUAITA, STANISLAS DE   A French occultist. Late in the nineteenth century he founded a Rosicrucian Kabbalistic Order.

GUARDED In astrology, this term is applied to one or more elevated planets guarded on the East by the Sun and on the West by the Moon.

GUARDIAN According to a tradition in the Eastern Orthodox Church, every person has, in addition to a guardian angel, a guardian devil as well.

GUILLAUME DE PARIS A medieval sorcerer. He was credited with producing, by Satanic aid, statues that were endowed with human speech.

GUILLAUME DE POSTEL (1510-1581) A French Kabbalist and astrologer. The son of poor peasants, he succeeded in becoming a master of Oriental languages. He engaged in diplomatic missions and was later appointed professor of Oriental languages and mathematics.

He gave up his position, however, and traveled and lectured. Claiming to have received revelation in the stars, he adopted certain Gnostic beliefs, asserting that the male and female principles were incorporated in himself. Imprisoned by the Inquisition, he escaped and finally returned to his professorship in Paris. His lectures, however, full of mysticism, compelled him to flee to a convent, where he spent the rest of his life.

He wrote The Key of Things Kept Secret from the Foundation of the World.

GULDENSTUBBE, BARON A necromancer who belongs in the nineteenth century. He evoked the spirits of many historical personalities. He also wrote a treatise on spiritualistic phenomena, and on the validity of spiritualism itself.

GUNAS (TRIGUNAS) In occult philosophy, differentiated matter is assigned three essential qualities, and these are known by their Sanskrit names: *Sattwa, Rajas,* and *Tamas* (truth, passion, and illusion).

GURU   The Sanskrit word for teacher. According to the ancient occultists, the guru is the midwife who helps to bring into the active life of the chela the spiritual powers of the disciple.

GURU-PARAMPARA   A Sanskrit compound meaning an uninterrupted series or succession of teachers. In ancient occultism, each school was headed by a teacher who passed on his mystical authority to a designated successor. The Great Brotherhood of the Sages and Seers of the world, conceived esoterically as the Holy Association of the Masters of Wisdom and Compassion and Peace, is one example of the Guru-parampara. The Theosophical Society is supposed to be a copy or reflection of the esoteric Guru-parampara.

GYMNOSOPHISTS   The ancient Greek writers assigned this name to the naked mendicants of India who were reputedly endowed with mystic faculties.

GYROMANCY   A form of divination by walking round in a circle.

GYUD   In Tibetan mysticism, this term denotes ritual magic, a phase in the initiatory progress of a mystic.

H

HACKS, CHARLES A physician of German extraction who flourished in the nineteenth century. Under the pseudonym of Dr. Bataille he was believed to have written Le Diable au XIX siècle. In this work the author relates strange personal occult experiences and discusses Satanism.

HAGGARD, SIR HENRY RIDER (1856-1925) English novelist. In his autobiography, he makes reference tu his experiences in previous reincarnations.

HAGITH In occult works, Hagith is listed as the ruler of Venus, whose day is Friday. He is one of the seven Olympian Spirits.

HAIR In occultism and mystic philosophy, the hair, both human and animal, is regarded as the receptacle of the vital essence. In the case of the Biblical Samson, his vital strength lay in his hair.

HALF CIRCLE In mathematical mysticism, this figure symbolized the soul.

HALL, MANLY P. A twentieth-century Canadian writer on occultism, in particular on the mystic symbolism of numbers.

HALLELUJAH A semi-Christian religion which originated among Carib-speaking peoples during the nineteenth century. The fusion of traditional beliefs concerning the

167

nature of spirit, particularly as manifested in culture heroes, and elements of Christianity resulted in the evolution of a flourishing religion, one practiced by the Akawaio today. The core of their religion is expressed in three words: *akwa* ('light'), *akwalu* ('spirit'), and *akwalupo* ('without life or light').

HALL OF REVELATIONS In China, an assembly place where spiritualistic phenomena appear through the aid of mediums.

HALLUCINATION A sensory experience arising quite apart from any corresponding external stimulation. It is usually an indication of a psychosis, delirium, or drug addiction. But it can also be produced as a test of hypnotic depth in normal persons.

HALOMANCY A form of divination by means of salt.

HANDS The study of the hands, with a view to determining character and abilities, is termed palmistry. This technique examines the shape of the hand, the position of the fingers, nails, the linear markings, the flexibility of the thumb and fingers, and other manual areas and conditions.

HANDWRITING The study of handwriting, which is termed graphology, proposes to interpret character by examination of the shaping of the letters, the linear slant, the size of the writing, flourishes.

HANSA In Oriental occultism, the name of a mystic bird.

HARE Among the ancient Egyptians the hare was held in sacred esteem. It was particularly associated with Osiris. It was also a symbol of the moon.

HATHA YOGA A form of Yoga embracing a number of postures or 'asanas' which are supposed to open up new spiritual perspectives. Various positions are supposed to enable the practitioner to influence certain nerve centers.

HAUNTED In Ireland and in country houses in England, in remote farms and in houses in old European towns, from Vienna to Italy, the traditional ghost is still active. The apparition appears in various guises, sometimes ectoplasmically, or as a dark flitting shape. On occasion only the being's voice is heard, uttering groans or lamentations or curses. The apparition may appear to more than one person at a time, at a specific hour, usually of the night. But in most cases scientific investigators and parapsychologists have exposed the phenomenon publicly as illusions or as circumstances that admit of sober rational and earthly explanation. But there is despite all this an almost continuous flow of accounts that appear to disprove the non-existence of the ghost. Day and hour are given, along with other evidences of the actuality of such manifestations. Such evidence, in most of these latter instances, assume some form of psychic operation. Questions still remained unsolved regarding the objective validity of all such spirit calls and spirit appearances. What connection is there, for example, in the opening of Egyptian tombs and in the doom that often awaits those who violate these ancient tombs? What relation is there between the opening of Tutankhamen's tomb in 1922 and the fate of the Earl of Carnarvon and Howard Carter? Was it a case of cause and effect? Or were the two situations merely sequential?

HAUSER, KASPAR (1812?-1833) A German foundling of mysterious origin. He had strange powers over animals. He is the subject of a novel by Jakob Wassermann entitled Kaspar Hauser.

169

HAWAIIAN MAGIC Necromancy, spiritualism, in its essential significance, and other occult arts were practiced for centuries by the Hawaiians. Divination and astrology were also in force.

HAWAIIAN RITES In funeral rites among the Hawaiians, the belief was that one of the deities associated with death helped the spirit of the dead person on the journey to the last home. This concept coincides precisely with the practice of Osiris and his attendant gods, as exemplified in the Egyptian guide for the deceased entitled The Book of the Dead.

HAWAIIAN SPIRITS The Hawaiian maintains that every person has two souls or spirits. In sleep, one spirit protects the sleeper, while the other can wander at will. This concept coincides with that of the Egyptian Ka, the astral body.

HAYZ In astrology, in Horary Questions, this term denotes a masculine diurnal planet above the earth in a day figure, and a feminine nocturnal planet under the earth in a night figure. This is called a Dignity of 1 degree, and is reckoned fortunate. The Arabs did not conceive a perfect Hayz except when the masculine planet was in a male sign, or the feminine planet in a female sign. A masculine planet in a male sign under the earth by day was considered to be only in his light, and the person denoted by it to be in a state of contentment.

HEAD In the Zohar, the Book of Splendor, a Kabbalistic treatise, the head is regarded as a symbol of astral light.

HEARN, LAFCADIO (1850 - 1904) Noted writer. Born in the Aegean Islands of Greek and Irish parentage. Spent some years in England and the United States. Finally migrated to Japan and identified himself with Japanese life and culture. Interested in Oriental occultism. Author of Karma, In Ghostly Japan, Gleanings from Buddha Fields, Kwaidan, Shadowings, Some Chinese Ghosts.

HEAVEN   In astrology, heaven is divided into twelve compartments, each marked by one of the twelve signs of the zodiac.

HEBRAIC PROHIBITIONS   In Hebraic mysticism there are four special prohibitions concerning what is above, what is below, what is before, what is behind. Whoever breaks these prohibitions, runs the admonition, should rather not have been born.

HEBREW ALPHABET   The Hebrew alphabet consists of twenty-two letters. Much Kabbalistic speculation was tied to this alphabet and its three 'mother' letters, Aleph, Mem, and Schin. Aleph, for example, corresponds to the number 1, the sign of fire, the heavens, summer, and the head. The seven double letters of the alphabet correspond to the seven planets, the seven days of the week, and the seven orifices of the head. The twelve simple letters correspond to the zodiac signs, the months, and various organs of the body.

HECKETHORN, CHARLES W.   Author of The Secret Societies of all Ages and Countries: first published in 1875.

HELIACAL RISING   In astrology, this term means a rising with the Sun. When a planet or a star, after it has been hidden by the Sun's rays, becomes again visible, that is a heliacal rising.

HELIACAL SETTING   In astrology, this expression is applied when a star is overtaken by the Sun and is lost in its rays. The heliacal rising or setting of the Moon occurs when it is within 17 degrees of the Sun: other stars and planets, when within 30 degrees distance.

HELIOCENTRIC ASTROLOGY   In this type of astrology the astrological interpretations are based on a Figure in which the solar system bodies are located according to their heliocentric longitudes.

HELIOCENTRIC LONGITUDE AND LATITUDE   This is based on the Sun as the centre. The Nautical Almanac gives the heliocentric positions of all celestial bodies. The astrologer's Ephemeris is now made from the Nautical Almanac by reducing these positions to their geocentric equivalent.

HELL   Demonologists and magicians reckoned the number of the inhabitants of Hell at 1,758,064,176. Modern theologians generally interpret Hell as the state of the damned. Like the Greek Hades and the Hebrew Sheol, Hell may also mean the abode of the human spirit after its separation from the body.

HENRY III (1551 - 1589)   The last ruler of the House of Valois was rumored to be a sorcerer. Pamphleteers accused him of conducting lessons in magic at the Louvre. He was also accused of procuring a prostitute for his favorite devil.

HEPATOSCOPY   A form of divination by observation of the liver of a sheep. This type of divination was practiced, among many nations, but largely by the Babylonians, Hittites, and Etruscans.

HERBAL EXORCISM   In the rite of exorcism of a house haunted by evil spirits, the herb abyssum was hung up at the four corners of the house.

HERMES TRISMEGISTUS This expression means Hermes Thrice Greatest. This is the name given by the Greeks to the Egyptian god Thoth. He was the master of knowledge. Reputedly he was the originator of treatises on magic, astrology, and alchemy. The collection of treatises is known as the Hermetica. These works, attributed to Hermes Trismegistus, were actually written by Greeks, in Egypt. Hence their association with ancient Egyptian wisdom.

HERMES UNVEILED A treatise on alchemy produced by Cyliani in 1782, in French. The book contains many autobiographical passages in which the writer describes how a woodland nymph, emerging from an oak tree, was his mentor in the transmutation of base metal into gold.

HERMETIC CHAIN The secrets of Hermes Trismegistus were handed down from pupil teacher to pupil in an unbroken succession. The ancient Greeks had a mystical tradition of a chain of living beings, reaching from the highest divinities downward through inferior gods, heroes, and sages to ordinary men and the beings below men. Each link in the Hermetic chain inspired and instructed the link below itself, communicating love, wisdom, and knowledge of the secrets of the universe.

HESYCHASM In Eastern Orthodoxy, a spiritual system which originated on Mt. Athos. The term means the condition of being quiet. The system advocates meditation, quietude, and certain bodily postures as a means of seeing the divine light. Hesychasm is still in force in the monastic life.

HEX To hex is a term used popularly to denote the practice of affecting a person malefically by magical devices. In recent times, in Pennsylvania, hexing was practiced with sinister, even disastrous results. A New England magazine currently advertises hex signs as adornments.

HEXAGON A line drawn between every second zodiacal sign forms a hexagon or sextile. The sextile is regarded astrologically as favorable.

HEXAGRAM A six-pointed figure: called the Shield of David or the Shield of Solomon. The hexagram was used in occult rites, particularly for the purpose of controlling demons.

HEYDON, JOHN An English astrologer who flourished in the seventeenth century. He wrote on the occult arts, and was himself a Rosicrucian.

HIDDEN SUN GOD During an eclipse of the sun, Hindus prayed that the Sun God be released from Rahu, the demon snake. Hindus feared that the duration of the phenomenon created a danger that the Sun God might be swallowed before prayers could save him.

HIERARCHY A word used in theosophy to signify the degrees, grades, and steps of evolving entities in the cosmos. Every part of the universe is under the vital control of a divine being and only material manifestations of the workings of the spiritual power appear on our plane. The series of hierarchies reaches infinitely in both directions.

HIGHEST GOOD In yoga mysticism, the supreme good is realization of the presence of the spirit and the real self.

HIGHER TRIAD The imperishable spiritual ego considered esoterically as a unity. The reincarnating part of man clothes itself in each earth-life in a lower quaternary. The Higher Triad is the unity of Aman, Buddhi, and the higher Manas; the lower quaternary includes the lower Manas, vitality, the astral model-body, and the cadaver.

174

HILDEGARD (c. 1100-1179) German nun. Abbess of the convent of Rupertsberg. She began to have visions at the age of three. She also became noted for her predictions.

HILYOD, RANGA An ancient Indian sage whose book, Illuminated Brahminism, sets forth the doctrine of reincarnation.

HINDU LEVITATION In Buddhistic tradition, a certain Rajah Kalasoka had a sister endowed with the power of levitating through the air.

HINDU WITCHCRAFT Even today witchcraft is practiced in some Hindu communities. By condemning socially undesirable traits in the individual, by putting blame for an unfortunate occurrence on an evil spirit rather than a person, and by upholding traditional values, witchcraft acts as a moralizing agent, sustains social equilibrium, and strengthens the traditional structure of society. Accusations of witchcraft usually involve persons who are on bad terms with each other. All accusations are against women and are intra-caste.

HITCHCOCK, E. A. An American who in 1865 wrote Remarks on Alchemy and the Alchemists. He postulated the mystical and allegorical significance of alchemy.

HITLAHAVAT A Hebraic term used in Chassidic mysticism. It denotes ecstasy or God-intoxication.

HOD In Kabbalistic mysticism is the name given to the number eight. It signifies eternity.

HODGSON, RICHARD (1855 - 1905) An Australian scholar and psychical researcher who exposed Mme. Blavatsky and cast doubt on the claims of Eusapia Paladino. His major research efforts centered on the investigation of the mediumship of Mrs. Piper, whom he knew through William James. He is reported to have received communications from the controls of Mrs. Piper after her death and to have communicated after his death with James Hervey Hyslop.

HOLZER, HANS A New York author who has made movies, records, and television shows, lectured, and written more than a score of books on the occult. In 'Window on the Past' he tells of his encounter with the ghost of Aaron Burr. In the recently published 'Psychic Photography' he claims to present pictures of 'ghosts and ectoplasmic Material.'

HOME, DANIEL D. An American medium who was notable in England in the nineteenth century. Apart from producing psychic phenomena, he was said to be capable of levitation.

HOMER In Homer's epics, the Iliad and the Odyssey, many magic and supernatural practices and phenomena appear. In the Odyssey an incantation stops the flow of blood in Odysseus' wound. Circe, an enchantress, transforms men into swine. She also instructs Odysseus how to summon the spirits of the dead.

HOMODROMI In astrology, this term, of Greek origin, means fellow-runners. It is applied to the internal or variously called minor or inferior planets Mercury and Venus, which have a maximum elongation from the Sun of approximately 28 degrees and 46 degrees respectively.

HOMUNCULUS The homunculus ('little man') theme may have originated with the Kabbalists, who were said to have the power to create artificial human beings (Golem). According to the alchemists, the homunculus had to be conceived without sexual intercourse, by artificial means. Paracelsus thought it possible to manufacture human beings, and Aurobindo believed that a 'supramental' race would reproduce itself through the power of sexless love.

HONORS   In astrology, honors refer to the Sun and Midheaven and their radical aspects, indicating the degrees of fame and honor to which a person is predestined. The luminaries in an angle and well-aspected are a sign of high honors. Jupiter rising, or in the Midheaven, shows a high degree of prestige. Saturn similarly placed denies credit and renown, however much deserved. Rising planets show aspirations to honors and high ambition, but the outcome of such aspirations depends on which planet first culminates. If the majority of the planets are oriental to the Sun and occidental to the Moon the native will arrive at authority and accumulate wealth. In modern astrology, the term is rare.

HORARY CYCLES   In astrology, the arcs, or circles, in which the planets appear to move around the earth by virtue of the earth's diurnal revolution. The cycles are either diurnal or nocturnal.

HORIMEA   In astrology, this term refers to the rays of the Hyleg after it has passed the Midheaven.

HORNED HAND   A sign of recognition between the initiated. The horned hand is made by raising the index finger and the little finger while turning down the middle fingers and thumb. Occultists have held that they can make the devil powerless by holding up a horned hand to the light.

HOROSCOPE   Astrologically, the rising sign of the zodiac in which the degree of the ecliptic lies is called the horoscope. Popularly, a horoscope is a diagram showing the relative positions of the planets and signs of the zodiac and providing a basis for predictions concerning an individual.

Hundreds of thousands of Americans now buy computer-produced 'personal' horoscopes for about $20.00 each.

HOROVITZ, ISAIAN HA-LEVI A seventeenth century Kabbalist. He became renowned in Poland for encouraging the study of the Kabbalah.

HOUSE In Astrology, every planet has two houses, one of the day, the other of the night.

HOUSEHOLD OF THE UPPER WORLD In Hebraic mysticism, this expression denotes the highest rank of angels.

HOUSE OF LIFE In astrology, this refers to all the influences, favorable or malefic, that affect the life of a person.

HOUSE OF WISDOM An esoteric sect of Moslems, founded in the ninth century in Egypt.

HOUSES, CLASSIFICATION OF In astrology, Houses are classed as follows:
Individual or Life Houses: I, 5, 9, representing respectively the body, soul, and spirit: the Trinity of Life.
Temporal or Possessive Houses: representing the temporal status of the native: 2, possessions and property: 6, comforts: 10, honor and credit, position in society: the Trinity of Wealth.
Relative or Association Houses: relating to human relationships: 3, ties of consanguinity: 7, conjugal ties: 11, friendship: the Trinity of Association.
Terminal or Psychic Houses: referring to eventualities, particularly the termination of conditions in the native's life: 4, environment in each period of life: 8, influence of others: 12, hindering influences: the Trinity of Psychism.

HOUSES, GROUPING OF   In astrology, Houses may be grouped by direction:

Eastern Houses: Those in the eastern half of the Figure, containing planets rising toward the Midheaven: that is, the third, second, first, twelfth, eleventh, tenth. Of these, the three above the horizon — containing planets which, moving clockwise against the order of the signs, are passing away from the horizon toward their culmination at the Midheaven — are considered to confer upon these planets added strength 'by position.'

Western Houses: Houses in the western half of the Figure — fourth, fifth, sixth, seventh, eighth, ninth. Posited in these Houses, malefic planets are said to be strengthened and benefic planets weakened — particularly regarding their influence on the native's health.

Oriental Houses: Houses which extend clockwise from the horizon to the meridian: the twelfth, eleventh, tenth, sixth, fifth, fourth.

Occidental Houses: Houses which extend clockwise from the meridian to the horizon: the ninth, eighth, seventh, third, second, first.

HSIANG   The four Hsiang (Symbols) of the I Ching consist of two undivided lines (the *Yang* in its major phase), two divided lines (the *Yin* in its major phase), a divided line over an undivided line (the *Yang* in its minor phase) and a divided line under an undivided line (the *Yin* in its minor phase). These four Hsiang give rise to the Eight Trigrams of the I Ching.

HSIAO   Straight lines which are arranged in various combinations of three to produce the Eight Trigrams (Pa Kua) of the I Ching.

HSIAO-TZ'U (HSI-TZ'U)   A commentary on each of the six lines of a hexagram in the I Ching. The Hsiao-Tz'u

(Appended Judgments) are attributed traditionally to Chou Kung, son of King Wen, author of the *T'uan* (Judgments). The trigrams, hexagrams, T'uan, and Hsiao-Tz'u became the basis of occultism as set forth in the I Ching.

HSIEN   Chinese mountain hermits who lived several centuries before the Christian era. They are said to have succeeded in prolonging life far beyond the ordinary span by means of physical exercises, dieting, and mental cultivation.

The word *hsien*, derived from two pictographic elements, 'man' and 'mountain,' was first applied to men who had retired from the world and confined their activities in the mountains to the gathering of herbs and roots, meditation, and cultivation of their physical and mental powers. They were often credited with supernatural powers besides the prolongation of life: control over the elements, rejuvenation, and the ability to move with great swiftness and to appear simultaneously in several places.

Later, hsien were classed according to their habitat: (1) celestial hsien, who dwelt in heaven; (2) terrestrial hsien, who remained on earth without aging; (3) aquatic hsien, purely *yin* or feminine; and (4) divine or spiritual hsien. demigods who dwelt on the Isles of the Blest.

HULDA   She was a Jewish prophetess who flourished during the period of the First Temple.

HUMAN LEOPARD SOCIETY   A secret society whose members were thought to be able to change at will into leopards. The secret brotherhood evolved from a Mendi medicine war into a cannibalistic institution.

HUMAN SOUL   The Greek philosophers, particularly Plato, divided the soul into the rational part, noetic, and the irrational, animal part, called agnoia.

180

HUMBLE The Humble Ones were a Hebraic esoteric sect of whom little else is known except that their mysticism involved prayers.

HUNG SOCIETY A Chinese secret society that has existed since 386 A.D. Closely associated with the White Lotus, it was founded by Eon or Hwui-Yin to spread the cult of Amitabha Buddha and has the largest membership of any secret society in the world. The initiation ceremony symbolizes the soul's journey through the underworld and paradise to the City of Willows, which is the abode of the gods. Allegorically, the ceremony depicts the experiences of the mystic in seeking to unite with the Supreme Being. The importance attached to the triangle is reflected in the alternate name of the brotherhood, the Triad Society.

HUNGAN A priest of the Voodoo cult.

HUNTING MAGIC Drawings which have existed in caves in France and Spain since prehistoric times suggest that hunting magic is inspired by belief in the supernatural. Even today, among the Iglukik Eskimos, drawings can be found which are inspired by belief in the supernatural.

HUTIN, SERGE Author of a book on Secret Societies, entitled Les Sociétés Secrètes: published since 1940.

HUYSMANS, JORIS KARL (1848 - 1907) French novelist. Author of Là-Bas, on a Satanic theme. Huysmans declared: The principle of Evil, and the Principle of Good, the God of Light and the God of Darkness, two streams contend for our soul. At the present time, it is quite evident that the God of Good is in eclipse, that Evil reigns over the world, as master. In Là-Bas he also describes a black mass celebrated in Vaugirard.

HYDESVILLE The small hamlet near Rochester, New York, known as the birthplace of modern spiritualism. It was there that the Fox Sisters heard uncanny sounds and tried to establish communication with the invisible world.

HYLEG In astrology, this term means: the giver of life. It denotes a planet so located as to have influence upon the longevity of the native. It is one of the most complex and controversial subjects in the field of astrology but which has fallen more or less in disfavor as a result of the concept that any attempt to predict the time of death is now considered unethical. The strongest planet that occupied one of the aphetic places became Hyleg, and was considered to be the Apheta, the giver of life. When it had progressed to an aspect to the place of the Anareta, the taker-away of life, the native was presumed to have run his span of life.

HYMN TO THE SUN Julian the Apostate, the Christian Roman emperor who turned to paganism, belongs in the fourth century A.D. He is the author of a Hymn to the Sovereign Sun, which is packed with astrological allusions.

HYPEROURANIOI In Neoplatonic philosophy, this Greek expression denotes the twelve super-celestial gods.

HYPOGEON This expression, of Greek origin, denotes: under the earth. In astrology, it generalizes the lower heaven: it includes the nadir, the *imun coeli,* and the Fourth House.

HYSLOP, JAMES HERVEY (1854-1920) A professor of logic and ethics at Columbia University, the greatest American propagandist of survival was at first the most skeptical of psychical researchers. In Life After Death he states: 'I regard the existence of discarnate spirits as scientifically proved.'

I

I One of the fundamental concepts of the I Ching. It means change, simplicity, and invariability.

IAO (IHAHO) A mystic name embodying the symbols of the male and the female generative principles. Clement of Alexandria stated that it was worn by the initiates of the Mysteries of Serapis.

I CHING In Confucianism, one of five books *(Ching)* in the canon known as the Five Classics. The *I Ching* (Book of Changes, or Book of Divination), traditionally ascribed to Wen Wang in the twelfth century, B.C., is based upon the figures of divided and undivided lines known as trigrams and hexagrams. There are eight diagrams of triplet lines, undivided and divided. These are expanded and doubled to produce sixty-four hexagrams. Each hexagram is followed by a short, enigmatic explanation of each line.
The most ancient of the Chinese Classics is at once an oracle, a philosophy, and a work of art. Confucius is reported to have said, at the age of seventy, that he would spend extra years, if they could be added to his life, studying the I Ching. Hermann Hesse tells of his initiation to the work in Magister Ludi. The work originated in connection with a process of divination based on the manipulation of milfoil stalks.

ICHTHYOMANCY A form of divination by observation of the entrails of fishes.

I-KIM An ancient and obscure Chinese text. It belongs reputedly in the fourth millennium B.C. Its subject is Kabbalistic mysticism. The Key to this work is called the Trigrams of Fo-Hi, after the name of the Emperor Fo-Hi, the putative author.

ILLUMINATED THEOSOPHISTS A branch of Masons that was founded in London in the eighteenth century.

ILLUMINATI This Latin expression means: The Enlightened Ones. It was applied in the fifteenth century to certain putative adepts in occult practices. The name was revived in the eighteenth century by a German professor named Adam Weishaupt, who added mystical concepts to the fraternity of Illuminati. This fraternity had associations with Freemasonry and became involved in political activities. The society was dissolved late in the eighteenth century.

ILLUSIONISTS A Gnostic sect that maintained that if Christ did die, his death was only an illusion.

IMMORTALITY In Hebraic thought, immortality was a basic belief in Talmudic days, accepted by Pharisees and rejected by Sadducees. Philosophers, from Maimonides to Spinoza, upheld the belief.

IMPEDED: IMPEDITED In astrology, these two synonymous terms refer to a luminary or planet when badly aspected, especially by the malefics. The terms are also used of the Moon when passing to a conjunction, square, or opposition to the Sun, Mars, or Saturn. The Moon when impedited by the Sun at birth was anciently said to produce a blemish in or near the eye.

184

IMPERATOR A famous control who, according to Stainton Moses, announced his presence on September 19, 1872, and later claimed to be Malchias, leader of a band of spirits working toward the elevation of the human race. This band, or a similar band, is said to have taken over control of Mrs. Piper in 1897. Several later mediums claimed to receive communications through Imperator.

IMPERFECT SIGNS: BROKEN SIGNS In astrology, these signs are: Leo, Scorpio, Pisces.

IMPS There was an age-old belief that witches suckled imps in animal shape. In William Congreve's play Love for Love reference is made to this belief.

IMUM COELI This Latin expression means: the lowest heaven. In astrology, the North Angle or cusp of the Fourth House.

INCOMMUNICABLE AXIOM The Incommunicable Axiom is a secret key to the occult. It is found embodied in the four letters of the Tetragram, in the Kabbalistic transcription of the words Azoth and Inri, and in the monogram embroidered on Constantine's standard (XP). One who succeeds in deciphering it is supposed to become omnipotent.

INCONJUNCT This term means: dissociate. In astrology, a planet is inconjunct when it forms no aspect and is not in parallel of declination or mutual disposition to another planet. Dissociate was formerly applied to the 150 degrees or Quincunx aspect, which was regarded as inconsequential. Now it is applied to any two signs or houses which have no familiarity with each other, that is, those which bear a twelfth, second, sixth, and eighth house relationship, as Taurus with Aries, Gemini, Libra, and Sagittarius.

INCUBUS   A male demon who copulates with women. Correspondingly, a female demon who copulates with men is called a succubus. The offspring are called cambions. The princess of all the succubi is called Nahemah. The belief in such spirits was current in the Middle Ages.

INFERIOR PLANETS   In astrology, these are the minor planets, those whose orbits are within that of the earth, namely, Mercury and Venus.

INFORTUNES   In astrology, this term is applied to Mars and Saturn.

INGRESS   In astrology, this term applies to the entry of any orbital body into a sign, or a quadrant. The Sun makes an ingress into the cardinal signs at the equinoxes and solstices. The planets also have their ingresses into the various signs, which result in certain alterations of their influence.

INITIATING SIGNS   In astrology, the first sign of each season of the year: the cardinal signs: Aries, Cancer, Libra, Capricorn, characterized by a constant state of mobilization for action.

INITIATION   In Hebraic mysticism, there were grades of initiations into the mysteries. These initiations entailed rigid preparations, both spiritual and ascetic.
In a general sense, initiations into secret cults were classified thus:
first stage: purification, directed toward perfection.
second stage: illumination, directed to the acquisition of universal knowledge.
third stage: reintegration: assimilation into a lost Golden Age.
Theosophy teaches that there were in ancient times seven

degrees of initiation. After passing through the three preparatory stages, the disciple was considered sufficiently cleansed, purified, and disciplined to enter the fourth stage and learn by the old mystical processes the secrets of the structure and operations of the universe. The fifth, sixth, and seventh degrees were supposed to help the disciple to develop his latent powers and faculties, and to penetrate more deeply beyond the veils of illusion and become a Mahatma (superman).

INNER GOD Mystics of all ages have taught the ever-present power of an individual inner god in each human being. Esoterically, this inner god is conceived as man's essential self.

INNER MAN In mysticism, this term refers to the essential spiritual entity of a person.

INSPIRATIONAL NATURES In astrology, this expression refers to the quality of sensory receptivity and reaction that characterizes those born with the Sun in Aries, Leo, and Sagittarius — respectively, the initiative, executive, and deductive types of the inspirational group.

INSTRUCTION IN WITCHCRAFT Training in occult practices and the Black Arts is publicly offered. This training includes making voodoo figures, producing ritual candles, performing spells. The invitation comes from the pseudonymous Satan's Daughters.

INTELLECTUAL NATURES In astrology, this expression refers to a quality of sensory receptivity through the mind that characterizes those born with the Sun in Libra, Aquarius, and Gemini — respectively, the initiative, executive, and deductive types of the intellectual group.

187

INTERCEPTED HOUSE In astrology, a House in which a sign is contained wholly within the House, which sign does not appear upon either cusp of the House. An intercepted House is generally either preceded or followed by one that has the same sign on both the cusps. The affairs of an intercepted House are generally complicated and the planets therein are of more than average importance.

INTERMEDIATE NATURE Theosophy teaches that the intermediate nature, offspring of the divine spark, enshrines the ray from the spark. An imperfect thing, it learns much in the sphere of universal life. Gods, monads, and atoms in the universe are copied in the essential trichotomy of man: spirit, soul, and body. The intermediate nature of man, commonly called soul, may also be referred to as his divine-spiritual and astral-physical parts.

INTERPOLATION In astrology, this term is applied to computing a planet's position for a given moment between two known positions, such as the noon or midnight position prior to and subsequent to the desired moment, as taken from an Ephemeris for that year. The term is also used to compute the house cusps for an intermediate latitude between two sets of tables computed for latitudes on either side of that for which the interpolation is required. In making the calculations necessary for an interpolation, use is frequently made of Tables of Diurnal Proportional Logarithms.

INTERPRETATION In astrology, this term refers to an individual judgment on the significance of a configuration of birth planets, or of transiting or progressed aspects to a birth configuration.

INUA   Among the Eskimos of Alaska the *inua* is a spirit in human form or a spirit that can assume such a form.

INVENTORS OF MAGIC   Apuleius, the Roman novelist and philosopher who belongs in the second century A.D., states that the inventors of magic were Zoroaster and Oromazus.

INVISIBLE WORLDS   Ancient occultism teaches that the universe is a living organism with invisible realms or spheres unknown to man. These inner realms interpenetrate and permeate our physical sphere. Our imperfect senses prevent our seeing them, for they arc built of a more ethereal matter than our universe. They are the fountainhead of all the energies of the whole physical world.

INVOLUTION   In theosophical writings, involution is considered to be the reverse of the process of evolution. Before death, for example, the material side of being weakens; faculties previously unfolded seem gradually to diminish.

IO-TE-PUKENGA   A Maori supernatural being conceived as the source of all things and omnipotent ruler of the world.

IPALNEMOHUANI   The name given by the ancient Aztecs to the sun, identified as the source of all vital force.

IROQUOIAN WITCHCRAFT   The Iroquoian peoples attributed disease to the mind of the patient himself, to witchcraft, and to physical injuries. The human body was thought to be inhabited by a single soul with several functions or capacities: animation, knowledge, judgment, willing, desiring, and separation from the body. The soul occupied all parts of the body and had the power to leave the body during dreams or after death. Witchcraft was used to introduce foreign articles into a victim's body thereby producing sickness.

IRUNGU The Nyoro spirit of the bush and wild animals. Irungu is one of several spirits involved in the Nyoro cult of spirit mediumship. When he is 'in the head' of a medium, Irungu may divine for clients willing to pay the fee for his services.

ISAAC OF HOLLAND An alchemist who reputedly belongs in the fifteenth century. Author of alchemical treatises.

ISAAC THE BLIND The French Jew credited with revealing the basic works and mystical teachings of the ancient rabbis. Isaac (fl. 1190-1200) initiated a renewal of interest in a mystical trend centered on two problems: how to reconcile God to the material world, and the origin of matter.

ISLES OF THE BLEST In the ancient Greek epic poet Hesiod these isles are destined for certain heroes exempted from death. A variant name for the Isles of the Blest is Elysium.

ISRAELI, ISAAC (c. 832-932) Famous physician, founder of an influential medical school. Also philosopher. Author of Kitab al Istiksat, written in Arabic and translated into Hebrew and finally into Latin under the title of De elementis. He made a distinction between the impression received by the five senses and the post-sensory perception. Israeli practiced medicine in Egypt and Tunisia. A Christian monk, Constantine of Carthage, translated several of Israeli's medical treatises into Latin in 1087, and used them as a textbook at the University of Salerno, the oldest university in Western Europe.

190

ISWARA This Sanskrit term means lord and is frequently applied to cosmic divinities and to the cosmic spirit in man. Iswara is the divine, individualized spirit in man, his own personal god.

ITALIAN BELIEF IN AFTER-LIFE In ancient Italian religious thought, the spirits of the dead, dwelling in the Underworld, can return only at certain times: as, for instance, at the feast of the Lemuria. This festival, celebrated in May, brought out hungry ghosts from the Lower Regions. They prowled around houses and were fed in order to get rid of them.

ITALIAN WITCHCRAFT In the late nineteenth century there were still old women in Italy who concocted potions or used occult amulets and had secret traditional knowledge of ancient pagan rites and invocations to pagan deities.

ITALY In the latter part of the nineteenth century spiritualistic phenomena acquired such influence that many notable personalities became deeply interested. Among these were King Victor Emmanuel and Garibaldi.

J

JACOBITES A Christian sect that flourished in Syria in the sixth century.

JACOB'S LADDER In Kabbalistic mysticism this vision symbolizes alchemical forces.

JAGEL, ABRAHAM BEN HANNANIAH DEI GALICCHI A Jewish-Italian Kabbalist who flourished in the sixteenth/seventeenth century.

JAGRAT A Sanskrit word designating the state of consciousness during wakefulness, as opposed to the dreaming-sleeping state of consciousness.

JAMES, WILLIAM (1842-1910) An American psychologist, philosopher, and founder of the American Society for Psychical Research, William James maintained throughout his lifetime an interest in the supernatural. He was responsible for the psychic research centering on Mrs. Piper, whom he credited with supernatural powers. In Contact with the Other World Hyslop discusses James' return after death.

JAPANESE EXORCISM One Japanese procedure involves rushlights, placed in a lantern, along with the recital of an incantation one hundred times.

JAPANESE NEW YEAR This festival involves banishing evil spirits from homes by throwing out peas and beans and also by the use of certain mystical numbers — 3, 5, 7.

JEANNE D'ARC (1411-1431) The Maid of Orleans heard voices from early childhood. Her exhibition of supernatural powers persuaded the Dauphin of her divine mission but led eventually to her burning. Her prophecies were realized after her death. She was canonized in 1920.

JEHOVAH'S WITNESSES A movement founded by C. T. Russell. The members conceive Jehovah as their Lord. They maintain a belief in a Messianic kingdom on earth, in a Last Judgment, and in resurrection. They have their own version of the New Testament.

JETTATURA This Italian expression denotes the casting of the Evil Eye on a person or thing or animal. The term is used in Southern Italy, where the practice is still in vogue.

JINN In Islamic demonology, the jinn belonged to an order of spirits lower than the angels. They had the power to appear in human or animal form, and to exert supernatural influence. They are represented as riding on porcupines, foxes, gazelles. They belong in Moslem demonology. In Malayan magic, there are 190 black jinn, who operate malevolently among the hills and forests.

JIVA A Sanskrit word meaning a living being divested of all attributes or qualities. It is equivalent to the theosophical term monad.

JIVANMUKTI In yoga, this term denotes the state of being liberated while still embodied. It is the state of a person who never, while conscious, loses sight of the atma or true self.

JOHN OF INDAGINE A German writer of Nuremberg who flourished in the sixteenth century. He was the author of a book on divination. He postulated the concept of divining human character from a physiognomical study of a person.

JOINED IN In astrology, this expression is applied to any body that is embraced within the orbs of any aspect to any other body: more specifically applicable to a conjunction.

JOLIVET-CASTELOT A high dignitary of the French Rosicrucian Society, Jolivet-Castelot helped to bring alchemy back into fashion. He is said to have used transmutation to produce gold.

JOSEPH BEN JACOB IBN ZADDIK A twelfth century Spanish-Jewish poet and philosopher. Author of Microcosm, a philosophy of religion based on Neoplatonism influenced by Aristotle.

JOSHUA BEN LEVI A Talmudic scholar of Lydda, in Palestine, who flourished in the third century A.D. In legend he became a heroic figure who robs the angel of his sword and reaches Paradise alive.

JOYS In astrology the planets are in their joys when they reside in the strongest and most influential houses: for example, when Mars is in Scorpio, or the Sun is in Leo.

JUDAIC MAGIC There are extant Greco-Jewish magical texts, discovered in Egypt. Invocations and supplications are made therein to the Hebrew Angelic Hierarchy and to the Hebrew name of God.

JU-JU A generic name for African magic practices. There are secret societies with strange initiatory rites, occult cults and brotherhoods that are, according to reliable evidence furnished by European government officials and others, able to enlist the services of powerful Ju-Ju men.

These latter are knowledgeable in ancient traditional secrets that may affect life and death. They are feared by their fellows and they have demonstrated, to the knowledge of physicians, engineers, administrators who are coldly objective, that they are capable of producing phenomena inexplicable to reason. They are reputed to protect a client by fashioning apotropaic amulets. The love potions that they prepare will win over a recalcitrant or forgetful lover. On the sinister side, they may prepare powders to induce sickness, even death. They can cause illness in a designated person who shows no external symptoms or other diagnostic evidence amenable to medical diagnosis. A Ju-Ju curse is a serious matter, and may bring agonies to the victim until it is broken by certain specific rituals. Ju-Ju is practiced by women as well as by the so-called 'witch-doctor' or medicine man. There is a special costume worn by the Ju-Ju man, a special cane. Devil masks are part of the equipment.

If an evil spirit enters a man, the Ju-Ju adept is called in, and in his own mysterious way he exorcises the diabolic creature as demons were exorcised since Biblical times. In the jungle and in forest areas, among the haunts of wild beasts, all kinds of hazards are to be encountered. But a medicine brewed by a Ju-Ju man is a sovereign remedy.

Witches abound, casting evil spells on an entire village, on women and cattle alike. But the superior skill and potency of the medicine man will subdue her, by remote control, by means that are telepathic and psychic. When the witch is caught, she may suffer the extreme penalty, being strangled or burned or drowned, as was the practice in the Middle Ages.

196

JULIAN THE APOSTATE (332-363 A.D.) Roman Emperor. He turned from Christianity and became a pagan. He was a mystic and while in Mesopotamia he participated in secret rites. He glorified Mithra, the Sun-God. He had been initiated into paganism in a ruined temple near Ephesus, long before he became Emperor. Before his death, he is supposed to have said, 'Why mourn for a soul ready to unite with the spirits of the stars?'

K

KABBALAH   A Judaic mystic esoteric body of lore, based on occult interpretations of the Bible. The Kabbalah, which is variously translated as 'tradition' or 'acceptance,' dates in the fourteenth century. It consists of ancient doctrines dealing with the mystic symbolism of numbers and letters. There are different views on the sources of the Kabbalah. It is referred to the Greeks and the Pythagorean interpretation of numbers. Again, it is associated with the Gnostics, an ancient esoteric sect.

The Kabbalah stresses light, its emanations, letter-mysticism, space and time, good and evil, man in the cosmos, angels and demons. These themes in the Kabbalah coincide in many directions with ancient Persian beliefs, especially the two opposing principles of good and evil, Ahura Mazda and Ahriman respectively.

The central area associated with the study of the Kabbalah was the Holy Land. Subsequently the centre was transferred to Mesopotamia, where it was developed systematically. In Babylonia it was studied intensely between the sixth and the eleventh century. The Kabbalistic system was cultivated in particular in the Academy of Pumbeditha. In the nineteenth century the Kabbalah became widely known in Europe, especially in Italy, Germany, and France. Those who were deeply versed in the text and its interpretation were known under various names, as Bearers of the Secret, Men of Action, Gnostics. Among the most noted Kabbalists were Aaron ben Samuel, Isaac the Blind, and Azriel.

The most sacred of all Kabbalistic writing was the Zohar, which was revealed to the public by Moses de Leon in 1300. With the appearance of the Zohar, the study of the Kabbalah spread, thereby losing something of its exclusively esoteric import.

KABBALAH OF THE NINE CHAMBERS In Hebraic mysticism, a secret kind of writing, intended for the eyes of the initiated only.

KABBALISTIC LITERATURE The literature of the Kabbalah, the body of mystical Hebraic writings, began in Palestine and Babylon. Among the systematic works of the early period are a treatise on the measures of God and the Book of Creation.

KABBALISTIC PRACTICES Kabbalistic practices involved magical rites, the use of amulets, exorcism of diabolic spirits, and mystic prayers.

KABBALISTIC SYMBOLS In Hebraic Kabbalistic mysticism there are four secret symbols attached to the four letters comprising the name of the Lord: the wand is related to I, the cup of libation to H, the sword to V, the shekel of gold to H.

KABBALISTIC THEME The theme of the Kabbalah, the body of mystical Hebraic writings, is God before creation and man after creation.

KABBALISTIC WRITINGS In the early Middle Ages the centre of Kabbalistic studies was established in the Mediterranean countries and in Germany. In that period the major works published in the field were: a treatise on emanations, the Book of Enlightenment, and the Zohar, the Book of Splendor.

KABOD In Jewish mysticism, this term means a materialization of the divinity in the form of a cloud.

KADO The sacred dance of the Kiowa Indians, performed annually in honor of the sun as a divine power.

KAHUNAISM In Hawaii the old indigenous magic system is still in vogue. The term kahuna signifies a sorcerer.

KAKATYCHE This Greek term, which means: ill fortune, is applied in astrology to the Sixth House.

KALPA A Sanskrit word meaning a period or cycle of time. Sometimes a Kalpa designates the great manvantara (Maha-manvantara) after which the globes of a planetary chain die; or it may mean a 'Day of Brahma' whose length is 4,320,000,000 years.

KAMA In Oriental occultism, the word kama ('desire') designates the fourth substance-principle of man's constitution, the seat of impulses, desires, and aspirations.

KANISCH, PETER The fifteenth century founder of a religious sect called Pikarti. One of the tenets was that God was indwelling in any person who served him.

KANT, IMMANUEL (1724-1804) The German philosopher analyzed the experiences of Swedenborg in Dreams of a Spirit Seer. He believed that departed souls could still act on the souls of the living.

KARDEC, ALLAN A pseudonymous name. He was a French spiritualist who belongs in the nineteenth century. He died in 1869. Kardec exerted a deep influence throughout Europe. Among his beliefs was a conviction of reincarnation.

KARSHIPTA　In Zoroastrianism, a sacred and mystic bird that symbolized the soul.

KEEMA　An animating principle identified by the Mossi with the dying. The keema of a dying man may wander around and frighten people. After a man dies, he ceases to be called by his name and is referred to as the 'keema.'

KERNER, JUSTINUS (1786-1862)　A German poet and physician who wrote many works on supernatural phenomena. The Seeress of Prevorst (1829), based on the experiences of a somnambulist, brought him acclaim. A new school of philosophy was based on its revelations.

KETHER　The first Sephira of the Tree of Life: the Crown, situated in the world of Atziluth. Known also as the Primum Mobile, the highest point in a Figure of the Heavens. The term refers chiefly to Hindu astrology.

KEY OF SOLOMON THE KING　A medieval treatise on magic falsely attributed to King Solomon and intended to serve as a guide to the discovery of treasure. The Lesser Key of Solomon dating from the seventeenth century contains conjurations used in controlling the offices of all spirits.

KEY WORDS　In astrology, certain key words are associated with the twelve zodiacal signs, as follows:
　　Aries: Aspiration
　　Taurus: Integration
　　Gemini: Vivification
　　Cancer: Expansion
　　Leo: Assurance
　　Virgo: Assimilation
　　Libra: Equilibrium
　　Scorpio: Creativity
　　Sagittarius: Administration

Capricorn: Discrimination
Aquarius: Loyalty
Pisces: Appreciation

KHALID IBN JAZID   An Arab occultist. He flourished in the seventh century and wrote on the mystic arts.

KHE-CHARA   A Sanskrit word meaning sky-walker. The term is used in mystical literature to signify one of the powers possessed by the yogi. It is the projection of the Mayavi-rupa to any part of the surface of the earth or beyond, at will.

KHUNRATH, HEINRICH   A German mystic, alchemist, and Rosicrucian. In 1601 he published an Amphitheatre of Eternal Wisdom.

KI   A human aura. The theory of the existence of a subtle emanation conveying mesmeric or similar influences has been investigated by parapsychologists.

KING OF THE SACRED RITES   The combination of priestly functions with royal authority was common in ancient Greece and Italy. The Sacrificial King, or King of the Sacred Rites, were titles accorded such men at Rome and in other cities of Latium.

KINGSFORD, ANNA   A nineteenth century theosophist, who had remarkable revelations and visions. These were often induced in a state of deep sleep.

KINGS OF THE WOODS   A line of priests descended from the mythical Virbius and linked with certain trees in the sacred grove at Nemi. They regularly perished by the swords of their successors.

KINKIRSE   Spiritual agents of the Mossi earth gods. They enter the wombs of women and emerge as children.

KIPLING, RUDYARD (1865-1936)   English novelist. One of his short stories, The Finest Story in the World, deals with the reincarnation of the principal character.

KIRCHNER, ATHANASIUS (1602-1680)   The German Jesuit is famous as the inventor of the magic lantern. His writings on occultism profoundly influenced the alchemists of his century.

KIRUBI   In Assyrian mythology, they were guardian beings at the entrances of temples. They correspond to the Hebraic cherubim.

KITAB-EL-HIKMET   This is the title of the basic book of the mystic sect of Druses who live on Mount Lebanon. It denotes The Book of Wisdom. The founder of the sect was Hamsa.

KLESHAS   In yoga mysticism the five kleshas are the five sources of human trouble: ignorance, self-personality, desire, aversion, possessiveness.

KNIGHTS TEMPLARS   A military-religious Order which flourished during the Crusades in the twelfth century. Their variant names were Knights of the Temple of Solomon and Poor Knights of Christ. Originally the Templars consisted of nine Knights, under the direction of Hugh de Payens. The purpose was to protect pilgrims on their way to the Holy Land. The Order expanded in time and became immensely powerful.

The Order was accused of many crimes, particularly the practice of Satanic rites and participation in ceremonials that were inimical to Christian doctrine. The Grand Master,

Jacques de Molay, was burned at the stake in 1314, at which time the Order was dissolved.

KNORR VON ROSENROTH, CHRISTIAN (1636-1689) A Kabbalist who in 1684 published his Cabala Unveiled. It is in the form of a dialogue between the Cabalist and the Christian Philosopher.

KNOTS The belief that knots obstruct human activity is widespread. The maleficent power of the physical act is manifested in the form of sickness, disease, and other kinds of misfortune.

KNOWING ONES The Knowing Ones is the name of an African secret organization reputedly skilled in the occult arts.

KONKOMBA SORCERY The Konkomba, a small tribe inhabiting the Oti Plain in the Gold Coast, believe that the *osuo* or sorcerer uses magical medicines to cause the death of a victim. The osuo may also cause death by sending snakes to lie in wait for the victim or by sending his shadow to devour the victim's shadow. A flaming stick may be used to drive away a sorcerer.

KOONS SPIRIT ROOM A room fitted out for holding spiritualistic séances. It was built from special measurements by Jonathan Koons, of Ohio, in the nineteenth century. Among the phenomena that were manifested were allegedly spirits who were pre-Adamites.

KRA In African belief, the kra is a kind of being dwelling within a man. It is virtually his double, and is of human form as well. The kra acts as a protective agent, like the Egyptian Ka.

KRAFFT, KARL A German astrologer who was attached to Hitler's headquarters. He guided Hitler's plans by observation of astrological phenomena.

KRISHNAMURTI Mrs. Annie Besant, who succeeded Madame Blavatsky as head of the Theosophical Society in 1907, thought that in Krishnamurti she had discovered the next in the series of great instructors who appear in the world at the opportune moment. Following a sensational guardianship trial in Madras, he was proclaimed the vehicle of the new Messiah. In 1929 he renounced his claim of messiahship and followed an independent course.

KSHETRA This yoga term, meaning the field, denotes the entire field of manifestation and all objects therein.

KUAS Sixty-four Kuas or hexagrams, themselves composed into six tendencies, yield a total of 11,520 different situations described in the I-Ching. Rings are used to interrogate the I-Ching in the Chinese system of divination.

KUKLOS ANANKES A Greek expression meaning The Cycle of Fate. A mystery cult in ancient Egypt and Chaldea. The rites and ceremonials of the cult were performed in subterranean crypts.

KUMBHAKA The Sanskrit designates a dangerous practice of the Hatha-Yoga system. It consists of breathing exercises involving closing the mouth and pinching the nostrils to shut off the supply of air in an attempt to evolve forth the powers of the inner divinity.

KUNDALINI The Sanskrit word Kundalini ('circular') is used esoterically to designate a hidden power working through man's Auric Egg and expressing itself continuously in many familiar phenomena of existence. In its higher aspect

206

kundalini is a force moving through winding or circular pathways and originating in the Higher Triad.

KWEI   In Chinese demonology, a spirit that takes possession of a living body. Akin to the medieval dybbuk.

L

LADDER OF LIFE   A theosophical term expressing the ascending grades or stages of manifested existences in the universe, which is embodied consciousness. It is marked at intervals by planes of being, or different spheres of consciousness.

LAGNA SPHUTAS   In astrology, this Hindu term denotes the calculating of the Ascendant.

LAMBE, JOHN   Dr. John Lambe was an English wizard who practiced prognostication. One of his adherents was said to be the Duke of Buckingham. In 1628 Lambe was stoned to death by a London mob.

LAMMAS   Celebrated as harvest, feast, or first-fruits day in early English history, Lammas is one of the old pagan 'sabbaths.' It was celebrated on August 1 by adherents of the Old Religion.

LANTOINE, ALBERT   Author of a book on secret societies entitled Les Sociétés secrètes en Europe et en Amérique: published since 1940.

LAPIS PHILOSOPHORUM   This Latin expression means The Philosophers' Stone. It refers to the alchemical concept of a universal solvent which ultimately produces pure gold.

LATIF, ISSAC BEN ABRAHAM IBN (died 1290)   A Kabbalist who was concerned with the divine emanations and expounded them in mathematical and metaphysical terms.

LAVATER, JOHANN KASPER (1741-1801) The Swiss poet, mystic, and theologian was widely read in his time. Best remembered as the originator of a system of physiognomy, he was assisted by Goethe in writing a four-volume work on the subject (Physiognomical Fragments for the Promotion of the Knowledge and Love of Man, 1775-78).

LAYA In occultism, that point where substance becomes homogeneous and is not able to differentiate.

LAYA CENTRES In astrology neutral states between solid, liquid and gaseous. They are said to be governed by Saturn.

LEE, ANN (1736-1784) An English religious mystic. Called Ann the Word and Mother Ann. Founder of the Shaker Society in New York state. She conceived herself as a reincarnated female messiah. The community that she established after her migration to the U.S.A. was dedicated to celibacy, chastity. It also rejected medical aid.

LEEK, SYBIL An English witch, by her own admission, who traces her ancestry back to 1134. She calls her witchcraft the Old Religion. She writes a column on astrology for a magazine, acts as a medium, and lectures and travels throughout the United States.

LEFT In occultism, the left side and the left hand are associated with sorcery, evil performances, and demoniac forces. The Latin term for left, sinister, has acquired in its English context a pejorative and malefic connotation.

LEIPPYA In Burmese belief, after the death of a person, the soul becomes an invisible butterfly.

LELU Among the Nupe of West Africa, the official head of all the witches and of all the women in town.

LEMURIA   A modern term adopted by theosophists to name the continent that preceded Atlantis.

LEO   In astrology, the Lion. The fifth, northern sign of the zodiac. It is equated with fire, with the power of the sun. In occultism, it symbolizes strength and courage. Kabbalistically, it signifies the heart of the grand old man of the heavens, the fire vortex of physical life, and the life center of humanity.

LESHY   In Slavic mythology, a wood spirit or sylvan deity. Leshies are depicted as having both human and animal characteristics. They run through the forests, imitate human voices, and lead the unwary into their caves.

LEVI, ELIPHAS (1810-1870)   The real name of this French occultist was Alphonse Louis Constant. He was trained for the priesthood, but was expelled for his views. After an unfortunate marriage, he dedicated himself to occultism, and also gave instruction to disciples. He professed to have conjured the spirit of Apollonius of Tyana. Among other writings, he produced a History of Witchcraft, in which he stresses mystical interpretation of the occult elements in Nature.

LEVIATHAN   A sea monster mentioned in Job and elsewhere. The expression occurs five times: in four cases, it denotes the crocodile, while in the fifth instance it refers to the whale. In Hebraic mysticism, on the day of resurrection, the righteous will partake of it.

LEVITATION   A term applied to the rising of the human body or of inanimate objects into the air, contrary to the laws of gravity. There is on record the case of a seventeenth century Italian monk, Saint Joseph of Copertino, who rose by auto-levitation from a church floor to the high altar, a distance of forty feet. This ability is also attributed to certain Tibetan lamas.

Simon Magus, who appears in Acts of the Apostles 8, was credited with the power of levitation. A painting by Benozzo Gozzoli, a fifteenth century Italian artist, depicts the scene.

LEWIS, MATTHEW GREGORY (1775 - 1818) The English author commonly known as Monk Lewis maintained a lively interest in the occult throughout his lifetime. His play Castle Spectre (1798), Tales of Terror (1788), and Tales of Wonder — an anthology of popular occult verses to which Sir Walter Scott contributed — won him great popularity among people interested in the supernatural.

LEYAK A bewitched spirit, according to the Balinese, who haunts lonely roads and deserted places. These spirits are responsible for the misfortunes that befall men.

LIBELLUS MERLINI The Latin tract on Merlin's prophecies (Little Book of Merlin) was written by Geoffrey of Monmouth about 1135.

LIBER LAPIDUM This Latin title means The Book of Precious Stones. It was written around 1123 by Marbod, bishop of Rennes. He describes each gem in symbolical terms. The onyx, for instance, brings nightmares. The sapphire is a protection against terror. The jasper aids childbirth, while the sardonyx is the symbol of the inner man.

LIBRA In astrology, the Balance. The seventh, southern sign of the zodiac. It symbolizes equilibrium in the material universe and in the psychic zone. Esoterically, and on the intellectual plane, it signifies external perception and intuition, united as reason and foresight. Kabbalistically, it represents the kidneys and loins of the grand old man of the heavens.

LIFE-WAVE   This term refers in occultism to the collective hosts of monads, the latter being in the spiritual realms of the Universal Life what the former are in the lower Planes of Form.

LIGHT, COLLECTOR OF   In astrology, a ponderous planet which receives the aspects of any two significators in some of their Essential Dignities. Both must be lighter planets than the Collector itself. It denotes a mediator who will interest himself in the affairs of both parties to bring to a favorable issue a desired result which could not otherwise be achieved. It is a favorable position for reconciling differences, quarrels, lawsuits: also for bringing about marriages and various agreements.

LIGHT PLANETS   In astrology, these are the Moon, Venus, Mercury, referring to their gravities and their consequent swiftness of motion. The nearer a body is to its gravitational centre, the more its motion is accelerated and its gravity proportionately diminished.

LIGHTS   This term is frequently applied to the Luminaries, the Sun and the Moon, as distinguished from the planets.

LILITH   A female demon associated with Assyrian demonology. In Talmudic legend she was Adam's first wife and bore him demons. She was represented with dishevelled hair, and winged.
The legend is that she was created out of mud.

LILITH: ASTEROID   The name Lilith is sometimes given to asteroid No. 1181, a minor planet, of magnitude 14.1. It is too faint to be seen except with the aid of a telescope. It is not a 'dark moon,' but a planet that shines by reflected light from the Sun.

LINGA (LINGAM) A Sanskrit word used esoterically to identify the symbol of every creative god in every nation.

LINGA SHARIRA In occultism, the astral body of man or animal. It is born before the body and fades out with the disappearance of the last atom of the body. It is the sixth substance-principle, counting downward, of man's constitution.

LI SHAO CHUN The first known Chinese alchemist. He lived during the Earlier Han Dynasty (203 B.C.-25 A.D.) and claimed to have acquired the art of transmuting cinnabar from An Ch'i. He insisted that cinnabar could be transmuted into pure gold which, when swallowed, would enable one to rise to heaven as a *hsien*. Shao Chun is said to have disappeared from his coffin, leaving the clothes in which he was wrapped 'like the slough of a cicada.'

LOBSTERS In Japanese thought, the lobster symbolizes longevity.

LOCI Astrologically, the twelve loci are divisions containing questions to be answered in accord with astrological calculations. They correspond to the twelve strips of the visible heaven.

LODGE, OLIVER (1851-1940) The famous English physicist and educator made studies in electromagnetism, light, space, etc., paving the way for modern theories about matter, including that of relativity. His interest in psychical research dates from 1883, when he studied thought transference. He investigated Eusapia Paladino, Mrs. Piper, and others, and attempted throughout his lifetime to reconcile science and religion. In Raymond, or Life and Death (1916) he records his supposed communication with his son, who died in World War I.

LOGOI The Greek plural form of logos, the word. In Hebraic mystical writing, this form is used by the Hellenized Jewish philosopher Philo. In this sense, the expression designates the angels.

LOKA In yoga, a level of existence of living beings. The loka of the physical world, realized by the senses. Another loka is that of the invisible world. The yogi who has mastered his thoughts and emotions can travel in the subtle or invisible world.
Another loka connotes the material heaven-world, the abode of ordinary people after death.

LOMBROSO, CESARE (1836-1909) The celebrated Italian criminologist took up the study of spiritualism a few years before his death and experimented with Eusapia Paladino, the famous medium. The results of his investigations are in several volumes, including After Death — What? (1909). Lombroso concluded that man, though probably not immortal, had a 'shell' or pattern of thought forces which survived him on earth for a considerable time.

LORD In astrology, this term is often used as a synonym of Ruler. More precise terminology would indicate the Ruler of a Sign and the Lord of a House.

LORD OF THE YEAR In astrology, this is the planet which has the most Dignities in a solar revolution Figure, or in an ingress Figure to be interpreted according to the rules of Mundane Astrology.

LORDS OF THE FLAME   In theosophical mysticism these are messengers sent from the planet Venus to guide the evolutionary process on earth.

LOTUS   In yoga, a lotus or a chakra is a psychic centre in the human body. There are seven such centres.

LOURDES   This town in the Hautes-Pyrénées, in Southwest France, is a place of pilgrimage. In 1858, in a nearby grotto, St. Bernadette saw a manifestation of Our Lady of Lourdes. Approximately a million pilgrims, in all stages of sickness, visit Lourdes seeking a miraculous cure.

LUGBARA WITCHES   The Lugbara, who live along the Nile-Congo divide, believe that the head of a family cluster has the power to cause ghosts from his special shrine to bring sickness to any member of his family who has misbehaved or acted improperly. The patient must then consult an oracle, for diagnosis of his ailment. A witch is associated with night creatures and looks like a corpse.

LULLY, RAYMOND   (1235? - 1315)   The famous Spanish philosopher was also the author of a number of alchemical works. He is reported to have made large amounts of Gold. Several of his alchemical works were quite popular. The two-volume Opera Alchima attributed to him was reprinted in London as late as 1673.

LUMINOUS MIRROR   In Kabbalistic mysticism, this expression denotes the faculty of prophecy and foresight. The name of Aeschylus' protagonist in one of his dramas is Prometheus, which in Greek means Foresight.

LUNAR GODS   In India, this expression is applied to the lunar ancestors, the Fathers.

LUNAR PITRIS   A term used in theosophy to name the seven or ten grades of evolving entities which pass into a state of nirvana at the end of the lunar manvantara and leave this state eons later as the hierarchy of beings which constitute the planetary chain of Earth.

LUNATION   In astrology, it is approximately used as a synonym for the New Moon. Specifically, it is the precise moment of the Moon's conjunction with the Sun — a Syzgy. The New Moon falling upon sensitive points in the Figure has much signification regarding events of the ensuing month.

LUNATION, SYNODICAL   In astrology, the return of the progressed Moon, after birth, to the same distance from the progressed Sun as that which the radical Moon was from the radical Sun at birth. This occurs approximately once every 29 ½ days.

LURIA, ISAAC   A noted Kabbalist who belongs in the sixteenth century. He was known to his disciples as the Master. Among his more practical acquirements was, from observation of a person's brow, the ability to describe his transmigratory soul, to reveal the past and to foretell the future.

LUZZATTO, MOSES CHAIM   (1707 - 1747)   Italian - Jewish philosopher. Excommunicated but remained devoted to Judaism. Studied Kabbalistic mystical writings. His own mystical treatises were composed in Aramaic.

LYCANTHROPY   This term relates to the changing of a human being into a wolf. The traditional belief is as old as Plato. Pliny the Elder, the Roman encyclopedist, in his Natural History, asserts that a certain member of a family in each generation, became a wolf for nine years. Other ancient writers testify to this phenomenon, among them the poet Vergil, Petronius the novelist, Strabo, Pomponius Mela the geographer. In France, in the sixteenth century, edicts were promulgated against the practice of lycanthropy. The subject appears nowadays in films and in popular literature.

M

MAAT KHERU   The Egyptian intonation recited by the dead to gain power in Amenti (Hell).

MACROCOSM   The universe. The theory that a single great pattern links every element of the macrocosm with the microcosm (man) is one of the basic assumptions of magic. According to Paracelsus, every magical or Kabbalistic figure used to compel spirits may be reduced to two — the macrocosm or the microcosm. A six-pointed star or Seal of Solomon, formed of two intersecting triangles, is an important magic diagram symbolizing the macrocosm.

MACROPROSOPUS   In Kabbalistic mysticism, this Greek term denotes the Great Countenance, symbolism of the Universe.

MADRE NATURA   The ancient Italian priesthood may have founded the powerful secret society known as Madre Natura. Adherents worshipped nature and accepted the Neo-Platonic interpretation of pagan creeds.

MAGIA POSTHUMA   This tract on vampirism was written by Ferdinand de Schertz and published at Olmutz in 1706.

MAGIC   Magic is a practice based on the assumption that certain causes will produce particular effects unaccepted by science. Magic also assumes that non-natural, abnormal occurrences and phenomena may be produced by the adept in collaboration with demoniac agencies.

MAGIC APPARATUS Among objects and instruments and other paraphernalia used in magic rituals are: candles made of the fat of a hanged criminal, magic circles, formulas, invocations, special robes, trinkets and amulets, mirrors, stones, herbs, wands, diagrams, incense.

MAGIC FEAT With the aid of boughs, Jacob produced a magic phenomenon whereby he gained an advantage over Laban: And Jacob took him rods of green poplar, and of the hazel and chestnut tree; and piled white strakes in them, and made the white appear which was in the rods.

And he set the rods which he had piled before the flocks in the gutters in the watering troughs when the flocks came to drink, that they should conceive when they came to drink.

And the flocks conceived before the rods, and brought forth cattle ringstraked, speckled and spotted.

And Jacob did separate the lambs, and set the faces of the flocks toward the ringstraked, and all the brown in the flock of Laban; and he put his own flocks by themselves, and put them not unto Laban's cattle.

And it came to pass, whensoever the stronger cattle did conceive, that Jacob laid the rods before the eyes of the cattle in the gutters, that they might conceive among the rods.

But when the cattle were feeble, he put them not in: so the feebler were Laban's, and the stronger Jacob's.
Genesis 30: 37-42.

MAGIC GIRDLES Girdles made of ferns gathered on St. John's Eve supposed to cure diseases. The ferns must be gathered at midnight and arranged in such a way as to form the magic character HVTY.

MAGIC NUMBERS In the occult arts, numbers play an important part and have a profound significance. The

220

number one, for example, denotes Unity, that is, the Deity. Two, a dual number, refers to Satan. The number four signifies stability. Five is the symbol of justice. Seven in particular has an occult connotation. Ten, the sum of all numbers, denotes completion. In the Middle Ages one of the regular occult practices was divination by means of numbers.

MAGIC ROBES In the performance of magic rites, special garments and other equipment were used by occultists as an aid in the effectiveness of the ceremonies. Among such requirements were a tunic of white linen, or a purple robe; garlands fashioned of various branches, of violet, or vervain; incense and perfumes; cedar, citron, amber; poplar or oak wreaths. Black robes too were in order in certain diabolic rites: also necklaces, bracelets, beads, rings.

MAGIC WINDS Witches were traditionally regarded as vendors of favorable winds to travelers and sailors, as the following lines suggest:
"In Ireland and in Denmark both, Witches for gold will sell a man a wind."

MAGNETISM In the seventeenth century magnetic force was attributed to Satanic origins by Athanasius Kircher, a German Jesuit and scholar.

MAHATMA In theosophy, one of a class of adepts reputed to possess superior knowledge and powers. These perfect men are also called Elder Brothers, Masters, Sages, Seers, etc. They founded the modern Theosophical Society through their Envoy, H. P. Blavatsky, in New York in 1875.

MAIER, MICHAEL (died 1622) German physician and alchemist. Wrote in defense of the Rosicrucians. He was acquainted with the English mystic Robert Fludd.

MAIMONIDES, MOSES BEN MAIMON (1135 - 1204) Born in Cordova, but forced to migrate to Morocco then to Egypt. One of the greatest medieval Jews, outstanding in philosophy, religion, and medicine. In his medical treatises, written originally in Arabic, he anticipated modern discoveries concerning the affliction of the body by psychic factors. He also asserted his belief in the actuality of angels and of prognostication.

MALEFIC In astrology, this term is applied to certain planets regarded as exerting a harmful influence: chiefly Mars and Saturn. The term is also loosely employed with reference to an inharmonious aspect with any planet, and to a conjunction with any malefic planet.

MALINOWSKI, BRONISLAW KASPER (1884-1942) Polish-born British anthropologist known especially for the depth and comprehensiveness of his studies of Melanesian society. His detailed study of the function of magic in the Trobriand Islands led him to the conclusion that magic fills a gap in tribal knowledge and provides an alternative means of expression for thwarted human desires.

MALLEUS MALEFICARUM A papal bull against witchcraft, issued in 1484, prompted two inquisitors to compile the celebrated work. In this large volume, Jacob Sprenger and Henricus Institor reduced the doctrine of witchcraft to a regular system.

MALPHAS In medieval demonology, the Grand President of Hell. He appears in the shape of a crow, builds impregnable fortresses, double-crosses those who offer him sacrifices, and speaks with a hoarse voice when he takes the shape of a human being. He commands forty legions.

MAMBO   A priestess of the Voodoo cult.

MAN   Esoterically, man is seen as a spark of the central cosmic spiritual fire, an inseparable part of the universe, a copy of the graded organism of consciousnesses and substances of the universe. He is composed of three essential upadhis (bases): the monadic or divine-spiritual; the intellectual and intuitive; and the vital astral physical. The lowest of his three aspects or planes of being comes from the earth, the middle from the sun, and the monadic from the supreme seed of the universal hierarchy constituting the universal cosmos.

MANA   In occultism, a power of force which affects both things and the actions of men.

MANASAPUTRAS   The Sanskrit word Manasaputras ('sons of Mind') designates our highest natures in theosophical writings. These spiritual entities quicken our personal egos.

MANDRAKE   A plant, mandragora officinarum, of the potato family. It is also called mandragore. It often grows in the shape of human limbs. In former times it was frequently used in love philtres, and is so mentioned in Genesis 30.14-15. It is also known as 'the plant of Circe,' because her witch-brews were reputedly infusions of mandrake.
In the Middle Ages, the mandrake was said to grow from the sperm of men who had been hanged. The plant was supposed to have the power to predict the future, open locks, and produce gold.

223

MANILIUS, MARCUS A Roman poet who flourished in the first century A.D. He was the author of Astronomica, a didactic poem on the subject of astrology. Five books of the poem are extant. The themes treated include: the creation of the universe, the starry heavens and their disposition, the zodiacal signs, with their characteristics, aspects and subdivisions, methods of determining a horoscope, and the influence of the zodiac on human life.

MANO In mystic Gnosticism, this term is applied to the Lord of Light.

MANSIONS OF THE MOON In astrology, this expression refers to a series of 28 divisions of the Moon's travel through one complete circuit of 360 degrees, each Mansion representing one day's average travel of the Moon, beginning apparently at the point of the Spring Equinox, or zero degrees Aries.

MANTICISM A state of prophetic frenzy. In antiquity, the pagan priests and others associated with religious cults were accustomed, while in this condition, to make prophetic pronouncements. The early Church Fathers condemned this practice.

MANTRA In yoga, a mantra is a form of speech which has a material effect on the mind, the emotions, the body or on objects. A concept or idea is considered to precede the spoken word, which in turn is creative.

MANU The fourteen Manus are the patrons or guardians of the race cycles in a Manvantara. In the esoteric system, Manu is the spiritual tree of life of any planetary chain of manifested being.

MANVANTARA In theosophy, a period of manifestation, in contrast to Pralaya, a period of dissolution or rest. It applies to various cycles, especially to a Day of Brahma (4,320,000 solar years), and to the reign of one Manu (308,448,000 years).

MAN-WOLF The ancient belief in men turning into wolves is reflected in many customs associated with mystery cults, in which the initiates assume wolf-skins and take to the woods. This is the case with the ancient Greek cult of Dionysus Bacchus and of the Moroccan tribe of Isawiyya.

MARCIONITES A Gnostic sect established by Marcion, who flourished in the second century A.D. He maintained that all the accepted incidents associated with the life of Christ were only allegorical concepts. He also maintained that all matter is of everlasting duration.

MARIA HEBREA A Jewess who was an alchemist. She flourished possibly in the first century A.D., in Memphis, Egypt. Her name has survived in the expression bain-marie, a term used in chemistry.

MARS The planet Mars takes 687 days to encircle the Sun, as astrologers have long known.

MARTIAN In astrology, this term is applied to a person under the influence of, or ruled by, a strongly placed Mars.

MARTINEZ, PASQUALIS (c. 1715 - 1779) A Portuguese Rosicrucian and Hermetic. In 1754 he founded a mystic order called The Chosen Coven.

MARTIN, SAINT   This fourth-century exorcist is credited with the performance of more than two hundred miracles, many of them recorded by his biographer, Sulpicius Severus.

MASTER   In theosophical teachings, a Master is one who has his higher principles awakened and lives accordingly. He has developed an individual consciousness of his oneness with the Boundless.

MASTER OF THE NAME   A title given to certain Kabbalists at various times, since the sixteenth century. They claimed to perform thaumaturgic acts by using the secret appellation of the Divinity. In a general sense, these men and their followers were and are still called Chassidim, Pious. On account of the enthusiasm and the widespread interest of the Chassidim Kabbalistic mysticism became popularized in Eastern Europe.

MASTERS OF THE TEACHING   In the Zohar, the Book of Splendor, which is the essence of Hebraic mysticism, this term is applied to certain Kabbalistic adepts.

MATERIALIZATION OF THOUGHT   Tibetan lamas consider that in the case of certain persons specially trained thoughts can be made visible and palpable by means of the creation of a phantom or vision.

MATUTINE: MATUTINAL   In astrology, these terms refer to the Moon, Mercury, and Venus when they appear in the morning. When a star or planet rises before the Sun in the morning, it is called matutine until it reaches its first station, where it becomes Retrograde. The Moon is matutine until it passes its first Dichotome.

MAU   An ancient Egyptian term for the cat. The expression means The Seer, and it is believed that cats are sensitive to clairvoyant phenomena and ghostly manifestations.

MAYA   In yoga, this term denotes illusion. The belief is that every experience in the manifested universe is illusion. The illusion is that we see correctly the true and essential Reality.

MAY-EVE   One of the pagan 'sabbaths.' Celebrated by adherents of the Old Religion, probably as a survival of prehistoric breeding practices, the day became the Roodmas ('Invention of the Cross') of the Christians.

MBWIRI   In Central Africa, this is a malefic demon that enters the victim's body. The demon is exorcised by the priest-doctor of the tribe. The rite is performed over a period of some ten days or more, to the accompaniment of drinking, eating, dancing, and music. This ritual coincides largely with the exorcism ceremony as practiced in Tibet and as described by the Abbé Huc in his Travels in Thibet.

MEASURE OF STATURE   In Hebraic mysticism, this is the title of a treatise dealing with the symbolism of numbers.

MEDIEVAL CURE   A boy was falsely accused of a crime and had his tongue cut off. He had heard of St. Olaf's miracles and tearfully on bended knees he appealed to the saint's tomb for help in restoring his speech. After a while he fell into a deep sleep and observed a man coming out of the casket. He was of medium height and comely in appearance. When he came near and opened the boy's mouth, he pulled out part of the severed tongue. In his sleep the boy cried out. Then he fell asleep again. On waking, he was healed.

227

MEDIEVAL DEVIL   In the Middle Ages black tom-cats were regarded as forms of the Devil in disguise.

MEDIEVAL FORECAST   In the twelfth century Jacques de Vitry, who died in 1240, was Cardinal Bishop of Tusculum. He is the author of several volumes of sermons. These sermons contain legends, stories, and illustrative material suitable for preachers. The anecdotes are intended to drive home some moral point or to exemplify a particular topic. Here is one of these anecdotes, translated from the Latin:

I have heard that a certain astrologer occasionally made true predictions, just like those demons who foresee the future. The king at that time, who was friendly with the astrologer, began to have great faith in him and confidence in his forecasts.

On a certain day he was standing, in a dejected mood, in the king's presence. When the king asked him why he was sad and depressed, the astrologer would not tell him. Finally, after much urging, with lamentation and grief he told the king confidentially:

"Your majesty, I looked at the astrolabe and from the disposition of the stars I have concluded, after deliberation, that your majesty will not live more than six months."

On hearing this, the king believed his words and as each day passed he became distressed and agonized, and he fell into a deep melancholy. His knights consequently were greatly amazed and grieved at his condition. For usually he appeared to them in a cheerful frame of mind. But now he did not want to see them or speak to them.

At last, after many insistent pleas on the part of one of his close advisers, the king admitted that his cleric who was also a very excellent astrologer had predicted his approaching death.

Then the knight, afraid that the king was sinking into a melancholic state and would die by dwelling on it (for many people die just through fear of death), summoned the astrologer into the presence of all the courtiers and said to him:

"How can you be sure of the king's death?"

To which the astrologer rejoined:

"I am sure of his death. I have determined it by my skill, which is infallible."

The knight retorted:

"You must know about yourself, then, better than about another person. Do you know how long you will live?"

"I know," said the astrologer. "I am sure that I won't die for another twenty years."

The knight rejoined:

"You are wrong about your own life."

And, drawing his sword, he killed the astrologer in the presence of all the courtiers.

Then the king, now that the astrologer's forecasts were proved to be false, recovered his health and lived for a long time afterward.

MEDIEVAL SPACE FLIGHT   In a traditional and legendary sense, the life of Alexander the Great is packed with strange manifestations and miraculous exploits. Some of these are related by Ekkehart of Pau, an abbot who belongs in the late eleventh century. The incidents are part of Ekkehart's Universal History:

When his warriors came to the Red Sea, they discovered a very high mountain. On climbing it, they felt as if they were in heaven. With his companions, Alexander planned how he could mount to heaven, to test whether what we see is really heaven. So he made a car and taking his two griffins tied them with chains and put poles in front of them and on the top he put their fodder. Thus they started to mount upward, until the whole earth below seemed to him like a threshing-floor, and the sea like a dragon whirling it around. Under the protection of the divine agent the griffins came down to rest in a plain ten days' march from the army. However, Alexander sustained no harm in this spot. When he was united with his soldiers, they rejoiced. Then they proceeded to another plain, where at the first hour of the day trees rose out of the ground and grew bigger until the sixth hour: then from the sixth hour to sunset they sank into the ground. These trees bore very fragrant fruit. Alexander ordered some of the soldiers to pluck some fruit. But no sooner did they approach than demons sprang out and whipped them. The soldiers also heard a voice from heaven forbidding anyone to cut anything off the trees on pain of death. There were also quite tame birds there, but if any of the soldiers wanted to touch them, flames came out and scorched them.

Then they came to a certain mountain, below which was a golden chain. The mountain itself had 2500 steps formed of sapphire. Alexander climbed the mountain with some of his soldiers and found a palace there, in which there was a temple all of gold, and in it golden drums and cymbals, and a couch with the most marvelous food. On the couch sat a very resplendent figure, robed in a white silk garment adorned with gold and precious stones, and beside him was a golden periwinkle bearing clusters of grapes formed of precious stones.

MEDITATION   A popular magazine publishes an advertisement that invites readers to acquire the art of meditation. The aids toward this tranquillity and inner harmony include the purchase of a meditation robe, a phonographic disc, a meditating figure, meditating incense, an incense burner, and two sets of prayers.

MEDIUM   A spiritualistic medium is supposed to be susceptible to supernatural agencies and to be able to communicate knowledge obtained from them or perform acts made

230

possible only by their help. In theosophy, a medium is one whose unstable inner constitution functions in magnetic sympathy with components of the astral light.

The medium is generally an extremely sensitive person who can be readily 'controlled' by spirits. Among the earliest mediums in America were Mrs. Fox and her daughters, whose seances consisted mainly of rappings to convey messages from the spirits to the sitters. The crowning achievement of later mediums was the materialization of hands, faces, and finally the complete forms of 'controls.'

Trance utterances dealing with life beyond the grave are stressed by those for whom spiritualism is a religion. Spiritualists claim that mediumistic phenomena result from the influence of the spirits of the dead on the sensitive organism of the medium.

MEGWA　A word used in the Trobriand Islands to denote either a spell or magic.

MEMPHIS　An ancient city in Lower Egypt that was regarded as the repository of the secrets of Egyptian magicians.

MENDES　The demon-goat who was reputedly the object of worship by the Templars.

MEN OF JESUS CHRIST　A mystic religious sect in Kenya: an offshoot of the sect known as the Isawiyya that originated in Morocco.

MERCURY　Apuleius, the Roman novelist and philosopher who belongs in the second century A.D., asserts that Mercury was the inventor of incantations in the practice of the occult arts.

231

MERKAVAH A Hebraic term meaning a chariot. It is particularly associated with the divine chariot of Ezekiel's vision.

MERLIN A magician fabled to have been the fruit of the union of a Welsh princess and a demon. The famous fifth-century prophet and enchanter lived at the court of King Arthur.

MERU In Hindu mythology, a mountain in the centre of the earth. It is the home of the Hindu deities.

MESMERISM The older term for hypnotism. Mesmerism is derived from Anton Mesmer (1733-1815), an Austrian physician who discovered what was called animal magnetism. The principles of his discovery are expounded in De Planetarium Influxu: (1) celestial, terrestrial, and animated bodies influence each other; (2) this mutual influence depends on a continuous, subtle, and universal fluid; (3) unknown mechanical laws govern this influence; (4) alternating effects are produced (flux and fluxes and refluxes); (5) the human body has magnetic properties, making it susceptible to various influences.

MESSENGER In the theosophical sense, a Messenger is one who comes at the bidding of the Lodge of the Masters of Wisdom and Compassion and Peace to accomplish a certain mission.

METAPHYSICAL COMMANDS In a popular magazine an advertisement announces that Metaphysical Commands will help a person to travel in his astral body, to rejuvenate the body cells, and to control people around one.

METATRON In Jewish mysticism, this was the form into which Enoch was changed when he reached the heavenly zones. He is the chief of all the angels. He records the deeds and misdeeds of men.

METEMPSYCHOSIS A doctrine held by the ancient Egyptians and accepted as a tenet of Oriental mysticism. The word denotes the passing of the soul at death into a different body. In theosophy, metempsychosis is the changing of souls or soul-sheaths through the ages; a monad during its evolutionary course periodically throws forth from itself new soul-sheaths or soul-garments.

METONIC CYCLE The discovery, about 432 B.C. by Meton, an Athenian astronomer, of the Moon's period of nineteen years, at the end of which the New Moon occurs on the same day of the year. Upon this are based certain corrections of the lunar calendar.

METONIC RETURN This expression refers to the recurrence of an eclipse on a given degree on the same date some nineteen years later.

MICROCOSM This term, which in Greek denotes a miniature world, refers to man, who is a reflection or mirror of the universe. Macrocosm, on the other hand, denotes the great cosmos and refers to the universe in relation to man.

MICROPROSOPUS In Kabbalistic mysticism, a term that denotes one of the basic cosmic elements.

MIDHEAVEN Variant names are medium coeli, Southern angle, South point, and cusp of the Tenth House. These terms apply to astrology. Midheaven is sometimes wrongly called the Zenith. More precisely, it is applicable to the South point of the Map, and what it indicates is dependent on the manner of interpretation. Sometimes, too midheaven is loosely applied to the whole of the Tenth House.

MIDIWIWIN A secret society of the Ojibway Indians. The initiate is instructed in the mysteries of the society as he progresses through several grades with the assistance of snake-spirits.

MIDPOINT In astrology, this term denotes an unoccupied aspected degree between and equidistant from two other planets, resulting in a symmetrical grouping, sometimes called a planetary picture. Such configurations are regarded as important by some astrologers, although there is some difference of opinion regarding the width of orbs across which there can result a 'transference of light' through the planet which aspects the Midpoint.

MIDRASH In Biblical literature, a body of interpretations containing legendary themes and also mystical doctrines.

MILK BATH In Southern India every twelve years the statue of the Rain God Gomateswara is anointed by pilgrims with milk curds, sacred water, and sandal paste. The statue is fifty-seven feet high and a thousand years old.

MILKY WAY In old folklore the Milky Way is known as the Road of the Gods. The spirit of a dead person crossed it on the way to its everlasting dwelling-place.
In theosophy, the Milky Way is viewed as a vast star-cluster of suns in various degrees of evolutionary growth and the matrix of celestial bodies still unborn. It is the cosmic nursery of future suns whose manvantaric evolutionary courses have not yet begun. An Elephantine myth-complex makes the Nile flow from the Milky Way, a river of milk that produced the sun-egg. In the Akkadian myth of Creation Apsu, the watery abyss, and Tiamat, the Milky Way, are mates.

234

MIMI SPIRITS The Australian aborigines living in Arnhem Land believe that the Mimi spirits, hidden from view on a rocky plateau, have sensitive hearing which enables them to detect a stranger's presence from afar, then disappear into a crack in the rock opened by their breath.

MIND CURE A system of healing developed by Phineas Parkhurst Quimby, a professional mesmerist. His theories, modified and expanded, became the tenets of Christian Science: God is in all, Good, and Mind; God, Spirit, being all, nothing is matter; Life, God, omnipotent good, deny death, evil, sin, disease.

MIND-READING An unusual case of thought-extension or extra-sensory perception is reported from England. The person concerned can give the right brand of cigarettes to a new customer before the customer gives the order. The shopman even gives him the proper change before the customer has offered money. When he ran a pub, the subject could anticipate what drink a new customer was going to order. He stated that as a child he had 'visions,' clear and accurate, of forthcoming incidents.

MIRABILIS LIBER This Latin expression means The Book of Wonders. It is the title of a fifteenth-century book of predictions relating to national events. Among other astonishing revelations the edition of 1452 contains a prophecy of the French Revolution.

MIRACLES Miraculous actions and other phenomena were, in pre-Christian and non-Christian cultures, attributed to particular personalities — holy men, priests, sorcerers — who were regarded as endowed with abnormal powers. Around certain names — Zoroaster, Lao-tzu, Buddha,

235

Confucius, Mohammed — legends spread with regard to their birth and death, the temptations that assailed them from Satanic, malefic sources.

Miraculous deeds were attributed even to the followers of these figures. Such miracles, contrary to the normal laws of nature, involved healing practices, escapes from incarceration, transportation and flight. The saints in Hinduism and Buddhism performed endless miracles. They traveled through the air. They transported people across rivers, without the aid of boats. They induced rain. They controlled storms and floods. They healed chronic sickness. They removed sterility. They could pass through the earth or through a wall. They assumed any form they desired. They could achieve invisibility and invulnerability. They could produce illumination by burning a finger. They remembered past lives. They also foresaw the future. At Buddha's birth the earth quaked. At his death flowers rained from heaven around the funeral procession and fire from the heavens lit the funeral pyre. Zoroaster again and again was rescued from evil spirits who were determined to destroy him. Moses, at the court of Pharaoh, performed miracles, and Elijah the Prophet was equally a thaumaturgist. In Moslem tradition, Mohammed's ascent to heaven is the predominant miracle. The Chinese immortals too possessed supernatural powers. In Christian religion the miracles performed by Jesus form an integral part of Christian faith.

MIRACULOUS RAISING OF THE DEAD   Bishop Gregory of Tours was a dominant figure in the sixth century. In his History of the Franks he relates the following incident: I do not think it will be considered out of place to relate how an appeal to St. Martin saved a man's life. In a certain place a man was caught stealing. He was whipped and led to the gallows to be hanged. With death so near, he begged leave to pray. Then, just as he was, with his hands tied behind his back, he cast himself on the ground and began tearfully to invoke the name of St. Martin, begging him, since he could not save him, to absolve him of his sins. After these prayers, the thief was hanged and the soldiers departed. With open mouth, the thief slowly moved his lips, still trying to implore St. Martin's aid. He had been hanging thus for two days, when a woman found him still alive. He was lifted off the gallows and brought safe and sound to church. Those who saw him were amazed and asked:

"How is it he is still alive?"

Then they asked the thief how he had been set free. He replied: "St. Martin saved me from death and brought me here."

St. Martin had raised him from dead and the thief is still living.

MIRIAM'S WELL A legendary well that accompanied the Hebrews on their march through the desert.

MIRZA ALI MOHAMMED Called Bab-ud-Din, the Gate of Faith. He was a Persian mystic who in 1844 declared himself as the twelfth Imam, that is, the prophet of Him who was to come. He attracted many followers, preached widely, and wrote a number of books. In 1850 he was condemned to death by hanging. As the executioner's rope broke, however, the mystic was shot.

MITHRA In Iranian mythology, Mithra was equated with the Sun and was worshipped as such.

MITHRAIC CONCEPT In the ancient Persian mystery cult of Mithra, the soul, in its effort to release itself from the body, crosses seven spheres.

MITHRAIC INFLUENCE In the ancient Mithraic mystery cult, the position of the planets and their relationships to each other and their powers were conceived as influencing all terrestrial phenomena.

MITHRAIC MYSTERIES The Mithraic rite of the sacrifice of the bull symbolized the reduction of the animal principle in man.

MODERATORS In astrology, this term was anciently applied by Ptolemy to the Significators: Sun, Moon, Ascendant, Midheaven, Fortuna. It implied that aspects from the Significators moderate or condition the influences of the planets, producing a different 'mode of motion' in the rays reflected. The term is now largely obsolescent.

MODUS RATIONALIS In astrology, this term, which is Latin, means Rational Method. It is applied to a method of locating the cusps of the intermediate Houses — those which lie between the angular Houses of a Figure — by dividing the Ecliptic by the Equator instead of the semi-arc. Its division into twelve equal parts was accomplished by circles, the cusps located where the circles cut the plane of the Ecliptic. This method has been superseded by the employment of Oblique Ascension under the Poles of the Houses for all but the fourth and tenth cusps.

MOISTURE In astrology, moisture is said to increase when planets are matutine, when the Moon is in her First Quarter, during the winter, and by night.

MOKSHA A Sanskrit word meaning to release or to set free. In theosophical teachings, the word means that when a monad has evolved and become, successively, a man, a Planetary Spirit, a Brahman, and the Parabrahman for its Hierarchy, then it is absolutely free and perfected.

238

MOLEOSCOPY A method of studying the shape and location of the moles on a person. This technique proposes to interpret character and to predict future events relating to the subject.

MONAD In Greek this term means a unit. In theosophical mysticism it is the Divine Spark, part of the Logos. In occult mysticism, it signifies Nature's pattern for each species, with reference to differences between contrasting characteristics. According to Giordano Bruno, it is the microscopic embodiment of the divine essence which pervades and constitutes the universe.

MONEN In Kabbalistic mysticism, a phase of magic concerned with predictions by observation of the celestial bodies.

MONTE ABIEGNO A mystic mountain. In Rosicrucian mysticism, it appears as the source from which emanate many Rosicrucian documents.

MONTESPAN, MADAME DE (1641-1707) The mistress of Louis XIV is supposed to have allowed the Abbe Guibourg to sacrifice a child over her body in order to enable her to retain the favor of the king.

MOPSES An esoteric society that involved the occult arts and the celebration of a Sabbat.

MORIENUS An alchemist reputedly of Arab origin. Putatively belonged in the twelfth century. Author of treatises on occult and hermetic subjects.

MOROCCAN SAINT The town of Beni Rachid, in Morocco, is associated with a certain saintly Ali ben Hamdush. The town was recently the scene of a pilgrimage to the Islamic holy man. A woman had suffered convulsions and paralysis as, it was reputed, the result of the malefic operations of Aisha Qaidisha, a camel-hoofed she-demon.

MORSE, J. J. The well known English medium began late in the nineteenth century to manifest the phenomenon of elongation. Later he developed the faculty of trance-speaking, and lectured widely on spiritualism.

MORTALISTS A religious sect that flourished in the seventeenth century. It rejected the concept of the immortality of the soul.

MOSES BEN NACHMAN Also known as Nachmanides. A Spanish-Jewish Talmudist. Born in Gerona in 1194: died in Acre, 1270. He was also a physician and a Kabbalist.

MOSES, WILLIAM STAINTON (1839-1892) One of the most successful mediums connected with modern spiritualism. He attended numerous seances, published automatic writings, and was credited with numerous apports, communications from the spirit world, and acts of levitation. After his death, others claimed that his control was Imperator.
He wrote Spirit Teachings, a collection of automatic writings, and helped to found the British National Association of Spiritualism.

MOSLEM CEMETERY Near New Delhi, in India, hundreds of white clay pots are placed by Mohammedans on sticks to remind the dead that they have not been forgotten by their relatives.

MOTHERS In Hebraic mystic numerology, the twenty-two letters of the Hebrew alphabet were divided into three groups called Mothers.

MOTHERS OF EXISTENCE According to Jacob Boehme, there are in nature seven active principles. These 'Mothers of Existence' or 'Fountain Spirits' are astringency, sweetness, bitterness, and the qualities of fire, love, sound, and essential substance. These antipathetic qualities interact to produce the Supreme Unity. They are both parent and child with respect to each other and are typified by the seven golden candlesticks of the Apocalypse.

MOUNTAIN COVE COMMUNITY Two mediums, James Scott and T. L. Harris, founded a spiritualistic community in Mountain Cove, Fayette County, Virginia, in 1851. Previously, they had attracted a considerable following in Auburn. Spirits commanded Scott to form the community at Mountain Cove and obliged the members of the association to give up their possessions. The community was dissolved in 1853.

MOURNERS OF ZION A pre-medieval sect in Jerusalem. They lamented the cataclysms that had befallen the Jewish people throughout the stream of history.

MOZART, WOLFGANG AMADEUS (1756-1791) When asked by a mysterious stranger to compose a Requiem for an undisclosed sponsor, Mozart set to work on the composition that was to occupy his thoughts until the moment of his death. He became obsessed by the notion that he was writing the Requiem for his own funeral. He continued even on his deathbed to write, dictate, or sing parts of the Requiem. When the mysterious stranger returned, Mozart was dead.

MU This term, frequently used in mystic writings, refers to the Lemurian epoch, an early period in the cosmic scheme when the moon left the earth.

MUDRA In devotional Yoga, a general name for certain positions of the fingers, found by some Oriental mystics to have esoteric significance.

MULAPRAKRITI A Sanskrit word meaning root-matter or root-nature. In Occultism, it stands as the active pole corresponding to Brahman, the neuter pole or the Unmanifest Logos. It is the undifferentiated primordial substance, the fountain or root of Akasa, the cosmic veil of the First or Unmanifest Logos.

MUMMIFICATION The Egyptians employed ceremonial magic in the ritual of mummification. 'Words of power' were uttered as each bandage was set in place. Perfumed liquid was smeared on the eviscerated body. The backbone was immersed in holy oil drawn from Shu and Seb. Precious stones, each possessing a magical property, were laid on the mummy.

MUMMU The creative utterance or life-force of Apsu, the husband of Tiamat, in the Akkadian Creation myth.

MUMUKSHUTWA In yoga, this term denotes the desire for liberation from the limitations of manifested or incarnate existence. It is a kind of awakening of spiritual hunger.

MUNDANE ASPECTS In astrology, the aspects formed by planets occupying cusps, whereby it can be said that from the tenth to the twelfth cusps is a Mundane Sextile, though it may be as little as fifty degrees or as much as eighty degrees.

MUNDANE ASTROLOGY In mundane astrology, the significance of the solar system bodies is as follows:
Sun: executive heads.

242

Moon: the proletariat.
Mercury: the intelligentsia.
Venus: ambassadors of good will.
Mars: military leaders.
Jupiter: judiciary.
Saturn: state executives.
Uranus: air and rail transport.
Neptune: social movements.
Pluto: organized labor.

MUNDANE DIRECTIONS Or: Directions in mundo. In astrology, these directions are based solely upon the axial rotation of the earth in relation to the circle of observation whereby planets are carried clockwise through the Houses of the Figure, from east to west, forming aspects to the Ascendant, Midheaven, Sun and Moon. Aspects formed by the opposite or Converse Motion are also employed. The use of spherical trigonometry and of logarithms is necessary for reliable use of this Primary System of Directing. Knowledge of the exact place, hour, and minute is also essential.

MUNDANE PARALLEL Or parallel in mundo. In astrology, a progressed position in which a Significator and a Promittor occupy points on opposite sides and equidistant to any of the four angles of the geocentric Figure: Ascendant, Midheaven, Descendant, or Imum Coeli.

MURRAY, GILBERT (1866-1957) The world renowned classical scholar was president of the Society for Psychical Research for 1915-1916. He experimented with thought transference, a faculty which he discovered in himself by accident. He regarded the 'fringe of consciousness' as the key to telepathy.

243

MUSIC OF THE SPHERES Theosophy teaches that every atom is attuned to a musical note and moves in constant vibration at speeds incomprehensible to man. If one had the power to perceive the music around him, he could hear the unison of the songs of all individual atoms (spheres).

MUTABLE SIGNS In astrology, some zodiacal signs are changeable or mutable, while others are fixed or stable.

MUTILATED DEGREES In astrology, certain degrees are said by some astrologers to indicate lameness if rising at birth, or if the Moon or the Ruler of the Ascendant is posited therein.

MUTUAL RECEPTION In astrology, this expression refers to two planets mutually posited in each other's essential dignities. For example, with Jupiter in Aries, the Sun's place of exaltation: and the Sun in Cancer, Jupiter's place of exaltation, Sun and Jupiter are said to be in mutual reception. This is accounted a configuration of singular amity and agreement. By some astrologers, the term is confined to the placement of the two planets, each in a house or sign ruled by the other.

MYERS, FREDERICK WILLIAM HENRY (1843-1901) In Human Personality and its Survival of Bodily Death, the English poet, essayist, and psychic researcher set forth the potential powers of the subliminal self. He viewed the subliminal consciousness as a vast region, beneath the threshold of ordinary consciousness, embracing many phenomena associated with the supernatural.

MYOMANCY A method of divination by observing the movements of mice or by an examination of the entrails.

MYSTERIES Cults characterized by secret religious rites to which only duly initiated worshipers were admitted. The chief Greek Mysteries were Eleusinian, Orphic, and Samothracian. The Lesser Mysteries comprised mostly dramatic rites; the Greater Mysteries involved study of the secret meaning of the mythologies of ancient religions.

MYSTICAL NIGHT In Oriental Sufi philosophy the mystical night denotes exclusion of all sense perceptions and emotions in order to achieve an inner illumination.
Adherents believed that they could attain the state of mystical contemplation by closing the physical senses and allowing the spiritual senses to function freely. The Mystical Night is the sealing off of all sense-impressions and emotions to permit clear perception of the inner light.

MYSTICISM The belief that spiritual truth can be attained by intuition, insight, or illumination. Theosophy teaches that a mystic is one who has inner convictions based on inner vision and knowledge of the existence of spiritual universes cloaked by our physical universe.

MYSTIC NUMEROLOGY Pythagoras, the Greek philosopher and mathematician, conceived that the notion of friendship could be represented by a pair of numbers: 220 and 280. They were called amicable numbers. The numbers are such that each of them is equal to the sum of all the exact divisors of the other number except the number itself.
For 2000 years no other pair of numbers with such qualities had been found. From 1636 on, mathematicians have discovered examples of amicable numbers to the extent of some 400 pairs.

MYSTIC REINCARNATION In Egyptian eschatology, the belief was that the spirits of the dead, in the form of birds, ascend to the heavens where the Sun-God Ra changes them into stars.

MYSTIC SYMBOLS Mystic symbols were, since proto-historical times, associated with religious cults and secret rituals. In The Alchemist Ben Jonson asks:
"Was not all the knowledge
Of the Egyptians writ in mystic symbols?"

N

NAASENIANS An ancient Christian sect of Gnostics who worshipped the serpent. The serpent was the symbol of everlasting wisdom.

NAGAL A term used by tribes of Mexican Indians. It is applied to the principal tribal sorcerer.

NAGALISM This term stems from the Sanskrit naga, a serpent. Nagalism denotes serpent-worship. In the East, in Burma, there arc serpent gods who are held in great reverence. In Egypt and ancient Greece, too serpent-worship was practiced.

NAGARI The alchemists' dragon uttered these words: 'I rise from death, I kill death, and death kills me. I resuscitate the bodies I have created and, alive in death, I destroy myself.'

NAGUAL In Mexico and Central America, the nagual is a personal guardian spirit, thought to dwell in the body of an animal. The term is employed in various ways by the Indians themselves and by ethnographers. The Nahuatl of Tepoztlán say that the nagual is a person who can change into an animal. In other contexts the word has been translated as guardian spirit, soul bearer, companion spirit, destiny animal, and transforming witch.

NALJORPA In Tibetan mysticism, a naljorpa is one who has acquired psychic faculties and has premonition dreams. In a trance-like state he may learn of incidents that occur at a distance.

NANAK (1469-1538) Hindu mystic and poet. In a vision he was offered a cup of water with which to slake men's thirsts. As a result, he dedicated himself to this symbolical purpose.

NAPOLEON Napoleon was reputed to have a daemon or spirit that attended him. This spirit was said to manifest itself in the corridors of the Tuileries in Paris.

NARJOL A Tibetan term applied to holy men and yogi who have acquired occult powers.

NATIVITY In astrology, the Birth Moment. The instant wherein the native first inhales, thereby beginning a process of blood conditioning that up to that point had been accomplished by the receptivities of another. During the first years of life there ensues a growth of channels of receptivity to cosmic energy which results in a life-pattern of cosmic stimulation. Nativity is also applied to a Figure, or Horoscope, cast for a date, moment, and place of birth, as distinguished from an Electional or Horary Figure.

NATS In Burmese demonology, nats are evil spirits that can be exorcised by women.

NAVAHOS A Navaho belief was that every human being, however good and virtuous in normal life, has an 'evil' portion as well. This evil portion, after a person's death, becomes a dangerous 'ghost,' endowed with malefic potentialities.

Ghosts of the dead, and living beings such as witches, who have special ritual knowledge, can cause disorder in the natural cosmic scheme. Winds, too, lightning, certain animals, have the same capacity for inflicting injury and bringing disaster on human beings.

NAWAL In the Tzeltal and Tzotzil Indian communities of Mexico, people believe that men have animal counterparts. These nawales may be domesticated animals or wild creatures. One nawal may converse with another. The nawal provides its owner with a source of power. Men who use this power to inflict sickness on others are witches.

NDEMBO A secret African society headed by the *ganga*, who instructs the neophyte in the secrets of the cult. Initiates undergo symbolic death, learn an esoteric language, and become *Nganga* (Knowing Ones).

NEBUCHADNEZZAR, TEMPLE OF A famous temple at Barsippa, which has been excavated. It constitutes a color chart of astrological symbols. It was built in seven stages, each marked by a different hue. The lower stage was black and symbolized Saturn: the second, orange, symbolized Jupiter: the third, red, Mars: the fourth, yellow, the Sun: the fifth, green, Venus: the sixth, blue, Mercury: the seventh, white or silver, the Moon.

NEBULAE These are star clusters in which the light of the individual stars, because of their distance, merges to give the impression of a cloud with a more or less well-defined centre. Great numbers of them are found in the heavens, and when one of them is rising at birth, or is in conjunction with the Moon, it is said to produce blindness or other ocular defects.

The principal nebulae noted in astrology are: Praesepe, the Hyades, the Pleiades, the Aselli, Aldebaran-Antares.

Ptolemy, referring to the possibility of blindness, mentions the cloudy spot of Cancer, the Pleiades of Taurus, the Arrow-head of Sagittarius, the sting of Scorpio, the parts about the mane of Leo, the urn of Aquarius. The Ascendant or Moon in any of these positions and afflicted by Mars indicates blindness from an accident: afflicted by Saturn, by a natural defect.

NECROMANCY The evocation of the spirits of the dead. With the help of the so-called witch of Endor, Saul used this technique in asking her to raise Samuel.
Among the Romans, the necromancers of Etruria, in Western Italy, were particularly known for their prowess. Among the techniques used in necromantic rites was a bell that was rung in order to conjure the dead.

NECTANEBUS An Egyptian king of the fourth century B.C. He was a renowned magician, skilled in divination and the concoction of philtres. By making wax figurines of enemy fleets and of his own forces, he was able in one case, while watching the manoeuvres of the figures in a bowl of Nile water, to forecast victory for his forces and to circumvent imminent disaster by a timely escape.

NEOMENIUM This term denotes the New Moon.

NEOPLATONIC PHILOSOPHY A revival of Platonic thought among the pagan scholars from the third century to 529 A.D. Two of the most eminent figures were the philosopher Plotinus and his pupil Porphyry. Plotinus is the author of the Enneads, a mystical philosophical-religious treatise.

NEPHEHS In Kabbalistic teachings, the lowest level of human existence. It is conscious of the physical world, feeds on its forces, and leaves to it its creations.

250

NERO   In Revelation, the number of the Beast, 666, has been applied to the Roman Emperor Nero.

NERO, WOULD-BE THAUMATURGIST   Pliny the Elder, the Roman author of the encyclopedic Natural History, writes of the Roman Emperor Nero's interest in occultism. Nero was eager to secure control over the acts of the gods and over familiar spirits. He had also an acquaintance with Tyndates, King of Armenia, who was regarded as a magician and who gave Nero instruction in the occult arts. He introduced Nero to sacred feasts, initiated him into arcane mysteries. Yet, despite all the opportunities thus offered to the Emperor, he had no skill in the active practice of magic.

NESHAMAH   The highest level of existence, according to the Kabbala. It looks on the divine world.

NETSILIK SHAMANISM   The Netsilik, or Seal Eskimos, live along the Arctic Coast of Canada. Their shamanistic practices involved direct intercourse with the world of the supernatural. The shaman had control of one class of spirits, the *tunraqs*. He could send these spirits on an aggressive mission, but if a spirit failed to accomplish its mission, it became a reversed spirit, a blood-thirsty thing that turned on its shaman. Sickness was caused by evil spirits who attacked the patient, usually after they had been angered by the violation of a taboo, and stayed in his body until exorcised by a shaman.

NEUMANN, THERESA (1898-1961)   Born on Good Friday, April 8, 1898, Theresa Neumann received the first stigmata on her feet and hands on Good Friday, April 2, 1926, and the second on Good Friday the following year. In subsequent years those on her side, brow, and shoulder became prominent. She is credited with many supernatural accomplishments, including that of repeating the language spoken at the time of Christ's crucifixion.

NEW THOUGHT A modern religion similar in some ways to Christian Science. It stresses the importance of the mind in the healing process but does not rule out the need for medical treatment. The doctrine was formulated by P. P. Quimby, who was the first to use the terms mental-healing and Christian Science.

NEW MOON CENTRE This Centre, with headquarters in Poona, Southern India, offers Spiritual Illumination.

NGWA A word used by the Sudanese to denote magic. The word generally means wood and is used to refer to magic only in special contexts. The material element in Zande magic, occult and known only to the practitioner, usually consists of rare roots and strange woods.

NICHUSCH In Kabbalistic teachings, all events are assumed to be interconnected and to interact upon one another. Any event, thing, or person can become a Nichusch or prophetic indication.

NICOLAI, CHRISTOPH FRIEDRICH (1733-1811) The German author and bookseller recounted his own supernatural experiences in a paper read before the Royal Society of Berlin. Nicolai reported that figures of deceased persons had appeared to him frequently and for long periods of time. He further reported that the apparitions vanished when his surgeon performed a blood-letting operation.

NINE In mystic numerology, the number nine is associated, both in antiquity and in modern times, with certain myths, rituals, symbolisms. The ninth hour was observed as a time for meditation. In Greek mythology, there were nine

Muses who presided over various intellectual and artistic activities. In Welsh tradition, Merlin had nine bards. King Arthur battled for nine days and nine nights.

NINTH HOUSE   In astrology, this term refers to the house of religion, knowledge. It is governed by the sign of Sagittarius.

NODES OF THE MOON   In astrology, variant names for the nodes are: the Ascending and Descending Nodes, the North and South Nodes, Caput Draconis or the Dragon's Head, Cauda Draconis, the Katababazon, or the Dragon's Tail. The Nodes regress about three degrees of arc per day. The Nodes of themselves merely point to places where an incident may happen at a particular time. Events occur because of the time, the place, and the planet, and the Node is often the middle factor in that formula.

NODES OF THE PLANETS   In astrology, the points at which the orbits of the planets intersect the ecliptic, because of the inclination of their planes to the plane of the earth's orbit. One astrological authority states that a lunation or eclipse on the South Node of a planet tends to release a destructive force of the nature of the planet involved.

NORTHERN SIGNS   In astrology, this expression denotes the Commanding Signs, Aries to Virgo, pursuing the order of the sign.

NORTH POINT   In astrology, this expression denotes the Imum Coeli or cusp of the Fourth House: placed at the bottom of the map.

NORTON, THOMAS   An English alchemist who flourished in the fifteenth century. Author of a treatise on hermetics and alchemy.

NOSTRADAMUS (1503-1566) A French physician, seer, and astrologer. His real name was Michel de Notre-Dame. He produced the Centuries, a series of versified prognostications on personal and national events. The actual occurrences coincided in a remarkable degree with his predictions. Nostradamus was attached to the court of Catherine de Medici. He there continued his cryptic forecasts, including his own death.

NOTARIKON In Kabbalistic mysticism, a technique, used in Biblical interpretation, of composing new words from the first or last letters of other words.

NOVEMBER-EVE One of the four pagan 'sabbaths,' also known as Halloween.

NOVIKH, GREGORI (1871-1916) A notorious Russian monk and cultist, known to millions by the name of Rasputin. Possessing what seems to have been a hereditary gift of mesmerism, he initiated a new cult in which dancing and debauchery were mingled with mystical seances. He gained power over the royal family of imperial Russia after he was alleged to have performed a miracle in restoring Alexis, the young ex-czarevitch, to health. After he was murdered, his body was buried in a silver casket.

NUMBER OF THE BEAST 'Here is wisdom. Let him that hath understanding count the number of the beast: for it is the number of a man; and his number is Six hundred threescore and six.'

Revelation 13.18

The number, 666, is the symbol of evil.

NUMBERS In societies in which man is dominant, odd numbers are regarded as masculine, even numbers as feminine. Here are the generally accepted characteristics of numbers:

One stands for originality and creativity as well as determination and ambition. Two represents companionship and cooperation. Three is associated with artists, adaptability, and frivolity. Four, symbolized by the square, represents the practical aspects of life. Five is the number of energy, adventure, and individual freedom. Six represents unselfishness, responsibility, and justice. Seven is the mystic's number, eight the entrepreneur's, and nine the philosopher's.

NUMBERS IN CHINA   In Chinese mysticism, numbers have metaphysical and cosmological implications. There are five canons of the Confucian classics. There are three kingdoms, eight Trigrams, four forms.

NUMEROLOGY   A technique of interpreting numbers and their combinations and relationships with a view to reading character and forecasting events. Pythagoras is often regarded as the father of numerology.

NUNS   The institution of nuns was in its essentials familiar to antiquity. A nun was dedicated to a divinity. She was virtually the 'bride of the god,' whether the god was Ammon in Egypt or whether in Peru the nuns were 'virgins of the sun.'

NUNS OF LOUDUN   Many nuns living in the Ursuline convent of Loudun in France began in the year 1633 to show signs of diabolic possession, eulalia, and hysteria. Their confessor, Urbain Grandier, was convicted of giving them over to the devil. His death at the stake did not stop the affair, however, and the obstreperous demons were not quieted until they were finally exorcised by a very holy monk called Surin.

NUTRIQUM   A Kabbalistic system which makes every letter in a Hebrew word the initial letter of a secret word.

NYIMA   In Tibetan astrology, this term refers to the Sun.

NYORO DIVINERS   The Nyoro in rural Bunyoro, Uganda, consult diviners whenever they are in trouble. The most common technique of divination is by cowry shells. Other mechanical techniques used by diviners include casting strips of leather on an animal skin, squeezing the juicy leaves of the *muhoko,* rubbing a moistened stick, and examining the pattern created by tossing twigs into water. The technique of divination through possession by a spirit is perpetuated by a cult of spirit mediumship based on the Chwezi spirits and/or later additions of non-Chwezi spirits such as Irungu, the spirit of the bush.

O

OANNES In Chaldean religion Oannes was Dagon, the man-fish. He rose out of the sea every day and, like Prometheus, taught mankind the crafts.

OBLIQUE ASCENSION In astrology, as it rises, a star or planet, not on the equator, forms an angle with that part of the equator which is rising at the same time. This is known as its Ascensional difference. This Ascensional difference, added to the rising ascension if it has South declination, and subtracted therefrom if it has North declination, gives its Oblique Ascension.

OBLIQUE DESCENSION In astrology, the complement of Oblique Ascension. One hundred-eighty degrees, minus the Oblique Ascension, equals the Oblique Descension.

OBSESSION A driving, sometimes irresistible, idea. When combined with an emotion, it can result in action. Obsessions have been classified as intellectual, inhibiting, and compulsive.

OCCIDENTAL OR ORIENTAL In astrology, these terms have various meanings when differently applied. The Moon is oriental of the Sun when it is increasing in light, from the lunation to the full: occidental of the Sun when decreasing in light. A planet is said to be oriental of the Sun when it rises and sets before the Sun. Planets are said to be stronger when oriental of the Sun and occidental of the Moon.

Applied to the Sun, a special significance is involved by the fact that when the Sun is setting in one hemisphere it is rising in the other. Therefore the Sun is said to be oriental in Houses 12, 11, 10, 6, 5, or 4; and occidental in the opposite Houses. Thus the oriental Houses are those which have passed the horizon and are culminating toward the meridian: the occidental Houses, those which have passed the meridian and are moving toward the horizon. Some astrologers speak of the Eastern Houses, the entire eastern half of the Figure, as the Oriental Houses: the entire western half, as the Occidental Houses.

OCCULT INFLUENCE   Three mystics, versed in the Kabbalah, were said to have exerted occult influence on the course of the Napoleonic Wars until the downfall of Napoleon himself.

OCCULTISM   This term is used in relation to esoteric and mystic cults and practices. It includes magic and witchcraft, astrology, alchemy, palmistry, both in their traditional aspects and in their practical applications.

OCCULTIST, NAMES FOR   Variant names, in antiquity as well as in contemporary times, have been applied to persons knowledgeable in occultism and mysticism. Among such names are maharishi, initiate, mahatma, adept.

OCCULT PHILOSOPHY   In his treatise on The Occult Philosophy Cornelius Agrippa von Nettesheim (1486-1535) gives interpretations of the significance of the primary numbers from 1 to 9.

OCCULT POWERS   In Hindu mysticism, there are eight psychic powers in relation to a person. They are produced at birth, or induced by drugs, or effected by incantations or extreme ascetic exercises.

OCCULTATION   When a planet or star is hidden or eclipsed by another body, particularly by the Moon, the result is termed an occultation.

OCCURSIONS   This term refers to celestial occurrences such as ingresses, formation of aspects, and conjunctions in astrological phenomena.

OCCURSOR   In astrology, a term applied by Ptolemy to the planet which moves to produce an occursion. This term is now superseded by Promittor.

OCH   In works on magic, Och is listed as one of the seven Olympian Spirits who rule the world. He is the master of the sun.

OCTAGONAL FLOWER   A symbol used in astrology to represent the totality of a man, or the human ego.

ODD NUMBERS   In the symbolism of most cultures, odd numbers are regarded as masculine. Plutarch assigned a 'generative middle part' to odd numbers.

OINOMANCY   A method of divination by observation of wine spilt into various forms.

OLCOTT, COLONEL HENRY STEEL   Founder, with Madame Blavatsky, of the movement of Theosophy. He died in 1906.

OLD RELIGION The name by which witchcraft is often called. In England the Old Religion persisted in spite of the efforts of inquisitors and persecutors until the eighteenth century. Vestiges of pagan practices survive today in France and England.

OLD TESTAMENT APOCRYPHA Writings of scriptural form or content, but excluded from the canon. The term apocrypha at first had a laudatory significance, meaning esoteric writings withheld from the uninitiated because of their mystic character. Later, it acquired, since the second century A.D., a sense of non-canonical untrustworthy, even heretical writings. Among the Old Testament apocrypha are Esdras, Tobit, Wisdom of Solomon, Ecclesiasticus, Baruch, Prayer of Manasses, Maccabees.

OLYMPIAN SPIRITS According to occult writers, seven Olympian Spirits rule the world. They are also called the Seven Stewards of Heaven.

OMEN Throughout Europe, particularly in Germany, Italy, and France, in old tales and traditional folk legends, the cat has been regarded as a portent of approaching death.

ONOMANCY A form of divination by observing the letters that form a person's name.

OPHIEL The spirit of Mercury, whose day is Wednesday. Ophiel is one of the Seven Olympian Spirits who rule the world.

OPHIOLATRY This term means serpent-worship. The cult of the serpent as a deity was prevalent in ancient Greece. Vestiges of the practice still remain in secluded villages and valleys of modern Greece. Ophiolatry was also practiced in South America and the West Indies.

260

In the ancient mystery cult of Mithra, in Persia, baskets were used to carry the sacred serpents.

OPHITES A Gnostic sect, probably of Egyptian origin, dating from the second century. They used symbols representing fire, purity, life, and spirit.

OPPOSITION Astrologically, when the zodiacal sign is opposed to Libra, this is called Opposition. This position is regarded as unfavorable.

ORACLE Delphi, a town in central Greece, was anciently an oracular center. The oracle of the god Apollo was located here. In his temple a priestess, the Pythia, delivered the responses of the god. In a trance-like state, she uttered incoherent phrases in reply to questions of visitants. The temple priest collated the utterances into a coherent sequence. The priestess-prophetess could be consulted on one day in each month.

In the course of time the oracular utterances acquired such a wide reputation in antiquity that no expedition or major activity of any kind was undertaken without consultation of the oracle.

ORBS In astrology, the space within which an aspect is judged to be effective. The term is used to describe the arc between the point at which a platic, or wide aspect, is regarded as strong enough to be operative, and the point of culmination of a partile or exact aspect.

ORDER OF THE TEMPLE Long regarded as the leading occult organization of the Christian West, the Order of the Temple was founded by Hughes de Payns and eight other knights, all companions of Godefroy de Bouillon, in 1118. Later Philippe le Bel accused the Order of worshipping Bahomet. Jacques de Molay defended the Templars against their accusers, who charged them with having participated in incredible orgies. Before his death, Molay is said to have condemned the king and the pope to appear before God for judgment. Both Philippe le Bel and Clement V died before the year had passed.

ORENDA Among American-Indian tribes this term is applied to occult spirit-forces.

ORGANIZATION WEREWOLF A German organization founded after World War I. It was a terrorist movement whose ruthlessness was intended to imitate the vulpine cruelties and bestialities.

ORI A word used by the Lugbara to denote ghosts and also shrines erected to their descendants. After death men and women who have produced children have shrines built for them by their children. These shrines are known as ghost houses (*ori* or *orijo*). Ghosts are supposed to live underneath these houses as well as in the air and to accept offerings placed in their shrines by their descendants.

ORIENTAL EXORCISM Evariste Régis Huc (1813-1860), the French missionary, in his Travels in Tartary, Thibet and China during the years 1844-1846, describes exorcism in an Oriental setting:
According to the religious beliefs of the Tartars, all illness is owing to the visitation of a Tchutgour or demon; but the expulsion of the demon is first a matter of medicine. The Lama physician next proceeds, as Lama apothecary, to give the specific befitting the case; the Tartar pharmacopoeia rejecting all mineral chemistry, the Lama remedies consist entirely of vegetables pulverized, and either infused in water or made up into pills. If the Lama doctor happens not to have any medicine with him, he is by no means disconcerted; he writes the names of the remedies upon little

scraps of paper, moistens the papers with his saliva, and rolls them up into pills, which the patient tosses down with the same perfect confidence as though they were genuine medicaments. To swallow the name of a remedy, or the remedy itself, say the Tartars, comes to precisely the same thing. The medical assault of the usurping demon being applied, the Lama next proceeds to spiritual artillery, in the form of prayers, adapted to the quality of the demon who has to be dislodged. If the patient is poor, the Tchutgour, visiting him can evidently be only an inferior Tchutgour, requiring merely a brief, off-hand prayer, sometimes merely an interjectional exorcism. If the patient is very poor, the Lama troubles himself with neither prayer nor pill, but goes away, recommending the friends to wait with patience until the sick person gets better or dies. But where the patient is rich, the possessor of large flocks, the proceedings are altogether different. First, it is obvious that a devil who presumes to visit so eminent a personage must be a potent devil, one of the chiefs of the Lower World, and it would not be decent for a great Tchutgour to travel like a mere sprite; the family, accordingly, are directed to prepare for him a handsome suit of clothes, a pair of rich boots, a fine horse, ready saddled and bridled, otherwise the devil will never think of going, physic or exorcise him how you may. It is even possible, indeed, that one horse will not suffice, for the demon, in very rich cases, may turn out, upon inquiry, to be so high and mighty a prince, that he has with him a number of courtiers and attendants, all of whom have to be provided with horses.

Everything being arranged, the ceremony begins. The Lama and numerous co-physicians called in from his own and other adjacent monasteries, offer up prayers to the rich man's tents for a week or a fortnight, until they perceive that the devil is gone — that is to say, until they have exhausted all the disposable tea and sheep. If the patient recovers, it is a clear proof that the prayers

263

have been efficaciously recited; if he dies, it is still greater proof of the efficaciousness of the prayers, for not only is the devil gone, but the patient has transmigrated to a state far better than he has quitted.

The prayers recited by the Lamas for the recovery of the sick are sometimes accompanied with very dismal and alarming rites. The aunt of Tokoura, chief of an encampment in the Valley of Dark Waters, visited by M. Huc, was seized one evening with an intermittent fever.

"I would invite the attendance of the doctor Lama," said Tokoura, "but if he finds that there is a very big Tchutgour present, the expenses will ruin me." He waited for some days, but as his aunt grew worse, he at last sent for a Lama; his anticipations were confirmed. The Lama pronounced that a demon of considerable rank was present, and that no time must be lost in expelling him. Eight other Lamas were forthwith called in, who at once set about the construction, in dried herbs, of a great puppet which they entitled The Demon of Intermittent Fevers, and which, when completed, they placed on its legs by means of a stick, in the patient's tent.

The ceremony began at eleven o'clock at night. The Lamas ranged themselves in a semi-circle around the upper portion of the tent, with cymbals, sea-shells, bells, tambourines, and other instruments of the noisy Tartar music. The remainder of the circle was completed by the members of the family, squatting on the ground close to one another, the patient kneeling or rather crouched on her heels, opposite the Demon of Intermittent Fevers. The Lama doctor-in-chief had before him a large copper basin filled with millet, and some little images made of paste. The dung fuel threw, amid much smoke, a fantastic and quivering light over the strange scene.

Upon a given signal, the clerical orchestra executed an overture harsh enough to frighten Satan himself, the lay congregation beating time with their hands to the charivari of clanging instruments and ear-splitting voices. The dia-

264

bolical concert over, the Grand Lama opened the Book of Exorcisms, which he rested on his knees. As he chanted one of the forms, he took from the basin, from time to time, a handful of millet, which he threw east, west, north, and south, according to the Rubric.

The tones of his voice, as he prayed, were sometimes mournful and suppressed, sometimes vehemently loud and energetic. All of a sudden, he would quit the regular cadence of prayer, and have an outburst of apparently indomitable rage, abusing the herb puppet with fierce invectives and furious gestures. The exorcism terminated, he gave a signal by stretching out his arms, right and left, and the other Lamas struck up a tremendously noisy chorus, in hurried, dashing tones: all the instruments were set to work, and meantime the lay congregation, having started up with one accord, ran out of the tent, one after the other, and tearing round it like mad people, beat it at their hardest with sticks, yelling all the while at the pitch of their voices in a manner to make ordinary hair stand on end. Having thrice performed this demoniac round, they re-entered the tent as precipitately as they had quitted it, and resumed their seats. Then all the others covering their faces with their hands, the Grand Lama rose and set fire to the herb figure. As soon as the flames rose, he uttered a loud cry, which was repeated with interest by the rest of the company. The laity immediately rose, seized the burning figure, carried it into the plain, away from the tents, and there, as it consumed, anathematized it with all sorts of imprecations. The Lamas meantime squatted in the tent, tranquilly, chanting their prayers in a grave, solemn tone.

Upon the return of the family from their valorous expedition, the praying was exchanged for joyous felicitations. By and by, each person provided with a lighted torch, the whole party rushed simultaneously from the tent, and formed into a procession, the laymen first, then the patient, supported on either side by a member of the family, and lastly, the nine Lamas, making night hideous with their music. In this style the patient was conducted to another tent, pursuant to the orders of the Lama, who had declared that she must absent herself from her own habitation for an entire month.

After this strange treatment, the malady did not return.

ORIGEN   A Christian religious philosopher who flourished in the third century. He thought that the stars were powerful personalities and that the word, when spoken by man, was equally potent.

ORINDI   The Lugbara believe that a ghost witch may take the shape of a night animal and enter a victim's hut. The everyday body of the witch remains outside the hut while his *orindi* or soul goes inside.

ORPHEAN EGG   The cosmic doctrine of the legendary Thracian sage teaches that the ether proceeded from God and that the chaotic mass was fashioned into the shape of an egg, from which all things proceeded. Everything in the universe strives to attain the same shape.

ORTIVE DIFFERENCE   In astrology, this term is sometimes applied to the difference between the primary and secondary distances, when directing the Sun at its rising or setting. It appears to indicate an effort to accommodate the fact of horizontal parallax. In modern times, the term is rarely used.

OUPNEKHAT   The Persian Oupnekhat (Book of the Secret) instructs the reader in the means of producing visions.

OWEN, GEORGE VALE   The Reverend George Vale Owen was an English vicar who in the 30's produced a book on the afterlife, in the form of revelations from spirits with whom the Rev. Owen had made contact.

OWEN, ROBERT (1771-1858)   The British philanthropist who expressed his social philosophy in A New View of Society (1813) embraced the doctrine of spiritualism in his eighty-third year and preached with sustained vigor the new faith which he viewed as the inauguration of a social revolution.

P

PAIGOELS   Some Hindus believe that the Paigoels were created as devils, others that they were expelled from heaven for their sin. They tempt men, enter into their bodies, and welcome into their ranks the souls of the wicked.

PA KUA   The Eight Trigrams making up the original corpus of the I Ching. They consist of various combinations of *hsiao* (straight lines), arranged in a circle.

PALACE OF LOVE   In Kabbalistic mysticism, the palace which is situated in the secret and most elevated part of heaven is called the Palace of Love. Here the heavenly King dwells with the holy souls and is united with them with a loving kiss. This kiss is the union of the soul with the substance from which it emanated.

PALADINO, EUSAPIA (1854-1918)   An internationally famous Italian spiritualistic medium. She performed in the major cities of Europe. She was investigated by many noted men, among them Professor Cesare Lombroso, the Italian criminologist and psychiatrist and representatives of the British Society for Psychical Research. She was able to produce spirit emanations but finally was caught using trickery. Yet some of the phenomena she produced, which were coldly and effectively tested and investigated, were beyond any one definitive and conclusive explanation.

269

PAPAL SORCERERS Among popes who were involved in occult practices was Sylvester II, who fashioned a head that uttered oracles. Others who had reputations as magicians were Benedict IX and John XX.

PAPUS (1865-1917), the pseudonym of Gérard Encausse, a French Kabbalist who also wrote on the Tarot.

PARABRAHMAN Esoterically, the Sanskrit word Parabrahman ('beyond Brahman') is used to designate that which lies beyond Brahman, the summit of a cosmic Hierarchy. The word is linked with Mulaprakriti, with which Parabrahman interacted to cause the first stirrings of the Universal Life when spiritual desire first arose in the beginning of things.

PARACELSUS (c. 1490 - 1541) Theophrastus Bombast von Hohenheim, known as Paracelsus, was a German physician, astrologer, and magus who wandered over Europe. He was interested in occult subjects, in prognostication, and in alchemy as a means toward human perfection. He wrote on nymphs, sylphs, pigmies, and salamanders, mingling the results of his mystic studies with the folklore of his native country.

Paracelsus is known for his magic mirror, used in divining future events.

PARADISE FOR ANIMALS In Hindu legend the cat is credited with a second existence in Heaven. Among other creatures so distinguished were the hound, the wolf, and the ass.

Goethe has some verses treating this theme.

PARALLEL In astrology, the parallel has the same nature as a conjunction. A mundane parallel is a parallel in mundo. It refers to the similarity of relationship between two

270

planets on opposite sides of the Equator. A rapt parallel is a mundane parallel by direction, formed after birth, as the result of the Earth's rotation.

PARAMATMAN The Sanskrit word designates the permanent self, the Brahman or Universal Spirit-soul, the Heart of the Universe.

PARANORMAL PHENOMENA There are countless instances of psychic or paranormal phenomena in relation to man and to the cosmos that have challenged scientific investigation. The East in particular is rich in such phenomena. Levitation is practiced by some Tibetan lamas. Hindus can pierce the body without the appearance of any blood or injury. Afghan mystics, holy men or gurus perform strange feats. Spirits are materialized: demons that pullulate in the air. Mystic shamans abound as healers, while evil spirits prowl the jungle depths.

PARAPSYCHOLOGY A branch of psychology that investigates psychical and psychophysical phenomena such as telepathy, apparitions, visions, premonitions, automatic writing, states of impersonation, clairvoyance, materialization of spirits, telekinesis. Supporters of parapsychological manifestations included the philosophers Fichte, Schelling, and Hegel. Some paranormal phenomena may have religious interpretations to persóns undergoing the experience. The source for an intensive study of this entire field is the London Society for Psychical Research. In the U.S.A. Dr. Rhine of Duke University has been internationally prominent in parapsychological investigations.

PART OF FORTUNE In astrology, this is the distance of the moon's position from the sun, plus the degrees of the ascendant.

271

PARVOS   In Tibetan mysticism these are psychic mediums.

PASSIVE   In astrology, the Sun and the moon are termed passive, as they take their coloring from the signs in which they are posited, or the planets with which they are in strongest aspect. The Passive Qualities are: Moisture and Dryness.

PASTOPROROI   This Greek term denotes the bearers of the sacred coffin of the Sun-gods. It was applied to candidates for initiation in the ancient mystery cults.

PATH   Theosophy teaches that Universal Nature, our Great Parent, exists everywhere, in each entity, and that no separation of the part from the whole, the individual from the cosmos, is possible. Mystics discover the Path to utter Reality by unfolding the intrinsic faculties within them.

PATIENCE WORTH   Many volumes written in late medieval prose and poetry are attributed to Patience Worth by Mrs. John H. Curran, a medium who first communicated with her by means of a ouija board. Patience Worth claimed to have lived in seventeenth-century England and to have been killed in America by Indians. Her works include The Sorry Tale, an account of the life and times of Christ.

PAWANG   An important functionary in Malay society. The Pawang concerns himself with taboos and is served by a hereditary demon known as *hantu pusaka.* He also falls into trances and acts as a medium.

PEDOMANCY   A method of divination by observation of a person's foot.

PEGNOMANCY   A form of divination by means of a wand.

PENUMBRAL ECLIPSE   In astrology, eclipses of the Moon, when the Moon approaches closely enough to the earth's shadow to cause an appreciable diminution of light though it does not directly touch it. These are frequently called appulses. They are not generally classed as eclipses, though from their close resemblance to eclipse conditions they often produce effects similar to those attending an actual eclipse.

PEREGRINE   This term, in astrology, denotes foreign, alien. It refers to a planet posited in a sign where it possesses no essential dignity: where it is neither dignified nor debilitated. It is employed in Horary Astrology, where it is usually reckoned as a debility. In a question of a theft, a peregrine planet in an angle or in the second house is the thief. However, no planet is reckoned peregrine if it is in mutual reception with another.

PERFECTION   In Kabbalistic mysticism, perfection is reached by prayers, fasting, ablutions, and ascetic exercises.

PERIODICAL LUNATION   In astrology, a Figure cast for the Moon's synodic period, when it returns to the exact degree held at birth. It is often employed for monthly forecasts in a way similar to the Solar Revolution for annual forecasts. A true Figure for the Moon's periodical return is difficult to construct, because of the Moon's acceleration from hour to hour.

PERNETY, ANTOINE JOSEPH (1716 - 1801)   A follower of Swedenborg the mystic. Pernety conceived all the mythology of antiquity as one concept, The Great Arcanum.

273

PERSIAN EXORCISM In ancient Persia, hair and nails of a person were used in performing a conjuration of the dead.

PETER OF ABANO A thirteenth century Italian philosopher and astrologer. Reputed to have had associations with Satanic forces. Wrote on magic, predictions, and geomancy.

PETRO In Voodoo cults, the dispenser of magic powers.

PETRONIUS In the Satyricon, a realistic novel of Roman life, Petronius, who belongs in the first century A.D., relates a story by a guest at a banquet. The tale concerns a soldier who, after certain ceremonies, turns into a wolf and runs off into the woods.

PHALEG In works on magic, Phaleg is listed as one of the seven Olympian Spirits. He is the prince of Mars.

PHILALETHEANS This expression etymologically means truth-lovers. It was the name of the Neoplatonist philosophers of Alexandria. The founder of the system was Ammonius Saccas, who flourished in the third century A.D.

PHILALETHES, EUGENIUS A seventeenth century alchemist. Author of a hermetic treatise entitled Light of all Lights. Also wrote in defense of the Rosicrucians.

PHILIP THE APOSTLE In Gnostic mysticism, he is the reputed author of the Gnostic treatise entitled Pistis Sophia.

PHILO Also called Philo Judaeus (c. 20 B.C. - c. 50 A.D.). He was a Hellenistic Jew who flourished in Alexandria. In his allegorical interpretation of the Pentateuch he attempted reconciliation between Hebraic and Greek philosophy.

274

Philo's mystical expositions are based on the concept of the divine Logos, the Word. Philo regarded Creations as an indirect operation of God, through the agency of his Potencies.

PHOENIX   A fabled bird of the eagle family. It was traditionally reborn from its own ashes. In legend and in early Christian thought it was conceived as the symbol of immortality.

PHRENOLOGY   The study of the relation of the conformation of the skull to mental faculties and traits of character. Robert Thidd foreshadowed phrenology in attempting to symbolize the 'mystery of the human head' and the manner in which 'the celestial word enters into the cranium.' Systems of phrenology were described by the Swiss mystic Johann Kaspar Lavater (in collaboration with Goethe) and by the German physician F. J. Gall. According to Lavater's system, the face is divided into three worlds: the forehead is the divine world; the triangle formed by the nose and eyes, together with the forehead and mouth, is the psychical world; the jaw and chin are the physical world.

PHUL   In treatises on magic, Phul is listed as the administrator of the affairs of the Moon. He is one of the Olympian Spirits.

PHYLLORHODOMANCY   A method of divination by the observation of rose leaves.

PHYSIOGNOMY   Divination by facial features is based on the notion of a connection between the human body and the universe. The art of discovering temperament and character from outward appearance enjoyed great popularity in the nineteenth century. As early as 1619, Robert Fludd had explored the interconnection between the microcosm of Man and the macrocosm of the universe.

PI The symbol of the sky, Pi, corresponds to hexagram number 1 in the I-Ching. It represents Yang.

PIKE, BISHOP JAMES A. In recent years Bishop Pike was the subject of violent controversy for his unorthodox views on the Church, its functions, and its effectiveness.
Ordained twenty-five years ago, Bishop Pike, until recently Bishop of the Protestant Episcopal Diocese of California, left the Church, accused of heresy. His 'open communion' policy was attacked, as were his sermons on doctrine and race.
With his wife, a former missionary, he founded in 1966 the New Focus Foundation, directed toward a fresh appraisal of Christian doctrine and its purposes.
Of immediate and particular interest is Bishop Pike's view of the life after death. In collaboration with his wife, he published The Other Side, an account of his communication with his dead son, only a few months before he perished on the Sinai desert.
Bishop Pike wrote for the popular press and appeared frequently on television, expounding his new religious orientation.

PINE BRANCHES In Japan, pine branches symbolize longevity.

PIPER, MRS. LEONORA E. An American spiritualistic medium. She possessed marked powers, particularly in the matter of communication with the dead. Among those who investigated her capacities were the noted psychologist William James and Sir Oliver Lodge. She first became entranced in the company of a professional clairvoyant,

276

in 1884. Later the famous trance medium was controlled by numerous spirits, including Bach and Longfellow.

PISCES   In astrology, Fishes. The twelfth southern sign of the zodiac. It represents dissolution of matter followed by resurgence. Esoterically, this sign represents the flood and is the last emanation of the watery trigon. Kabbalistically, it signifies the feet of the archetypal man and the mechanical forces of humanity.

PISTIS SOPHIA   The secret writings of the Gnostic sect.

PITRIS   In Oriental mysticism they are the primal creators of men. The pitris are grouped in two orders: corporeal and spiritual.

PK   This term, used in parapsychology, denotes psychokinesis. It refers to the extramotor aspect of PSI: a direct, mental, non-muscular influence exerted by the subject on an external physical process, condition, or object.

PLANCHETTE   A small heart-shaped board used in establishing communication with the spirit world. It is named for a French spiritualist who invented the instrument in 1853. When the fingers of one or more persons are rested on the board, it moves in such a way that a pencil automatically traces messages.

PLANES   The word is used in theosophy to denote the range of a state of consciousness or the perceptive power of special senses. The physical world is said to grade off into the astral world, which grades off into a superior world, and so on throughout the series of hierarchical planes of our universe.

277

PLANETARY AGES OF MAN In astrology, the ancients called the planets chronocrators, markers of time. It was presumed that different periods of life were ruled by different planets. The Moon was related to the infant. Mercury referred to the scholar. Venus was attached to the lover. The Sun denoted the citizen. Mars was interested in soldiers. Jupiter implied the judge. Saturn denoted resignation, age.

PLANETARY CHAIN Every cosmic body is composed of inner energies and invisible substances and of an outer vehicle or body which is visible to us, according to the teachings of theosophists. Every self-contained entity or individual life center consists of seven elements. Every physical globe seen in space is accompanied by six invisible globes, forming a Chain. Our Earth-globe is the fourth and lowest of the seven globes of the Earth-chain.

PLANETARY GODS In mysticism, they are representations of human characteristics. The planetary gods are: the Sun, the Moon, Venus, Mercury, Mars, Saturn.

PLANETARY INFLUENCE In astrology, the strongest planetary influence is that of the Sun, which governs the sign of Leo.

PLANETARY MOTIONS In astrology, certain motions are associated with the planets.
Converse — applied to a progressed or directed motion to a point of aspect, in a clockwise direction or opposite to the order of the signs.
Direct — the true motions of the planets in the order of the signs, or counter-clockwise, within the Zodiac. Applied to progressed or directed motion, it is the opposite of converse motion.
Diurnal — a diurnal planet is one that was above the

278

horizon at the time for which the Figure was cast. Such planets are said to be passive.

Rapt — the apparent diurnal motion of the heavens, in consequence of the earth's axial rotation.

Re-direct — applied to the reversal to direct motion following the second station of the retrograde.

Retrograde — the apparent motion in the Zodiac of certain planets, as viewed from the earth during certain parts of the year.

Slow of course — slow in motion. Applied to a planet whose travel in twenty-four hours is less than its mean motion.

Stationary — when a planet appears to have no motion, as when changing from retrograde to direct or the reverse, it is said to be stationary.

Stations, in retrograde — each planet has two stations, or stationary points: 1. the place in its orbit where it becomes stationary before it turns retrograde: 2. when it again becomes stationary preparatory to resuming its direct motion.

Swift in Motion — planets that at the moment are moving at a speed in excess of their mean motion are said to be 'swift in motion.'

PLANETARY PATTERN In astrology, a symmetrical arrangement of two or more planets or sensitive points around a common axis. A planetary picture as employed in Iranian Astrology represents the inter-activity of two planets, connected through a third planet or sensitive point at or in hard aspect to their midpoint.

PLANETS In astrology, the planets are the most important heavenly bodies. They have signs attached to each of their names. The names are as follows: Saturn, Jupiter, Mars, Sun, Venus, Mercury, Moon. The planets and the signs of the zodiac are always present in the heavens but not all are visible. Some lie above and some below the horizon.

PLANETS AND SPIRITS   In a medieval grimoire, a manual of magic practices, the Olympic spirits are mentioned as being in control of the planets. Bethor governs Jupiter: Phaleg, Mars: Och, the Sun, and Aratron, Saturn.

PLANETS, CLASSIFICATIONS OF   In astrology, planets are classified as:

barren and fruitful: barren planets are Mars, Saturn, Uranus. Fruitful: Sun, Moon, Venus, Jupiter, Neptune.

androgynous: Mercury, which is both dry and moist.

benefic and malefic: e.g. benefic — Venus and Jupiter. malefic — Mars and Saturn.

cold and hot: Cold: the Moon, Saturn. Hot: Sun, Mars.

diurnal and nocturnal: nocturnal — the Moon, Venus. Diurnal — those which at birth were above the horizon.

dry and moist: Dry — Sun, Mars, Saturn. Moist — Mercury, the Moon.

electric and magnetic: electric — Sun, Mars, Jupiter. Magnetic — Moon, Mercury, Saturn.

masculine and feminine: Masculine — Sun, Mars, Jupiter. Feminine — Moon, Venus, Neptune.

morning and evening 'stars,' although all the planet terms refer particularly to Mercury and Venus, as morning and evening 'stars', although all the planets become morning and evening stars at some part of the year.

superior and inferior. The major or superior planets are those that have orbits larger than that of the earth and which lie at a greater distance from the Sun. They are: Mars, Jupiter, Saturn, Uranus, Neptune, and Pluto. They are also called the Ponderous or ponderable planets.

The minor or inferior planets are those that have orbits

smaller than that of the earth, and which lie closer to the Sun. They are Mercury and Venus.

PLANET VENUS In alchemy, this planet is associated with copper. Astrologically, it is related to the Moon and to Mars.

PLATONIC COSMIC YEAR The sun rises every year in a slightly different position in the Zodiac, during the equinox. In 25,920 years this changing movement of the sun completes a circuit, appearing once again at the equinox. The 25,920 years constitute a Cosmic Year, in Platonic philosophy.

PLAYING CARDS Such cards, used in fortune telling, were according to tradition, brought into Europe by gypsy tribes in the fourteenth century.

PLEROMA This Greek term denoting fullness was applied in Gnostic mysticism to the Divine World.

PLOTINUS (c. 204 - 270) The most famous of the Neo-Platonists taught that one must withdraw into his inmost self, into his own essence, in order to know God intimately and infinitely.

PODOVNE VILE Water sprites that deal kindly with men on the shore but may be treacherous away from the land. They constitute one of three major classes of Slavonic spirits. The others include the earth-dwelling and the aerial spirits.

POETIC ASTROLOGY There are versified characterizations of the zodiacal signs composed, among others, by Addison, Milton, as well as by the ancient Greek poet Aratus and the Roman poet Manilius:

Who works from morn to set of Sun,
And never likes to be outdone?
Whose walk is almost like a run?
  Who? Aries.

Who smiles through life — except when crossed?
Who knows, or thinks he knows, the most?
Who loves good things: baked, boiled or roast?
  Oh, Taurus.

Who's fond of life and jest and pleasure:
Who vacillates and changes ever?
Who loves attention without measure?
  Why, Gemini.

Who changes like a changeful season:
Holds fast and lets go without reason?
Who is there can give adhesion
    To Cancer?

Soon as the evening shades prevail
The Moon takes up the wondrous tale,
and nightly to the listening Earth
Proclaims the story of her birth.
                    — Addison.

Who praises all his kindred do;
Expects his friends to praise them too —
And cannot see their senseless view?
  Ah, Leo.

The Lion flames: There the Sun's course runs hottest.
Empty of grain the arid fields appear
When first the Sun into Leo enters.
                    — Aratus.

Who criticizes all she sees:
Yes, e'en would analyze a sneeze?

282

Who hugs and loves her own disease?
  Humpf, Virgo.

But modest Virgo's rays give polished parts,
And fill men's breasts with honesty and arts;
No tricks for gain, nor love of wealth dispense,
But piercing thoughts and winning eloquence.
                              — Manilius.

Who puts you off with promise gay,
And keeps you waiting half the day?
Who compromises all the way?
  Sweet Libra.

...Now dreadful deeds
Might have ensued, nor only Paradise
In this commotion, but the starry cope
Of heaven perhaps, or all the elements
At least had gone to wreck, disturbed and torn
With violence of this conflict, had not soon
The Eternal, to prevent such horrid fray,
Hung forth in heaven his golden scales, yet seen
Betwixt Astraea and the Scorpion sign.
                    — John Milton, Paradise Lost.

Who keeps an arrow in his bow,
And if you prod, he lets it go?
A fervent friend, a subtle foe —
  Scorpio.

Bright Scorpio, armed with poisonous tail, prepares
Men's martial minds for violence and for wars.
His venom heats and boils their blood to rage,
And rapine spreads o'er the unlucky age.
                              — Manilius.

Who loves the dim religious light:
Who always keeps a star in sight?

283

An optimist, both gray and bright —
  Sagittarius.

Midst golden stars he stands resplendent now,
And thrusts the Scorpion with his bended bow.

—Ovid.

And, what was ominous, that very morn
The Sun was entered into Capricorn.

—Dryden.

Who climbs and schemes for wealth and place,
And mourns his brother's fall from grace —
But takes what's due in any case?
  Safe Capricorn.

. . . Pitiless
Siroccos lash the main, when Capricorn
Lodges the Sun and Zeus sends bitter cold
To numb the frozen sailors.

—Aratus.

Who gives to all a helping hand,
But bows his head to no command —
And higher laws doth understand?
Inventor, Genius, Superman — Aquarius.

Man's fate and the stars:
Men at some time are masters of their fates;
The fault, dear Brutus, is not in our stars,
But in ourselves, that we are underlings.

—Shakespeare.

Who prays, and serves, and prays some more;
And feeds the beggar at the door —
And weeps o'er loves lost long before?
Poor Pisces.

Westward, and further in the South wind's path,
The Fishes float; one ever uppermost

284

First hears the boisterous coming of the North.
Both are united by a band.
Their tails point to an angle
Filled by a single goodly star,
Called the Conjoiner of the Fishes' Tails.

— Aratus.

POINT OF LIFE In astrology, a progressed point, obtained by advancing zero degrees Aries at the rate of 7y per sign. A planet at this point is presumed to affect the native according to its nature and strength.

POINT OF LOVE In astrology, as this represents the position of Venus in a solar figure, and as Venus never has a greater elongation from the Sun than 48 degrees, the Arabian Point can never be in other than the 11th, 12th, 1st or 2nd Houses.

POINT OF THE FATHER In astrology, this appears to be the Point of Sudden Advancement, except that if Saturn is combust Jupiter is to be taken as the Ascendant in considering the House-position of the Sun.

POLAR DAY In occultism, the Polar Day is the cycle of duration of any life-wave on our planet. It equals 2,592,000 years.

POLAR ELEVATION In astrology, the elevation of the Pole, or the Pole of the Descendant, is relative to the north or south latitude of the place for which a map is erected.

POLTERGEIST A poltergeist is a being that makes its presence felt to presumably psychic persons by creating noises and disturbances, such as the transference of objects from one spot to another, or throwing furniture around a room. The poltergeist has a long tradition that runs through many

285

centuries, but no rational explanation has been forthcoming regarding the source of its operations.

POPULARITY OF ASTROLOGY In the United States alone there are more than 2000 periodicals and newspapers that publish regular columns or articles on astrological subjects: advice and guidance in terms of personal horoscopes and predictions based on astrological calculations.

PORPHYRY (c. 232 - 305 A.D.) A Neoplatonic philosopher: pupil of the great Neoplatonist Plotinus. Like the early Greek philosophers, Porphyry had a profound belief in demons and in their malefic practices which required secret rites and formulas, invocations and conjurations to dispel them. Among Porphyry's works is a mystical treatise On the Return of the Soul.

PORTA, GIAMBATTISTA DELLA (c. 1518 - 1615) Italian physician and scientist. He founded the first scientific society. He was also involved in magic and alchemy. He established the practice of interpreting character by observation of the physiognomy.

PORTENTS In Greek antiquity priests, after sacrificing an animal, sought, by examination of the entrails and similar means, to interpret the will of the gods in relation to approaching events.

POSTEL, GUILLAUME A sixteenth-century French visionary who believed that God had commanded him to reunite all men under one law.

POWER OF PROJECTION In alchemy this is a variant name for the Philosophers' Stone.

POWER OF MEDITATION The Hindu mystic Patanjali, who flourished in the second century B.C., asserted that through the use of mind-poise certain powers may be acquired: among them, knowledge of former states of life: power of invisibility: knowledge of the time of one's death: power of clairvoyance: power of levitation: power of clairaudience: astral traveling: power of the mind over matter.

POWER OF SHAMAN Among the Eskimos of Greenland and Baffin Land the shaman could make an animal figure composed of bones, parts of infants' corpses, and other materials, and endow it with supernatural powers of flight and injury.

POZEMNE VILE Earth-dwelling spirits that give good counsel to mortals. Southern Slavs regard them as companionable spirits.

PRAJAPATI The Sanskrit word meaning 'master of progeny' is applied to several Vedic gods, but particularly to Brahma, the Emanator, in theosophical writings. Prajapati often refers to the seven Givers of Life on the Earth's Planetary Chain.

PRAKRITI Esoterically, the Sanskrit word means the primordial essence of things, or Nature in general, as opposed to Purusha. Prakriti and Purusha together make up the primeval aspects of the one unknown God.

PRALAYA In theosophy, a period of obscuration or repose, whether planetary, cosmic, or universal. Its opposite is Manvantara.

PRANAYAMA   A distinctive feature of yoga, pranayama is a special method of attaining samadhi. Pranayama means regulation of breath in order to control the life force of the body.

PRECIPITATION OF MATTER   Attempts to explain the passing of one solid through another include that of precipitation of matter. This theory assumes that the atoms of a body 'dissolve,' pass through the other solid, and reassume their original form by 'precipitation.'

PRECOGNITION   Foreknowledge. In its essence this concept coincides with the Platonic Theory of Pre-Natal cognition. In parapsychology, it is the prediction of random future events the occurrence of which cannot be inferred from present knowledge.

PREDICTION   The passion for probing into the future is so intense nowadays that all sorts of techniques, both old and more recent, have been revived and promoted. A large number of such procedures concern the daily routine, domestic affairs, personal situations. One of the most popular methods in common vogue is the use of numerology. Interpretation of numbers and their impact on persons and events have become a major issue. Gambling, especially in races, appeals to practitioners in numerological calculations.

A trip taken for business or pleasure is conditioned by consultation of certain numbers and combinations of such numbers. Numbers too affect the good or unfavorable days for moving to a new location, a new apartment. Lucky days are determined similarly by numerical observation. These practices are referred back to antiquity, to ancient procedures among the Egyptian priesthood, among Chinese wizards, and among the priests of the pagan mystery cults of Phrygia and Mesopotamia.

PREDICTIVE ASTROLOGY The branch of astrology that deals with Directions, the methods by which future influences are ascertained.

PRE-EXISTENCE A philosophical concept that posits the existence of the human soul prior to the physical birth of a person. This is associated with the Platonic Idea of Precognition, knowledge acquired in the life prior to actual physical appearance in the material world. A poetic exposition of this theory appears in William Wordsworth's Ode on Intimations of Immortality: 'Our birth is but a sleep and a forgetting.'

PRETU The Hindus believe that the soul takes the form of a pretu ('departed ghost') after the body death and inhabits a body the size of a man's thumb. It remains in the keeping of Yama, the judge of the dead, until its punishment is completed. Then it is delivered from this state by the performance of the Shraddhu, received in the heaven of the Pitris, and rewarded for its good deeds.

PRIESTLY TABOOS In ancient Rome, the high priest of Jupiter was subject to many traditional restrictions. He could not observe an army in battle array. He was not permitted to touch or ride a horse. His hair had to be cut with a bronze knife. He was not allowed to eat beans or bread made of wheat.

PRIMARY DIRECTIONS In astrology, any method for determining the changing influences of the altered relationship between the cuspal and the planets' places on successive days or years after birth that is based on the diurnal rotation of the earth upon its axis is known as Primary Direction.

PRINCE OF THE PRESENCE In Hebraic mysticism, this expression refers to the chief attendant on the Supreme Divinity.

PRINCIPAL PLACES In astrology, these are the five places in which the luminaries are said to have the most beneficial effects in a Nativity: the hylegiacal places: the 1st, 11th, 9th, and 7th Houses.

PRINCIPLES OF MAN The seven principles of man are viewed by occultists as a copy of the seven cosmic Principles. The seven fundamental and individual aspects of the One Universal Reality in the cosmos and in man are the basic differentiations which constitute all things. The seven aspects in their manifestations in the human being are: divine, spiritual, psychic, astral, physiological, and physical.

PROFECTIONS In astrology, a term used by Ptolemy to indicate the successional rising of the signs, hence of the Sun and other Significators, at the rate of one sign per year.

PROGRESSED HOROSCOPE In astrology, a horoscope erected for a date that is as many days after a given birth date as the native's age in years.

PROGRESSIONS In astrology, alterations in the birth chart aiming to show the changing influences that result from motions of the celestial bodies after birth.

PROMISE OF AFTER-LIFE The Greek mystery cult of Eleusis, in the sixth century B.C., promised its initiates happiness in an after-life. Other tenets of this cult were: the divinity of the soul and metempsychosis.

PROMISES MADE BY CULTS The ancient mystery cults of Dionysius and Sabazius, of Attis and Isis and especially of Mithra promised its followers a happy life after death.

PROMITTOR In astrology, a planet to which a significator may be 'directed' in order to form an aspect between the 'progressed position' of the significator and the 'birth position' of the promittor, whereby certain events or conditions are promised as concern the significator so directed. The distance the significator must travel to form this aspect is termed the 'arc of direction,' to be reduced to time, usually at the rate of one degree for a year.

PROPER MOTION In astrology, this expression refers to the motion of a planet in space, as compared with any apparent motion which results from any movement of the earth: either axial rotation, annual revolution, or the motion through space of our entire solar system. The term is also loosely applied to the direct motion of a planet through the signs, in distinction to the diurnal rising and setting caused by the earth's rotation.

PROPERTIUS In one of his poems Propertius, the Roman poet who belongs in the first century B.C., refers to spells capable of changing a man into a wolf.

PROROGATOR In astrology, this term was used by Ptolemy in connection with a method of direction, effected by proportion of horary times — semi-arcs. The Prorogator is the Apheta or Life Giver, in contrast to the Anareta. By day and in aphetical places, the Sun holds the position of Prorogator: by night, the Moon.

PROTOLOGOI This Greek term, which means First Words, is in mysticism applied to the seven primal forces that materialized into archangels.

PSEPHOMANCY A form of divination by observing pebbles drawn from a heap.

PSI In parapsychology, these initials represent a general term to identify a person's extrasensorimotor communication with the environment.

PSI PHENOMENA In parapsychology, occurrences which result from the operation of PSI. They include the phenomena of both ESP, including precognition, and PK.

PSSR In the Rosicrucian mystic system, these letters represent the Latin words: Per Spiritum Sanctum Reviviscimus — Through the Holy Spirit we Live again.

PSYCHAGOGUES This expression, of Greek origin, means conjurer of the spirits of the dead.

PSYCHEDELIC EXPERIENCE A state of heightened awareness resulting from the use of mind-expansion chemicals, drugs, or plants. Experimentation with LSD (lysergic acid diethylamide), psilocybin, mescaline, etc. is now prohibited except under the supervision of psychiatrists working in a mental hospital setting.

PSYCHIC This is a bi-monthly magazine, published in California, which has just made its appearance. It is devoted to every aspect of psychic phenomena and related topics. It is designed to present material of substance to the general public and bring about open discussion among proponents and detractors.
The first issue includes an interview with Jeane Dixon,

who has been called the "seeress of Washington": an article on ESP in Eastern Europe and Russia: and a piece on the Lost Continent of Atlantis.

PSYCHIC ABILITY   It appears that a psychic person is not necessarily born so. Advertisements in popular magazines offer instruction to the aspirant wishing to acquire such power.

PSYCHIC DOMINANCE   In a popular magazine a course is offered which professes to train in acquiring psychic control over others.

PSYCHOMANCY   This is the practice of divination by conjuring the spirits of the dead. In ancient Greece psychomancy was a common practice.

PSYCHOMETRY   The faculty of reading a person's character by holding in one's hand an object belonging to that person. J. R. Buchanan is supposed to have discovered this faculty which many mediums possess.

PSYLLI   A class of persons thought in ancient times to have had the power of charming snakes.

PTOLEMY   Claudius Ptolemy of Alexandria, geographer and mathematician, flourished in the second century A.D. He is the author of a basic treatise on astrology.

PUEBLO CULTS   The Pueblo Indians in the American Southwest practiced a polytheistic and animistic religion. Their major deities were the sun, the earth-mother, and two hero twins. There were many cults, and the main aim of all these cults was to establish harmony in society and increase the fertility of crops. Their ceremonies were closely linked to rain, the symbol of goodness, health, and fertility. Since the rain came from the clouds, a major cult centered around worship of the *shiwana,* with whom the clouds were identified.

PURIFYING FIRE, THE   This is the title of a Kabbalistic treatise belonging in the sixteenth century. It deals to a large extent with alchemy.

PURRAH   An African secret society. A Tulka-Susus tribesman who seeks membership in the society must pass a severe test. His relatives first must swear that they will kill him if he fails the test or reveals the mysteries of the society.

PURUSHA   The Sanskrit word meaning Ideal Man is used esoterically to designate the Spiritual Man in each human being.

PYRAMIDS   Apart from the intricate mathematical and architectural calculations involved in the building of the Egyptian pyramids, these structures have been mystically and symbolically interpreted in terms of man, his spiritual ascent, and, in general, the evolutionary process of mankind.

PYROIS   In astrology, this term, of Greek origin, refers to Mars and its fiery nature.

PYTHAGOREAN COMMUNITY   A community, founded in the sixth century B.C., in Southern Italy, by the Greek philosopher and mathematician Pythagoras. The members studied mathematics as a mystical means of interpreting man and his place in the cosmos.

PYTHONESS The most famous evocation of the dead in biblical times was accomplished through the intermediary of a pythoness. Saul conjured up the shade of Samuel through necromancy.

Q

QUADRANTINE LUNATION   In astrology, this term is sometimes applied to the conjunctions, squares and oppositions of the Sun and the Moon.

QUADRANTS   In astrology, the four quarters of the celestial figure, representative of the four quarters of the heavens, measured from the cusps of the four angular Houses. The oriental quadrants consist of Houses X to XII inclusive, and IV to VI inclusive. The occidental quadrants, of Houses I to III inclusive, and VII to IX inclusive. If applied to the zodiac, the oriental quadrants are from Aries to Gemini and from Libra to Sagittarius inclusive, the occidental quadrants consisting of the opposite signs.

QUADRUPEDAL   In astrology, the four-footed signs: Aries, Taurus, Leo, Sagittarius, Capricorn, all of which represent quadrupeds. Those born when these ascend were said by the ancient astrologers to have the qualities of such animals: as bold as a lion, as lustful as the goat.

QUADRUPLICITY   In astrology, the zodiacal signs are classified in groups of four, called quadruplicities, as follows:
cardinal signs: Aries, Cancer, Libra, Capricorn
fixed signs: Taurus, Leo, Scorpio, Aquarius
mutable signs: Gemini, Virgo, Sagittarius, Pisces

QUESITED In astrology, this term is employed in horary astrology to indicate the person or thing that is the subject of an inquiry.

QUIMBY, PHINEAS PARKHURST (1802-1866) An American mystic who practiced mesmerism. He maintained that he could cure sickness by mental treatment, even at a distance from the patient. It is thought that from these beliefs stemmed Christian Science. Two of Quimby's patients continued his work after his death and established the movement known as New Thought.

QUINARY Mystically, a group of five: for example, five colors, five planets, five occult innovations.

QU-TAMY This Chaldean term is applied to the mystic who receives revelations from the moon goddess.

R

RADA In the Voodoo cult, the rada is the royal rite of the sun. It bears the name of the snake which personifies Dangbe, the supreme deity.

RADEWYN FLORENTIUS (1350-1400) A Dutch leader of the Brothers of the Common Life. This sect merged with the religious Order of Mendicants.

RADICAL POSITION In astrology, this expression refers to a planet's position in a birth horoscope: as distinguished from the transitory or progressed position it occupies at a later date.

RADIX In astrology, this term denotes the radical map: the horoscope of birth, the root from which everything is judged. The term is also applied to the radical or birth positions of the planets, as distinguished from their progressed or directed positions. Progressed aspects can never entirely contradict or negate a radical aspect, but must be interpreted only as modifying or mitigating the influences shown in the Radix.

RAINBOW In mysticism, the rainbow has various significations. Among the Chinese it represents a communion of heaven and earth. In the Biblical context, it symbolizes a pact between the divinity and the Israelites.

In the Orient a popular belief was that the rainbow was a bridge. On a person's death, his spirit crossed this bridge in order to reach his heavenly dwelling.

RAIN-MAKING   One of the chief functions of the public magician is to control the weather for the good of the tribe. Most methods of rain-making are based on imitative magic: sprinkling water, ploughing, mimicking clouds, etc. Frogs and toads have earned a widespread reputation as custodians of water. Some Orinoco Indians consider the toad to be the lord of the waters and refrain from killing it.

RAJU, SATHYANARAYANA   An Indian mystic and miracle worker, known to his followers as Baba. Born in 1917, he claims to be the reincarnation of Krishna. He is reputed to have performed many miraculous cures, to have produced sandalwood statuettes of Krishna from the sand by magic, to have turned water into gasoline, and to have cured himself of heart attacks which he had taken on himself in order to spare the life of another person. His goal is to restore justice to the world by teaching men how to follow the 'moral path.'

RAPP, GEO.   A Gernah peasant who, after persecution in his own country, fled to the United States. There he founded the sect of Harmonists, in 1803.

RAPPORT   The name used by spiritualists to denote a community of sensations that links the medium and someone actually present at a seance or represented by some personal object.

RAPS (RAPPINGS)   Sounds produced by an assumed supernatural agent or agency. Modern spiritualism traces its origin to raps heard at Hydesville in 1848.

RAPT PARALLEL   In astrology, two bodies, which by rapt motion are carried to a point where they are equidistant from and on opposite sides of the meridian or the horizon, are said to be in Rapt Parallel.

RASPUTIN   An opprobrious nickname, derived from the Russian word meaning 'dissolute, licentious, profligate,' and applied to the notorious Russian monk Gregori Novikh.

RAUWOLFIA SERPENTINA   From the dried root of Rauwolfia Serpentina a drug known as Rauwiloid is extracted. It is used to reduce high blood pressure. Rauwolfia Serpentina has been used in India for thousands of years. In Sanskrit the plant is known as sarpagandha. The plant was named after Leonhard Rauwolf, a sixteenth century German botanist. Serpentina refers to the snaky roots of the plant. The active principle, rauwolfia, is extracted from the powdered roots. The dried root was chewed by holy men in India as an aid to contemplation. Mahatma Gandhi used it regularly. The plant also grows in the Philippines, China, Java, and South America. In Guatemala it is known botanically as Rauwolfia Heterophylla and is natively called calchapa.

RAYS, UNDER THE   In astrology, a planet is 'under the rays' of another when it is within orbs of an aspect. This term is rarely used in modern astrology.

REAPERS OF THE FIELD   In the Zohar, the Book of Splendor, which is the essence of Hebraic mysticism, this term is applied to certain Kabbalistic adepts.

RECEPTION, MUTUAL   In astrology, this term refers to two planets when they are in each other's sign or exaltation.

RECORDI, PETER A fourteenth century Carmelite monk. He was imprisoned for life on the charge of conjuring demons and seducing women by fashioning wax images as a phase of sympathetic magic.

RECTIFICATION In astrology, the process of verification or correction of the birth moment or ascendant degree of the map, with reference to known events or characteristics relating to the native.

RED DRAGON One of the key books of Occidental practitioners of black magic. 'Red Dragon' and 'The Secret of Secrets' were the bibles of the adepts.

RED SEA To cross the Red Sea, in alchemical mysticism, denotes a hazardous undertaking. It also represents a spiritual transformation.

REFRENATION In astrology, this term is used in horary astrology when one of two planets applying to an aspect turns retrograde before the aspect is complete. It is taken as an indication that the matter under consideration will not be brought to a successful conclusion.

RELIABILITY OF MEDIUMS Exposés have repeatedly revealed trickery perpetrated by mediums in the course of their practice. They claim clairvoyance and ability to predict and to communicate with the dead. Most of such cases are flagrantly the result of quackery. Yet parapsychologists and scientific investigators acknowledge that in some instances there is acceptable evidence of such capacities. Names are listed, and evaluations are given of such professional and reliable psychics, who appear in New York, London, Paris, and other large cities.

RELIGION DEFINED   Alfred N. Whitehead (1861-1947), the English mathematician and philosopher, says: Religion is what the individual does with his own solitariness.

On the other hand the dramatist G. B. Shaw asserts that religion is that which binds men to one another.

To Höffding (1843-1931), the Danish philosopher, religion is faith in the conservation of values.

Salomon Reinach (1858-1932), the French scholar, declared that religion is a body of scruples which impede the free exercise of our faculties.

John Dewey (1859-1952), the American philosopher, stated that whatever induces genuine perspective is religion. The ethnologist and anthropologist R. H. Lowie (1883-1957) finds the essence of religion in the sense of something transcending the expected or natural, a sense of the extraordinary, mysterious, or supernatural.

RESCUE CIRCLES   Circles of spiritualists formed for the purpose of awaking the dead and liberating them from this earth. In Wanderings of a Spiritualist, Sir Conan Doyle describes the work of a Melbourne circle.

RETROGRADE   In astrology, this term is applied to an apparent backward motion in the zodiac of certain planets when decreasing in longitude as viewed from earth.

REUCHLIN, JOHANN (1455-1522)   A Christian German Hebraist. He was deeply interested, like Pico della Mirandola, whom he knew, in the esoteric Kabbalistic writings. He himself wrote two treatises: The Kabbalistic Art, The Mirific Word.

REVIVAL OF INTEREST IN AFTER-LIFE   During the first century B.C. there was in classical antiquity a profound revival of interest in the life after death.

RHABDOMANCY   The art of water divining is known by the technical name of rhabdomancy. Divining rods were used in Germany in the sixteenth century to locate coal seams. Earlier, only a forked hazel twig was used in divining. Malebranche and others insisted that it was an instrument of the devil.

RHASIS   An Arabian alchemist born c. 850 in Khorassan. He claimed to be able to transmute metals and wrote many treatises on this and other occult subjects. He held that the planets influenced metallic formation under the surface of the earth.

RHINE, JOSEPH B.   Dr. Rhine of Duke University is a parapsychologist of international reputation. He has studied psychic phenomena, particularly ESP — extra-sensory perception, and has made vital and unique contributions in this field. It is a comparatively new field, and it is rich in possibilities. Dr. Rhine has demonstrated the fact of telepathy as a scientific reality. He has written extensively on his researches, among his books being New Frontiers of the Mind, published in 1937, and Parapsychology, Frontier Science of the Mind, which appeared in 1957.

RHYTHM AND MEMORY   The human memory is more retentive of the matter to be memorized when this act of memorization is linked with certain rhythmic formulaic devices: such a stamping with the feet, chanting, and a variety of similar mnemonic techniques.

RIGHT-ANGLED TRIANGLE   To the Egyptians the right-angled triangle was mystically associated with the deities Osiris, his consort Isis, and the son Horus. The geometric figure represented the cosmic scheme.

RIGHT-HAND PATH   In mystical and esoteric writings, two opposing schools of occult training are recognized: 'The Path of Light,' and 'The Path of Darkness.' These paths are more commonly called the 'Right-hand Path' and the 'Left-hand Path.' In the mystical language of Greece, the Brothers of Light ascend to Olympus whereas the Brothers of the Lefthand follow the path leading downward to spiritual obscuration.

RING-PASS-NOT   In occultism, a mystical term signifying the circle of bounds containing the consciousness of those deceived by the illusion of separateness. It is said that any entity, once it has reached a certain stage of the unfolding of consciousness, is blocked by some delusion from passing into a higher state.

RIPLEY, GEORGE   An English alchemist and occultist who belongs in the fifteenth century. He was reputed to have transmuted base metal into gold.

RISHIS   In Hinduism, a holy sage, an inspired poet, or a man of supersensuous experience.

RISING SIGN   In astrology, the sign of the subdivision of the sign which was rising on the eastern horizon at the moment of birth is regarded as exercising a strong influence on the personality and physical appearance of the native.

RITUAL MURDERS   The Druids practiced ritual murder in their cult. In pre-Columbian Mexico, human beings were sacrificed to Centocotl, the corn goddess. The Aztecs tore the heart from the victim placed on the sacrificial altar of Teotihuacan. Carthage was notorious for its mass burning of children. The practice of ritual murder reflects the belief that in this way the living may be protected from the dead, or made to prosper, or absolved of the wrongs they have committed.

RIVER BRETHREN A religious sect in the United States which emphasized baptismal immersion in a river.

ROCHESTER RAPPINGS An outbreak of rappings which occurred near Rochester, New York, in 1848, and which inaugurated modern spiritualism. The family of John D. Fox, disturbed by sounds manifesting signs of intelligence, called in neighbors who finally established communication with the unseen agent, who answered questions affirmatively by rapping and negatively by remaining silent.

ROMAN ASTROLOGY The ancient purpose of astrology was to reduce the notions of the heavenly bodies to mathematical precision. It was concerned with the influence of these bodies on human life.

The temples of Mesopotamia were the earliest to regard this view. When the Orient came into contact with Greece, and later on Rome came in contact with Hellenic culture, the emphasis on astrology grew until it reached its height in Roman Imperial times. The astrologers who practiced their skill in casting horoscopes were called Chaldaei and Mathematici. A major field of knowledge that was deeply affected by astrology was the practice of medicine.

ROMAN GHOSTS In Book 7 of his Letters, Pliny the Younger, the noted Roman man of letters, asks a friend whether he believes in ghosts. Then he relates the following incidents:

What particularly inclines me to give credit to their existence, is a story which I heard of Curtius Rufus. When he was in low circumstances and unknown in the world, he attended the newly-made governor of Africa into that province. One afternoon as he was walking in the public portico he was extremely daunted with the figure of a woman which appeared to him, of a size and beauty more than human. She told him she was the tutelar Genius that presided over Africa, and was come to inform him of the future events of his life:—that he should go back to Rome, where he should hold office, and return to that province invested with the proconsular dignity, and there should die. Every circumstance of this prophecy was actually accomplished. It is said farther, that upon his arrival at Carthage, as he was coming out of the ship, the same figure accosted him upon the shore. It is certain, at least, that being seized with a fit of illness, though there were no symptoms in his case that led his attendants to despair, he instantly gave up all hope of recovery; judging, it should seem, of the truth of the future part of the prediction, by that which had already been fulfilled; and of the misfortune which threatened him, by the success which he had experienced.

To this story, let me add another as remarkable as the former, but attended with circumstances of greater horror; which I will give you exactly as it was related to me. There was at Athens a large and spacious, but ill-reputed and pestilential house. In the dead of the night a noise, resembling the clashing of iron, was frequently heard, which, if you listened more attentively, sounded like the rattling of fetters; at first it seemed at a distance, but approached nearer by degrees; immediately afterward a phantom appeared in the form of an old man, extremely meagre and squalid, with a long beard and bristling hair, rattling the gyves on his feet and hands. The poor inhabitants consequently passed sleepless nights under the most dismal terrors imaginable. This as it broke their rest, threw them into distempers, which, as their horrors of mind increased, proved in the end fatal to their lives. For even in the day time, though the spectre did not appear, yet the remembrance of it made such a strong impression upon their imaginations that it still seemed before their eyes, and their terror remained when the cause of it was gone. By this means the house was at last deserted, as being judged by everybody to be absolutely uninhabitable; so that it was now entirely abandoned to the ghost. However, in hopes that some tenant might be found who was ignorant of this great calamity which attended it, a bill was put up, giving notice that it was either to be let or sold.

It happened that Athenodorus the philosopher came to Athens at this time, and reading the bill ascertained the price. The extraordinary cheapness raised his suspicion; nevertheless, when he heard the whole story, he was so far from being discouraged, that he was more strongiy inclined to hire it, and, in short, actually did so. When it grew towards evening, he ordered a couch to be prepared for him in the fore-part of the house, and after calling for a light, together with his pen and tablets, he directed all his people to retire within. But that his mind might not, for want of employment, be open to the vain terrors of imaginary noises and apparitions, he applied himself to writing with all his faculties. The first part of the night passed with usual silence, then began the clanking of iron fetters; however, he neither lifted up his eyes, nor laid down his pen, but closed his ears by concentrating his attention. The noise increased and advanced nearer, till it seemed at the door, and at last in the chamber. He looked round and saw the apparition exactly as it had been described to him: it stood before him, beckoning with the finger. Athenodorus made a sign with his hand that it should wait a little, and bent again to his writing, but the ghost rattling its chains over his head as he wrote, he looked round and saw it beckoning as before. Upon this he immediately took up his lamp and followed it. The ghost slowly stalked along, as if encumbered with its chains; and having turned into the courtyard of the house, suddenly vanished. Athenodorus being thus deserted, marked the spot with a handful of grass and leaves. The next day he went to the magistrates, and advised them to order that spot to be dug up. There they found bones commingled and intertwined with chains; for the body had mouldered away by long lying in the ground, leaving them bare, and corroded by the fetters. The bones were collected, and buried at the public expense; and after the ghost was thus duly laid the house was haunted no more. This story I believe upon the affirmation of others; I can myself affirm to others what I now relate. I have a freed-man named Marcus, who has some tincture of letters. One night, his younger brother, who was sleeping in the same bed with him, saw, as he thought, somebody sitting on the couch, who put a pair of shears to his head, and actually cut off the hair from the very crown of it. When morning came, they found the boy's crown was shorn, and the hair lay scattered about on the floor. After a short interval, a similar occurrence gave credit to the former. A slave-boy of mine was sleeping amidst several others in their quarters, when two persons clad in white came in (as he tells the story) through the windows, cut off his hair as he lay, and withdrew the same way they entered. Daylight revealed that this boy too had been shorn, and that his hair was likewise spread about the room. Nothing remarkable followed, unless it were that I escaped prosecution; prosecuted I should have been, if Domitian (in whose reign these things happened) had lived longer. For an information lodged by Carus against me was found in his desk. Hence it may be conjectured, since it is customary for accused persons to let their hair grow, that this cutting of my servant's hair was a sign I should defeat the peril that hung over me.

ROMAN HOROSCOPE   Under the Roman emperor Tiberius, who belongs in the first century A.D., astrologers who cast horoscopes were condemned to death.

RONACH The middle level of existence, according to the Kabbala. It looks out to the astral world.

ROOT-RACES Theosophy teaches that mankind as a Life-wave passes through seven evolutionary stages, or Root-races. Each Root-race is marked by the occurrence of a Racial Cataclysm after it has completed half of its cycle. The next Cataclysm is supposed to cut our Fifth Root-race in two some eighteen thousand years from now, just as one cut in two the Fourth-race Atlanteans and the Third-race Lemurians before them.

ROSE In many traditions of magic the rose symbolizes self-fulfillment and the blossoming of the personality.

ROSENKREUTZ, CHRISTIAN He founded the mystic Rosicrucian Order in the fifteenth century.

ROSICRUCIANS A fraternal organization whose purpose is the investigation and study of cosmic and natural laws. Centuries old, it aims to awaken the faculties and talents of man for greater personal attainment.
It is not a religious or sectarian body, nor has it political ambitions. It does not promulgate concepts that are contrary to accepted public morals and customs. The headquarters are in California, with branches in New York and Pennsylvania. The symbol of the organization is a Rosy Cross. The organization is also concerned with the symbolism of the swastika and the pyramids.
The name of the order derives from that of the founder, Christian Rosenkreutz, who is said to have died in 1484, after being initiated into the order in the Holy Land. The Danish astrologer Max Heindel claimed to have been visited in Berlin by invisible spirits who instructed him to reestablish the old secret society. He completed construction of a Rosicrucian Temple south of Los Angeles in 1920.

ROUND The doctrine of the seven Rounds means esoterically that the Life-cycle or Life-wave begins its evolutionary course on globe A, goes down to B, C, D (our Earth), then on the Ascending Arc to E, F, and G, completing the series of seven rounds. Seven Planetary Rounds equal one Day of Brahma.

ROWAN-TREE In folk legend, it was a belief that the rowan-tree could ward off malefic influences.

RUMINANT SIGNS In astrology, this expression denotes Aries, Taurus, Capricorn.

S

SABBATHS Assemblies or Sabbaths took place four times a year: Candlemas, May-eve, Lammas, and November-eve (Halloween). These joyous gatherings were attended by worshippers of all ages. Celebrations began in the evening and lasted until dawn.

SABBATICAL YEAR This was the seventh year, the year of rest. In the Mosaic code, the year had a sacred association. The land remained uncultivated, and the poor were helped.

SACRED MOUNTAIN During the pilgrimage to the Sacred Mountain, the Chinese practice vegetarianism.

SACRED NUMBERS In antiquity the number seven was associated with the planets. The dead and the gods were invoked three times. Incantations were repeated thrice. The god Apollo was associated with the number seven.

SACRED OGDOAD In Gnostic mysticism, they were the eight great gods.

SADRIPU The evil in human nature, according to the Balinese. Many rituals are designed to protect both sexes against sadripu.

SAFED A city in Palestine. In the sixteenth century Safed became the centre of Kabbalah, the Hebraic mystical system.

SAGITTARIUS In astrology, the Archer. The ninth, southern sign of the zodiac. It represents the corporeal and the spiritual elements constituting man. Esoterically, it represents the organizing power of the mind as well as retribution. Kabbalistically, it signifies the thighs of the old man of the heavens and represents stability and authority.

SAINT-GERMAIN The Count of Saint-Germain was an eighteenth century Man of Mystery. He was attached to the court of Louis XV of France. He claimed that he was 2000 years old and could recall in detail remote historical events. He was known to speak and write a dozen Western and Oriental languages. He had mastered alchemy and the transmutation of metals, could make himself invisible, and even corresponded, after his putative death, with the French nobility. He wrote an occult treatise entitled La Tres Sainte Trinosophie.

SAINTLY LEVITATION Among those who reputedly had the faculty of levitation were a number of saints, among them St. Albert of Sicily, St. Dominic, and St. Dunstan.

SAINT-MARTIN, LOUIS CLAUDE DE (1743-1803) Known as The Unknown Philosopher. A French mystic and Gnostic.

SAKTI A Sanskrit term used esoterically to designate one of the seven forces of nature, Universal Energy, which is the feminine aspect of Fohat.

SALAMANCA In the Middle Ages Salamanca, in Spain, had institutions where the occult arts were taught.

SALEM The great Salem witchcraft tragedies were inspired by the teachings of Cotton Mather, who was a strong believer in the superstition. Twenty victims were executed before the delusion ended.

SAMADHI A Sanskrit word meaning intense contemplation, with consciousness directed to the spiritual. In theosophy, Samadhi is the highest form of self-possession. One who has developed this power has complete control over all his faculties in this state, which is the highest state of Yoga. The initiate who has attained Samadhi is conscious of the inner and spiritual realms of nature and that he becomes practically omniscient for the solar universe in which he lives.

SAMBHALA A Sanskrit place-name mentioned in the sacred writings of the Hindus and identified in theosophy as the seat of the greatest Brotherhood of spiritual Adepts on the earth today.

SANASEL A sacred musical instrument that was anciently the Egyptian sistrum. It is used in Ethiopia to exorcise devils.

SANGHYANG DELING A Balinese trance dance, one of many rituals dramatizing the awareness of the supernatural world prevalent among the Balinese.

SARGON OF AKKAD This Babylonian king, who belongs in the third millennium B.C., was reputed to have in his possession a treatise on astrological calculations.

SAROS In astrology, a Chaldean and Babylonian interpretation of a cycle of sixty days as sixty years. The interpretation also denotes sixty sixties or 3,600. Also a lunar cycle of 6,585,32 days — 23 lunations.

In this period the centres of Sun and Moon return to so nearly the same relative places that the eclipses of the next period recur in approximately the same sequence.

SAR PELADAN A grand master of the Third Order of the Catholic Rosicrucians, Sar Peladan, along with La Rochefoucauld and Elémir Bourges, founded Rosicrucian salons, very fashionable Parisian centers.

SATAN In the Middle Ages the Satanic concept was very real. Satan was personalized under a number of different and significant names. He was Belial, and Beelzebub, and Lucifer. To those who paid homage to him he was generous. He aided alchemists to consummate the transmutation of base metal into gold. He showered riches on adherents. He granted vast powers to those whom he favored. He broke all human restraints, setting men free, but ultimately binding them to him, making them subservient everlastingly to his fiendish domination. That is the theme of medieval legends and poems, of dramas, sermons, miracle plays that appeared so abundantly in the middle centuries.

SATANIC MUSIC The demons have crept into the musical context. In 1830 Hector Berlioz the French composer produced a Symphonie Fantastique: it contains a musical interpretation of a witches' Sabbath.

SATANIC POSSESSION In 1968, in Zeitoun, a suburb of Cairo, in Egypt, a case of diabolic possession occurred. An Arab declared he had been possessed by a spirit for twenty years. The Coptic priest attached to the local church took the matter in hand. After many exhortations and much questioning, he succeeded in exorcising the diabolic visitant, to the clamorous joy of the spectators.

SATANIC SYMBOL In occultism, the cat was the sacred symbol of the Archfiend himself.

SATANIC TEMPTATION The devil and his diabolic minions are particularly hostile to saints, holy anchorites, devout hermits. St. Theophilus was attacked by Satan but he was rescued by the Virgin. St. Anthony suffered torments at the hands of the Fiend. In visions and during night vigils many saints were confronted by the Evil Fiend, who thrashed and tormented them. Among such victims were John of Damascus, St. Giles, St. Martin, St. Everard, and St. Eustochium.

SATANIST William, Lord Soulis, was a Scottish noble who belongs in the fourteenth century. Known as the Black Lord of Hermitage, he was a professed Satanist and was reputed to have performed human sacrifices to the Archfiend. Lord Soulis was also credited with having made a pact with the Devil. His fiendish acts and sinister ceremonials appeared to confirm that belief.

SATELLITIUM: STELLIUM In astrology, a group of five or more planets in one sign or House. In an angle it portends great changes of fortune, the good and the bad coming in patches. Heavy falls are succeeded in due course by a spectacular comeback, and vice versa.

SCHMID, CONRAD A monk who, in 1360, inaugurated a sect of Flagellants. He died in 1368.

SCHOOL OF THE SECRET FOREST A mystic, religious-philosophical school attached to a monastery in Ceylon. The members of this School, according to tradition, were persecuted and forced to migrate to the region of the Himalayas.

317

SCHROPFER, JOHANN GEORG (1730-1774) A German necromancer. In Leipzig and throughout Germany he acquired an awesome reputation as an occultist. He practiced witchcraft against his enemies and initiated many disciples. He died a suicide.

SCIENTOLOGY The Church of Scientology is a comparatively new sect. The founder is L. Ron Hubbard. Scientology is asserted to be applied religious philosophy.

SCIOMANCY A form of divination associated with shadows or ghosts.

SCORPIO In astrology, the Scorpion. The eighth, southern sign of the zodiac. It represents the human span of life. Esoterically, the Scorpion signifies death and deceit, the allegorical serpent that tempted Eve. Kabbalistically, it represents the procreative system of humanity.

SCORPION In medieval Christian art the Scorpion, the eighth zodiacal sign, symbolized treachery.

SCOT, MICHAEL (c. 1175 - 1232) A Scottish magician. Astrologer at the court of the Emperor Frederick II, Scot wrote numerous books on the occult, ranging from necromancy to alchemy, dream-interpretation, divination. He was himself credited with magic potency. Many legends were current about his skills in sorcery. He is mentioned by Dante.

SCOTTISH INCIDENT In 1596, in the Scottish town of Aberdeen, the local witches, according to folk tradition, were charged with assuming feline form in order to participate in the rituals of the Sabbat.

SEAL OR STAR OF SOLOMON   A six-pointed star symbolizing the macrocosm. It is formed of two intersecting triangles and emphasizes the double three rather than the number six.

SEANCE   A meeting of spiritualists held for the purpose of communicating with the dead. At least one member of the group must have mediumistic powers. The seance-room is generally darkened and the actual seance may be preceded by music. Sitters take their places around the table and join hands, forming a chain. Each person puts his thumbs together and allows his little fingers to touch the person on either side of him. The sitters are at the mercy of spirits, who announce their presence by rappings, tilting the table, etc., until the chain is broken.

SECONDARY PROGRESSIONS   In astrology, zodiacal aspects formed by the orbital motions of the planets on successive days after birth, each day accounted the equivalent of one year of life. Aspects are calculated to the birth positions of the luminaries, planets, and angles, and mutual aspects are formed between the progressed planets.

SECOND DEATH   This phrase is used by mystics to describe the dissolution of the principles of man after the death of the physical body. The second death occurs when the lower Duad is cast off by the upper Duad, which has already incorporated the Reincarnating Ego.

SECOND-SIGHT   The faculty of seeing a vision of a future event. The phenomenon is common in some northern countries, in Scotland, Ireland, and Scandinavia. In Scotland, second-sight often appears in a succession of families. Persons so gifted are called 'fey.'

SECRET OF SECRETS A combination of two ancient books, one of them attributed to King Solomon. 'The Secret of Secrets' was also known as 'The Clavicle of Solomon' and 'The Veritable Black Book.' Together with 'Red Dragon,' it constituted the bible of Western practitioners of black magic.

SECRET SOCIETIES In the ancient world secret societies were chiefly religious. They centered around the mysteries of Osiris and Serapis in Egypt, Orpheus and Dionysus in Greece, Mithras in Persia, and Cybele in Phrygia. The secret societies of the North American Indians are also chiefly religious. Those of Melanesia, and Africa, on the other hand, are primarily social or political. Most secret societies may be the outgrowths of puberty rites. Van Gennep believes that initiation rites symbolize a process of rebirth or separation from the outer world and entrance into full membership into the tribe.

SECRET TRADITION Occultists have long insisted that adepts have handed down their esoteric lore from generation to generation since prehistoric times. Mystic societies of the Middle Ages, for instance, seem to have descended from the older classical and Egyptian mysteries.

SEEGA An entity assumed by the Mossi to reside in all living beings. This spiritual essence or animating principle leaves the body during sleep. Its adventures are known to the sleeper through his dreams. If the seega is captured and eaten by a sorcerer, its owner will die.

SENA An island off the coast of Brittany. According to the Roman geographer Pomponius Mela it was inhabited by nine women, called Gallicenae. They practiced occult arts and were capable of raising winds and storms. They also had the faculty of transforming themselves into animals.

320

SENSES, SIGNIFICATORS OF   In astrology, the significators of the five physical senses are:
Mercury: sight.
Venus: touch.
Mars: taste.
Jupiter: smell.
Saturn: hearing.

SENSITIVE   A person who is susceptible to supernatural influences. A medium is sometimes, and perhaps more accurately, called a sensitive.

SENZAR   A mystic name applied to the universal sacred language of initiates.

SEPARATION OF SOUL   In Kabbalistic mysticism, the three parts of the soul become separated during sleep.

SEPHER YETZIRAH   In Kabbalistic mysticism, this Hebraic expression means the Book of Formation, symbolized by the ten numbers and twenty-two letters of the Hebrew alphabet.

SEPHIROTH   In the Sepher Yetzirah, an ancient Kabbalistic treatise that discusses the creation of the universe through the symbolism of the ten numbers (sephiroth) and the twenty-two letters of the Hebrew alphabet. Together, the ten numbers and the twenty-two letters are called the thirty-two paths of wisdom.

SEPTENARY SERIES   In occultism, seven worlds are presented in a septenary series. The present known world is regarded as the lowest in the cycle.

SERAPHITA A mystical Rosicrucian drama by Honoré de Balzac, the great French novelist. In seven parts, Seraphita stresses Love that triumphs over Desire.

SERIES In parapsychology, several runs of experimental sessions that are grouped in accordance with the stated purpose and design of the experiment.

SETHOS A diviner put to death by Emperor Manuel. Sethos is said to have predicted the death of Emperor Andronicus Comnenus by hydromancy.

SETON ALEXANDER One of the few alchemists credited by his contemporaries with the transmutation of metals. Early in the seventeenth century, Seton Alexander, who took for his first name the designation of a fishing village near Edinburgh, traveled widely in Europe and convinced many observers of his rare ability to change lead into gold.

SEVEN The number seven is esoterically associated with various phenomena, personalities, concepts. The seven deadly sins are traditional. Medically, seven is linked with the healing rhythm. The Bible contains many references to seven: Balaam's seven altars, seven years served by Jacob, seven kine. The seventh day of the seventh month was, among the Israelites, a time when a seven-day feast began. Physiologically, there are seven internal organs, seven tissue systems, seven compartments of the heart. In mythology and folklore, spells last for seven years. Ancient India had seven gods. The mystery cult of Mithra involved seven gates, seven altars. Among the Israelites, oaths were confirmed by seven witnesses. There are seven penitential psalms, seven sacraments.

SEVEN ANGELS In the pseudepigraphical Ethiopic Book of Enoch, there are seven angels who keep watch in the seventh heaven.

SEVEN OLYMPIAN SPIRITS This is another name for the Seven Stewards of Heaven.

SEVEN PLANETS In antiquity, the seven planets were considered the most powerful forces in influencing human life.

SEVEN SACRED PLANETS The seven sacred planets of the ancients (Saturn, Jupiter, Mars, Sun, Venus, Mercury, and the Moon) are viewed esoterically as members of a septenary chain. Each globe in each chain has six superior globes of more ethereal matter above the physical sphere.

SEVEN STEWARDS OF HEAVEN Works on magic list seven stewards of heaven by whom God rules the world: Bethor, Phaleg, Och, Hagith, Ophiel, and Phul. Magicians use special ceremonies to invoke each of these seven celestial spirits. They are also called the Olympian Spirits since they rule over the Olympian Spheres, embracing 196 regions.

SEVENTH HEAVEN In Hebraic mysticism, this is the highest heaven, the seat of the Throne of God.

SEVENTH HOUSE In astrology, this term refers to the house of love and marriage. It is governed by the sign of Scorpio.

SHABBATAI ZEVI (1626 - 1676) He was the most influential of medieval false Messiahs. He was excommunicated from Judaism and became a wandering leader. Multitudes accepted him at his own divine appraisal. When given the choice of conversion or punishment, he accepted Mohammedanism.

323

SHABDA In yoga, this term denotes sound. To attain the ability to hear the sound of the cosmos — the music of the spheres, in Platonic terminology — a yogi must listen to his inner voice in some five or ten different ways.

SHAMIR In Jewish legend, a worm that could split rocks and iron by its glance. It was reputed to have done the work of prohibited iron tools in the erection of the Temple.

SHELLEY, PERCY B. (1782 - 1822) Astrologically, the poet Shelley's horoscope showed the constellation Argo in the eighth house, which is the house of death. Argo is associated with ships and the sea, and the poet died by drowning.

SHIH I Commentaries and appendices which were added to the I Ching. The Chinese words mean 'Ten Wings.'

SHIP OF THE DEAD The indigenous tribes of Borneo conceive the spirits of the dead as being transported to their final haven in a ship shaped like a bird.

SHIWANA Deities associated with the Pueblo rain dances. The Shiwana were identified with clouds, as were the souls of the dead.

SIBYLLINE BOOKS Three books said to have been brought from the sibyl of Cumae by Tarquin the Proud, deposited in the Capitol, then stoned in the Temple of Apollo Palatinus. A second collection of prophetic books, brought from Asia Minor to replace the lost ones, was finally destroyed by Stiliko about 400 A.D.

SICUN The Dakota Indian deity whose substance is never visible but whose potency is shared by men.

SIDGWICK, HENRY (1838-1900)   The first president of the London Society for Psychical Research, Professor Henry Sidgwick filled the chair of moral philosophy at Cambridge. He conducted many investigations but never espoused the cause of spiritualism. He took a leading part in the exposure of Eusapia Paladino.

SIGNIFICANCE   In parapsychology, a numerical result is significant when it equals or surpasses some criterion of degree of chance probability.

SIGNIFICATOR   In astrology, a planet may be taken as a significator of a person or an event, or of affairs ruled by a House. Its strength by virtue of its Sign and House position and its relationship by aspects are then consulted in arriving at a judgment concerning a desired condition. In general the strongest planet in the Figure, usually the ruler of the Ascendant, is taken as the Significator of the native. Similarly the Ruler of the Sign on the cusp of the Second House is taken as the Significator of wealth, of the Seventh House of the partner, of the Eighth of the partner's wealth, and so on.

SILENT ONES   The Silent Ones were an ancient Hebraic sect who practiced religious mysticism.

SILENT WATCHER   A graphic phrase used esoterically to signify the summit of a spiritual hierarchy. He can learn nothing more from the sphere of life through which he has already passed. He has renounced further evolution for himself in order to help those beneath him.

SILVESTRIS, BERNARD   Author of De universitate mundi, Le Mégacosme et Le Microcosme. These works, which appeared in the middle of the twelfth century, present the

325

history of mankind in symbolical form. They include Creation, the Twenty Mountains, the appearance of the Twin Sisters, and Crossing the Spheres.

SIMON MAGUS   A sorcerer who bewitched the Samarians and claimed to have divine power. He is supposed to have learned magic from Dositheus, who posed as the Messiah foretold by the prophets. This first-century gnostic was said to have raised himself into the sky in Rome, as Jesus had done in Judaea. He claimed to be the supreme power of God. He traveled throughout the Roman Empire with a Tyrian courtesan whom he identified as Helen of Troy, Minerva, the first intelligence, and the mother of all things.

SINISTER   In astrology, a left-handed aspect — not, however, with reference to the proper motion of the aspecting body, but to its apparent motion.

SISHTAS   A Sanskrit word meaning anything that is left or remains behind. Esoterically, the term designates the superior classes left behind on a planet that has gone into obscuration. The Sishtas serve as the seeds of life when a new Life-wave initiates a new manvantara on that planet.

SIXTH HOUSE   In astrology, this term refers to health. It is governed by the sign of Virgo.

SIXTH SENSE   The faculty of spiritual perception possessed by the medium, or a keen intuitive power enabling its possessor to perceive or comprehend things not grasped by the other five senses.

SKANDHA   The Sanskrit term is used in theosophy to designate the five attributes of every man: form, perception, consciousness, action, and knowledge.

326

SKOPTSI   This Russian term means: castrated. The Skoptsi were members of a secret society founded in 1722 by a Russian peasant named Kondrati Selvinanov. Membership spread from Russia to other countries in Eastern Europe. Castration was a primary religious tenet, as it was among the Galli, the priests of the Phrygian goddess Cybele in ancient paganism.

In the nineteenth century the sect acquired many new adherents.

SKY WALKER   In yoga mysticism, this term refers to a yogi who can leave his corporeal body and travel in astral from.

SLATE WRITING   A popular spiritualistic performance in which writing mysteriously appears on a slate. The medium and the sitter occupy opposite ends of a table in a typical seance. Both hold an ordinary slate and pencil pressed against the underside of the table and wait for a message from the spirit-world to be inscribed on it. Spiritualists themselves admit that genuine mediums, owing to the uncertainty of their powers, may at times be forced to resort to fraud.

SLEEP   During sleep mysterious phenomena occur. The tale of Rip van Winkle has astounding counterparts in actuality. Cases have been reported in many countries of strange conditions and consequences associated with sleep. A child feel asleep for thirty years. A girl of nineteen continued in her trance-like slumber for fifty years. A man slept for four years on end and on waking predicted a national calamity. An accident caused a sailor to sleep for three years.

SNAKES   In Hong Kong old traditional Chinese ways are still in force. There is a particular snake-eating season. Snake stew, snake steaks, snake soup are highly popular, not only in a culinary sense, but for healing purposes as well. The gall bladder of the snake is considered a specific against winter cold.

The sea snake in particular is regarded as a cure for rheumatism. Transplanting of organs, in cases of sickness, is deprecated by older Chinese. The belief is that after death the body should remain intact in order to serve the deceased in the next life.

SOCIALIST COMMUNITY OF MODERN TIMES A community established on Long Island in 1851. Many spiritualists were members of the community.

SOCIETIES FOR PSYCHICAL RESEARCH The phenomena associated with clairvoyance, premonitions, telepathy and similar practices were known in proto-historical times. But organized research into such occurrences did not begin until the middle of the nineteenth century. In 1882 the Society for Psychical Research was established in England. It has investigated mediumship, precognition, and clairvoyance.

In 1885 an American Society for Psychical Research was founded, but it was dissolved in 1905. A similar society, the American Institute for Scientific Research, was established in 1904. In 1922 the Institute changed its name to the American Society for Psychical Research.

Similar societies have been established in other countries, notably in France, where the Institut Métaphysique International was founded in 1920.

SOCIETY OF HEAVEN AND EARTH One of the many aliases of the secret Chinese brotherhood known as the Hung or Triad Society.

SOCIETY OF THE MYSTIC SPIRAL   An esoteric organization that flourished in the eighteenth century. It was concerned with necromancy, levitation, and other occult practices.

SOD   A religious mystery. The mysteries of Baal, Adonis, and Bacchus involved sun-gods having serpents as their symbols. The word is of Hebraic origin.

SODALIAN OATH   The Secret Mysteries of the Torah were known earlier in occultism as the Sod. The Sodalian Oath was the most sacred of all oaths. The breaking of the oath meant death to the offender.

SOHRAWARDI   Born in 1155, he was put to death by Saladin in 1191. He was a prophet whose book, Hikmat el-Ishrah, proclaimed a resurrection. His concepts included elements of Zoroastrianism, Platonism, and Hermetic mysticism.

SOLAR EQUILIBRIUM   In astrology, a term used recently by astrologers with reference to the solar Figure: one cast for sunrise on a given day, but with Houses of uniformly thirty degrees each.

SOLAR REVOLUTION   In astrology, a horoscopical figure erected for the moment in any year when the Sun has reached the exact Longitude it occupies in the Radix. From this figure and from aspects of Radical planets to significators — Sun, Moon, Ascendant and Midheaven degrees — in the Solar Revolution map predictions are made covering the ensuing year.

SOLAR SYSTEM BODIES, INFLUENCE OF   In astrology, in external affairs, the solar system bodies exercise influence as follows:
Sun: leaders in authority.
Moon: public life.

Mercury: business.
Venus: social activities.
Mars: weapons of war.
Jupiter: material wealth.
Saturn: poverty, decay.
Uranus: power, authority.
Neptune: popular movements.
Pluto: idealistic organizations.

SOLOMON'S MIRROR   A well-polished steel plate especially treated for use in divination.

SONS OF FAITH   In the Zohar, the Book of Splendor, which is the essence of Hebraic mysticism, this term is applied to certain Kabbalistic adepts.

SONS OF THE BOOK   They are Karaites, a Jewish sect in the Middle East that originated in the eighth century A.D. They accept the Bible but reject the Talmud.

SONS OF THE PROPHETS   In Jewish mysticism, the reference is to a peripatetic body of men inspired with the faculty of prophecy.

SONS OF TWILIGHT   In mystic Christianity, this term was applied to the angelic beings.

SOOTHSAYING   This is the practice of foretelling events and the interpretation of dreams, visions, omens and portents by priests who were considered under the immediate influence of the gods. In Babylonia, soothsaying was closely associated with astrology and hepatoscopy. Under the Roman Empire, too, soothsaying was widely influential and frequently affected imperial policies.
Among the ancient Arabs, it was believed that persons with familiar spirits possessed powers of prediction. Among

330

the Hebrew the nabi was a form of soothsaying. The nabi or speaker was the herald or messenger of the deity or the spirit.

SOPHISIANS   The name of a French religious sect that flourished late in the eighteenth century. Its purpose was the interpretation of the Egyptian Pyramids.

SORCERY DEFINED   In 1591 Johann Georg Godelman published an occult treatise entitled De Magis. He defines therein sorcerers as those who by evil spells, dire curses, and the sending of foul spirits, by potions prepared by the Devil or through illicit arts from corpses of hanged men, harm and destroy the health and lives of men and beasts.

SORTILEGE   Divination by lots. It is one of the most ancient and common practices.

SOUTH AMERICA   The Indian tribes of South America, particularly those who inhabited Brazil, Patagonia, the Chilean archipelago, conceived that various nature spirits, pervading the universe, could threaten human beings and cause injury if they were not supplicated.

SOUTH AMERICAN INDIANS   Among the indigenous tribes of South America, sacred masks were used to impersonate supernatural beings. Secret rituals were also in force, from which women and uninitiated children were excluded. Among the Tucanoan tribes of the North-West Amazon, there was a cult of the dead. Bark cloth masks were used to impersonate ancestors, and secretly played trumpets imitated their voices.

SOUTH LATITUDES In astrology, the latitudes south of the celestial equator. In using the Table of Houses, for South Latitudes, signs are changed to their opposites: for instance, Aries becomes Libra.

SPECULUM In astrology, a table appended to a horoscope, comprising its astronomical elements: the planet's latitude, declination, Right Ascension, Ascensional Difference, Pole and Semi-arc. It is employed in the practice of directing by Primary Directions as taught by Ptolemy.

SPELL A spoken word or formula to which some magical power is ascribed. The uttering of words in a set order, generally one prescribed by tradition, is the essential part of magic in many cultures. In the Trobriand Islands, for instance, the word for spell (*megwa*) also means magic. Great importance frequently is attached to the exact wording of a spell, but individual changes within the prescribed frame are sometimes permissible.

SPHERES Spiritualists claim to have identified seven spheres in the spirit world: Hell, Summerland, Mind, Abstract, Sphere of Desires, Meeting of the Sexes, and Union of the Sexes. The ultimate realm of the blessed lies beyond these spheres, in the boundless expanse of the supernal heavens.

SPIRIT GUARDIANS Among the Eskimos the guardians of human life were the supernatural spirits. This belief gave a unity to communal relations, as associations of a friendly nature with the Supernatural thus conditioned the general welfare.

SPIRITISM The French form of spiritualism, particularly as developed from the doctrines of Allan Kardec. One of its main tenets is the doctrine of reincarnation.

SPIRIT PHOTOGRAPHY The practice of producing spirit photographs is regarded as a common trick perpetrated by fraudulent mediums.

SPIRITUAL FRONTIERS FELLOWSHIP Arthur Ford helped to found the Spiritual Frontiers Fellowship in order to bring psychic phenomena back to the church, where it started in the first place. The fellowship boasts membership from more than five thousand religious leaders, representing every major faith.

SPIRITUALISM This is a cult devoted to the study of psychic phenomena. The belief is that such phenomena can be explained in terms of incarnate or discarnate spirits who are interested in the living. The inception of spiritualism in modern times is assigned to the year 1848, when the Fox sisters gave fantastic exhibitions of their power to evoke spirits of the dead. In 1893 the cult was organized as the N.S.A., with headquarters in Washington.

The spiritualist seminary at Morris Pratt Institute in Whitewater, Wisconsin, is the first of its kind. A famous spiritualist camp is Lily Dale, in New York State. Harry Houdini, the magician and contortionist, devoted considerable time to an investigation of the claims of spiritualism. He conducted a rousing, publicized campaign. He repeatedly exposed fraudulent practices of mediums and publicly denounced them. His conclusions led him to reject totally and categorically all such claims of communication with the spirits.

On the other hand, Sir Oliver Lodge, the English physicist who died in 1940, pursued psychical research that induced him to a belief in communication between the living and the dead. In *Raymond, or Life and Death*, he published an account of his experiments in which he described his communication with his dead son Raymond.

Sir Arthur Conan Doyle, too, who died in 1930, was in

his later years deeply interested in spiritualism. He lectured and wrote passionately and sincerely on the subject.

More recently Bishop Pike has published an account of his communication with his dead son.

SPONTANEOUS PSI EXPERIENCE In parapsychology, natural, unplanned occurrence of an event or experience that seems to involve parapsychical ability.

SPURZHEIM, JOHANN KASPAR (1776-1832) An Austrian physician who, in cooperation with Franz Gall, founded phrenology.

ST. ANTHONY (1195 - 1231) St. Anthony of Padua was a Franciscan monk. He was reputed to have experienced bilocation: that is, he was said to have appeared in two churches at the same time.

STAR OF BETHLEHEM This star is commonly conjectured to have been the conjunction of Saturn, Jupiter, and Mars, which occurred about 2 B.C. It is assumed that the astrologers, the 'wise men of the East,' were trying to locate a child born at the point in terrestrial latitude and longitude from which this triple conjunction would occur in the same celestial latitude and longitude, and in the midheaven of that particular geographical location. As this was one of the grand mutations, it was presumed that a child born at the exact place and hour that would posit this important satellitium at the cusp of the Tenth House would be marked by Destiny to become the initiator of a new epoch in world history.

STARRY INFLUENCE In astrology, some astrologers credit the stars with an influence of their own, when in conjunction and parallel with a planet, either at birth or in transit. A star of the first magnitude on the Ascendant or Midheaven at birth is said to indicate that the native will become illustrious within his sphere of life. The two large stars, Aldebaran and Antares, which are in the tenth degree of Gemini and Sagittarius respectively, when directed to the angles of the horoscope, are said to produce periods of severe stress. They are considered more powerful when in the angles.

STATIONS   In astrology, stations are those points in the orbit of a planet where it becomes either retrograde or direct. So termed because it remains stationary there for a few days before it changes its course. The first station is where it becomes retrograde: the second station, where it abandons retrograde and resumes direct motion. From these stations orientality is reckoned. From apogee to the first station it is matutine, because it rises in the morning before the Sun, hence it is in the first degree of orientality. From the first station to perigee, the lowest apsis, it is vespertine, because it rises in the evening before Sunset, hence it is the first degree of orientality.

STATIONS OF THE MOON   In astrology, the Moon is never retrograde, but in a different sense her first and second dichotomes are often loosely termed her first and second stations.

STAUS POLTERGEIST   A small village on Lake Lucerne was the scene of a remarkable poltergeist search that began in 1860. The family of M. Joller, a distinguished lawyer, was disturbed by repeated knockings and other supernatural occurrences. Curious crowds are reported to have seen the opening and shutting of windows as well as other proofs of the presence of a discarnate intelligence or poltergeist.

STEINER, RUDOLPH The founder of the Anthropological Movement believed in reincarnation and was once a theosophist. Rudolph Steiner conceived the role of Christ in human developments in a unique way. His book 'Initiaton' was published in 1908, but his most original thoughts are contained in his second book, 'Occult Science.'

STEPHANUS OF ALEXANDRIA An alchemist and mystic. He flourished in the seventh century A.D., and wrote Nine Lessons in Chemia, an alchemical treatise.

STICHOMANCY A form of divination by haphazard reference to a passage or line in a book.

STIGMATA Wounds which sometimes bleed or marks similar to those on the body of Christ that manifest themselves in human beings. St. Francis of Assisi experienced stigmata and so also in the twentieth century did the German peasant Theresa von Konnersreuth.

ST. JANUARIUS A saint who was martyred in the reign of the Roman Emperor Diocletian. In Catholicism, there is a miracle associated with this saint. On certain feast days the congealed blood, preserved in the cathedral at Naples, is placed in two phials near the saint's head on the altar. After prayers, the blood is seen to become liquified and to flow as if newly shed from the veins.

STORMS In the Middle Ages storms were believed to be the work of demons. The Liber Penitentialis of St. Theodore, who was Archbishop of Canterbury (668-690), was the first ecclesiastical law. It was aimed at anyone who conjured demons in order to create storms.

STREET OF GOLD   In medieval Prague the Zlata Ulicka or Street of Gold was noted as an occult center where witches and alchemists plied their trades.

STUDIES IN ALCHEMY   In the Middle Ages, during the ninth and tenth centuries, there were academic institutions in Spain where the principles of alchemy could be studied.

ST. YVES D'ALVEYDRE   A twentieth century mystic who developed an esoteric system involving numerology, letter-mysticism, planets.

SUBCONSCIOUS   The Tibetans believe that the real nature of a person is manifested in dreams. The reaction of a person in a dream, therefore, coincides precisely with this reaction when awake. Hence sleep releases the mind from its corporeal environments and gives free play to a person's true nature.

SUCCEDENT HOUSES   In astrology, those which follow the angular Houses: 2, 5, 8, and 11.

SUMMA PERFECTIONIS   This Latin expression means the Sum of Perfection. It is the title of a manual on alchemy, composed by the Arab mystic and Hermetic Geber. Geber's real name was Abu Musa Djafar.

SUN AND MOON   In astrology, the Sun and the Moon have each one house only. The sun resides in Leo. The Moon resides in Cancer.
In the Mithraic mystery cult the two luminaries were the object of worship.

SUN DANCE   A dance performed in honor of the sun as a divine power, at the time of the summer solstice, by many of the Plains Indians.

SUPERIOR PLANETS In astrology, those planets which lie outside of the earth's orbit.

SUPERNATURAL GUARDIAN Among the Eskimos there was an assumption that a person had a supernatural guardian who protected him in his everyday life.

SUPERNATURALISM IN ANTIQUITY In ancient Greek and Roman times the supernatural included prodigies, portents, apparitions of the dead, miraculous occurrences, intrusion of some demonic agency into normal affairs, eclipses. The Greeks conceived the world as full of spirits, of malefic character, operating at all times, everywhere.
In Book 19 of Homer's Iliad, a horse Xanthus speaks to the Greek hero Achilles in a human voice. Divinities appear to mortals, but the latter are not startled as though it were a remarkable phenomenon. When the goddess Aphrodite, daughter of Zeus, enters the Trojan conflict, Diomedes calls to her: Go back, daughter of Zeus, go back from the battle. That is, he addresses her as though she were an ordinary mortal.
Again, in Homer's epic, the Odyssey, there is a vision of Theoclymenus the seer. 'The earth is full of phantoms,' he declares. At the moment of death, Hector the Trojan warrior is endowed with second-sight. He predicts to Achilles his enemy the fate awaiting him at the hands of the Trojan Paris and the god Apollo.

A wound is healed with an incantation. The use of spells was a regular technique in Greek medical practice.
The Greek cyclic poets use supernatural elements quite freely in their descriptions of incidents. Telephus is miraculously healed by Achilles. Lynceus is possessed of vision that travels any distance and penetrates stone and wood.
The spirit of Achilles appears above his tomb in the presence of the assembled Greeks.

338

In tragic drama, in Aeschylus' Persae, the spirit of the dead king Darius appears, summoned by incantations or invocations. This spirit talks to the living, then departs to its prison-house.

In the Hecuba of Euripides, the shade of Polydorus delivers the prologue.

Transformations are frequent. Cadmus is turned into a snake. Procne becomes a swallow. Such phenomena of transformations were popular in local legends and folklore. Witchcraft appears in the Idylls of Theocritus. In Apollonius Medea the sorceress appears.

The goddess who presides over magic, over the dead is Hecate, who is often invoked by the poets.

Thessaly was the ancient home of witchcraft. In the Roman poet Lucan's Pharsalia, Sextus Pompeius asks a Thessalian sorceress to bring back a dead man to life and to force him to predict the future. Magic spells, continues Lucan, can prolong the night, arrest the revolution of the stars, induce thunder and storms and rain, change the course of rivers.

The Roman poet Horace relates incidents in which witches appear, but he believes that the gods have no contact with them. 'I have learned that the gods spend their days in peace.'

The epic poet Vergil uses the divinities as friends, sometimes as enemies, of mortals. In a restricted sense, a supernatural instance occurs in Book 9 of the Aeneid, where the ships of Aeneas slip their cables and are transformed into sea-nymphs.

There are, too, apparitions of the dead — the dead father of Aeneas, the dead Queen Dido, Trojan and Greek heroes slain in battle. To the ancients, such spirits were not a subjective projection: they constituted objective reality. Patroclus appears to Achilles after his death. The slain Hector appears to Aeneas. Deiphobus dead is beheld by Aeneas.

In the Mostellaria, a comedy by the Roman playwright

339

Plautus, there is mention of a ghost, but it is a hoax perpetrated by the wily slave Tranio. Lucian, the Greek satirist, has a character Philopseudes, in a conversation, describe a ghost: 'an unkempt figure, blacker than the pit, long-haired. He can turn into a dog, a bull, or a lion.'

SUPERNATURAL POWERS In primitive society, disabled people and animals and mentally sick persons were credited with supernatural powers.

SUSUPTI In yoga, this term denotes a state of deep sleep, in which there is largely an inactive consciousness.

SWEDENBORG, EMANUEL (1688-1772) Swedish scientist and philosopher, who was born in Stockholm. He visited Europe in the eighteenth century, claiming to be an intermediary between the visible and the invisible world. He also claimed converse with God and the angels, and expounded enlightenment on the future life. In 1788 his disciples formed a congregation in London with the purpose of continuing his views.

SWIFT IN MOTION In astrology, this expression is applied to a planet whose travel in twenty-four hours exceeds its mean motion.

SWIFT, JONATHAN (1667-1745) Dean Swift wrote a satire on astrological predictions. It is entitled Predictions for the Year 1708, by Isaac Bickerstaff. It was directed in particular against an almanac maker named Partridge.

SWORD OF MOSES   In Hebraic mysticisms an esoteric treatise dealing with magic formulas. The manuscript was discovered and edited by Dr. Moses Gaster.

SYBALLINE ORACLES   Fragments of ancient oracles collected by Jewish editors between 200 B.C. and 200 A.D. and supplemented by Christian accounts of prophetic utterances concerning the life and work of Christ.

SYCOMANCY   A method of divination by writing on fig leaves questions that are to be solved.

SYMBOLIC DREAMS   The interest in dreams and their symbolic content goes back to antiquity. The dreams described in the Bible, the ancient dream book of Artemidorus Daldianus, and the interpretative manuals of the Chaldeans and Egyptians and Arabs testify to the importance of dreams as revelations of hidden truths about the life of the psyche. Oneiromancy is the technical term given to the divinatory technique relating to dreams.

SYMBOLISM OF ADAM   As the primal source of all human life, Adam symbolizes in Hebraic tradition the basic unity and equality of all mankind. Jewish theology treated Adam's fall as a parable of the imperfections which are inherent in all humanity.

SYMBOLISM OF THE ZODIAC   In astrology, the four signs of the zodiac that represent Ezekiel's vision of the living creatures are Taurus, Leo, Aquarius, and Scorpio.

SYMPATHETIC MAGIC   In ancient Rome, in periods of drought, the Romans practiced sympathetic magic as an inducement to rain conditions. They poured water over a stone, hoping for rain clouds.

SYNTHESIS In astrology, the art of blending together separate influences in a nativity, and deducing a summary thereof. The ability to synthesize a nativity is the mark of an experienced astrologer.

SYZGY In astrology, this term, of Greek origin, means a yoking together. It is often loosely applied to any conjunction or opposition: particularly of a planet with the Sun, and close to the ecliptic whereby the earth and the two bodies are in a straight line. In its use in connection with the calculations of Tide Tables it applies to the conjunctions and oppositions of Sun and Moon near the Node.

T

TABERNACLE OF PEACE An ancient ascetic community in Safed, Palestine. It was dedicated to Kabbalistic doctrines.

TABLES OF HOUSES In astrology, tables showing the degrees of the signs which occupy the cusps of the several Houses in different latitudes for every degree of Right Ascension, or for every four minutes of Sidereal Time.

TABLET OF CAMBYSES An astrological chart belonging in the sixth century B.C. Cambyses was a king of Persia.

TABLE TURNING Movements of tables or other objects during a seance. Attributed to the agency of spirits by practitioners, the phenomenon has been explained rationally by Faraday and others as the result of unconscious motor action.

TADIBE The Samoyeds believe in the existence of invisible spirits that constantly menace human beings and must be propitiated through the intervention of a *tadibe* or sorcerer. The tadibe, whose office is hereditary, is capable of producing many striking illusions.

TAIGHEIRM A magical sacrifice of black cats to the devils of the underworld, formerly practiced in Scotland. In the seventeenth century two exorcists, Allan and Lachlain Maclean, were supposed to have held a Taigheirm in Mull and to have received the gift of second sight.

TAI-ME The central figure in the *kado,* or Sun Dance, ceremony of the Kiowa Indians. It is a small image of dark green stone, rudely resembling a human head and torso, and dressed in white feathers. It was exposed to view only at the annual Sun Dance.

TANCHELM A Flemish heretic, notary of Robert II, Count of Flanders. Tanchelm gathered together some twelve disciples called Tanchelmians. He himself, the Master, the mystic consort of the Virgin Mary, was assassinated in 1115.

TAO The *hsien* of ancient China believed that Tao, the ultimate principle of the universe, would impart its immortality to its creatures if they were brought into complete harmony with it. A two-fold process was supposed to enable man to become immortal: (1) cultivation of the mind to achieve the quietude, passivity, gentleness, and self-effacement of Tao; and (2) a gradual refinement of the bodily substance by means of dieting, drugs, and exercises.

TAOISM Taoism is a Chinese religious system founded by Lao-Tse in the seventh century B.C. It requires its adherents to practice vegetarianism.

TARGET In parapsychology, in ESP tests, the objective or mental events to which the subject is attempting to respond. In PK tests, the objective process or object which the subject tries to influence.

TAROT A pack of cards, based on occult symbols and interpretations. One set of twenty cards is called the Major Arcanum. The rest of the cards, fifty-six in number, constitute the Minor Arcanum. The use of tarot cards rests on the assumption that every incident in the universe is the result of a causal law and that there is no haphazard chance.

344

TARTINI, GIUSEPPE (1692-1770)   The Italian violinist dreamed that the devil played a melody for him in order to make him appreciate the services he could expect from the devil. Upon awaking, Giuseppe Tartini could not get the melody out of his head. He wrote down the notes of the exquisite sonata, which today is known as 'The Devil's Sonata.'

TASSEOGRAPHY   This term denotes the reading of leaves, their shape and position, in a teacup, with a view to predicting the subject's future and coming events.

TAURUS   In astrology, the Bull. The second, northern sign of the zodiac. Taurus is equated with the procreative function. In occultism its genius is symbolized as Aphrodite. Kaballistically, the sign represents the ears, neck, and throat of the grand old man of the skies. Thus Taurus is the silent, patient principle of humanity.

TELEKINESIS   The faculty of moving objects by thought alone is called telekinesis. The theory of telekinesis resembles that of the magnetists who made energetic emanation the cause of levitations and apports.

TELEPATHIC INSTRUCTION   In Tibetan mysticism, candidates for initiation have been taught telepathically. The Master may teach the novice silently: or by means of signs and gestures, unaccompanied by speech.

TELEPATHY   There is a belief that cats have telepathic sympathy. It is said that the father of Alexandre Dumas the French novelist was in close telepathic communication with his cat.

TEMPON-TELORIS The Dayaks of Borneo believe that Tempon-Teloris pilots the Ship of the Dead to the golden shores of the Blessed.

TEMURAH In Hebraic mysticism, this term, used in Biblical interpretation, denotes the alteration of a word by transposition of the letters. The transformation may produce a new significance in a context.

TEN EMANATIONS In Kabbalistic mysticism, God manifests himself in ten emanations or Sephiroth. His divine attributes are: Wisdom, Reason, Knowledge, Greatness, Strength, Beauty, Eternity, Majesty, Principle, Sovereignty.

TENGA The personification of the earth itself in the religion of the Mossi. Tenga is considered the wife of Winnam, the supreme deity and god of the sun.

TENGKOUGAS Local deities of the Mossi, the Tengkougas are associated with ancestors as propitiatory agents. *Tengsobas*, or earth priests, appeal to these earth gods for help. When proper sacrifices are made to the Tengkougas, *kinkirse*, or spiritual agents, enter the wombs of women and are born as children.

TENGSOBAS Earth priests of the Mossi. They conduct rituals to propitiate the *Tengkougas*, or earth gods.

TENTH HOUSE In astrology, this term refers to ambition, prestige. It is governed by the sign of Capricorn.

TEPHRAMANCY A technique that examines ashes of tree bark and other materials for the purpose of divinatory interpretation.

TERMINAL HOUSES In astrology, the fourth, eighth, twelfth Houses, corresponding to the signs of the Watery Triplicity. So called because they govern the terminations of three occult or mysterious phases of life: the fourth, the end of physical man: the eighth, the liberation of the soul: the twelfth, the liberation of the hopes to which the native secretly aspires.

TERMS OF THE PLANETS In astrology, these terms comprise a system of subrulerships of portions of a sign by different planets, whereby the nature of a planet posited in a sign is altered to that of the planet in whose term it happens to be posited.

TESTAMENT OF ABRAHAM A Jewish apocryphal book which describes Abraham's death and ascent to heaven. It was probably written in Hebrew in the second century A.D. The author was possibly Jewish or a Jewish Christian.

TESTIMONY In astrology, a partial judgment based on the influence of a certain planet as conditioned by sign and House, strength of position and aspects, or of a certain configuration of planets in a Figure. The synthesis of several testimonies constitutes a judgment. The term, as used by Ptolemy, is approximately synonymous with Argument.

TESTIMONY ON ASTROLOGY Many famous personalities, both in antiquity and in modern times, have testified to their interest, and often to their belief, in astrological phenomena. To Dante, the author of the Divine Comedy, astrology was "the noblest of the sciences." He declares:

> I saw
> The Sign that follows Taurus, and was in it.
> . . . O light impregnated
> With mighty virtues, from which I acknowledge

All my genius, whatsoe'er it be.

John Ruskin stated:
The greatness or smallness of a man is, in the most conclusive sense, determined for him at his birth.

Tycho Brahe was quite categorical in asserting:
The stars rule the lot of Man.

Johannes Kepler the astronomer:
An unfailing experience of mundane events in harmony with the changes occurring in the heavens has instructed and compelled my unwilling belief.

Sir Walter Scott:
Do not Christians and Heathens, Jews and Gentiles, poets and philosophers, unite in allowing the starry influences?

Francis Bacon:
The natures and dispositions of men are, not without truth, distinguished from the predominances of the planets.

St. Thomas Aquinas:
The celestial bodies are the cause of all that takes place in the sublunar world.

John Milton:
Knowledge by favour sent
Down from the empyrean, to forewarn
Us timely.

Hippocrates:
A physician without a knowledge of astrology has no right to call himself a physician.

Benjamin Franklin predicted a future event by astrological calculation:
by my calculations. . . on October 17th . . . at the instant of the conjunction of Sun and Mercury.

Theodore Roosevelt:
> I always keep my weather-eye on the opposition of my Seventh House Moon to my First House Mars.

Goethe:
> These auspicious aspects, which the astrologers subsequently interpreted for me, may have been the causes of my preservation.

Shakespeare:
> The stars above govern our conditions.

TETRABIBLOS This term, of Greek origin, denotes four books. It is the title of the oldest record of the astrological system of the ancients which has survived. It dates from about 132-160 A.D. Here the author, Claudius Ptolemy, says that it was compiled from 'ancient' sources.

TETRAGONUM In astrology, a line drawn between Aries, Cancer, Libra, Capricorn forms a tetragonum or quartile. This figure is regarded as unfavorable.

THAUMATURGIST In Greek this term denotes a wonder-worker. It has been applied to various reputed magicians and also the various saints noted for miraculous phenomena. Among these saints were St. Gregory Thaumaturgus and St. Philomena, who is called the Thaumaturga of the nineteenth century.

THEOMANCY A form of divination by oracular utterances.

THEOPOEA This Greek term is applied to a magic art which endows inanimate objects with life, movement, and speech.

349

THERAPEUTAE An ancient Jewish sect of Alexandria that flourished in the first century A.D. One of their characteristics was the practice of vegetarianism. They are described in a book attributed to Philo Judaeus, the Hellenistic-Jewish philosopher.

THESSALY In antiquity this district in Northern Greece was reputed to be the home of magic. Necromancers and other practitioners of the black arts were regarded as being natives of Thessaly or as having been trained there. The Greek dramatist Sophocles and the comic writer Menander, along with the Roman poets Vergil, Horace, Ovid, Lucan describe Thessaly as the seat of occultism.

THEURGY A mystic cult established by Iamblichus, a mystic and Neoplatonist philosopher who flourished in the fourth century A.D. The theurgists were the priests associated with the temples of Egypt and Greece and the Middle East. They practiced ceremonial magic and evoked the images of the gods.

THIAN-TI-HWII An ancient esoteric group, said to have survived in China until 1674.

THIRD HOUSE In astrology, this term refers to the house of possessions. It is governed by the sign of Taurus.

THIRTEEN In Kabbalistic mysticism, the number thirteen is equated with Unity.

THOMAS, JOHN An American preacher who founded the Christadelphians, a religious sect, in the 1840's. Among the tenets of this sect were a belief in the coming Reign of Christ and in the immortality of those within the Kingdom.

THRASYLLUS OF ALEXANDRIA (died 36 A.D.) A noted astrologer who taught the art to the Roman Emperor Tiberius. Thrasyllus is the author of treatises on astrology.

THREE LITERATURES In Hebraic tradition, next to the Bible and the Talmud, the body of mystical writings is called the third great literature.

THRONE In astrology, a planet is said to be on its throne when in a sign of which it is the Ruler. In a more ancient usage it was applied to a planet posited in that part of a sign wherein it had more than one Dignity.

TI A supernatural power worshipped by the ancient Chinese. Formerly a tribal Lord, Ti became the God for all, an anthropomorphic deity who presided over the activities of men. Great ancestors were identified with Ti. Finally, Ti was replaced by the concept of Heaven (*T'ien*) as the supreme spiritual reality.

TIBETAN APPARITIONS In the process of initiation into Tibetan mysticism, apparitions frequently appear to the novice. Some Tibetans explain the visions as subjective only, as the result of the intense concentration on the novice's part, leading into a trance state. Others, however, consider such apparitional phenomena as the result of a magic creation, produced by the externalization of the novice's thought.

TIBETAN BOOK OF THE DEAD Ostensibly a description of the experiences to be expected at the moment of death, during the seven weeks following death, and during rebirth into another vehicle, the Tibetan Book of the Dead uses the symbolism of Bonism and Buddhist conceptions, according to some interpreters, to cloak the mystical teachings of the ancient Tibetan gurus. The esoteric meaning is that of the death and rebirth of the ego. Known in its own language as the Bardo Thödol (Liberation by Hearing on the After-Death Plane), the book stresses that the ego has only to hear and remember certain teachings in order to gain its freedom.

TIBETAN MAGIC In the French Abbé Huc's Travels in Tartary, Thibet and China during the Years 1844-1846, there is much matter on the occult arts:

"Doubtless," said we, "some grand solemnity calls you together?"

"Yes, tomorrow will be a great day: a Lama Boktè, that is, a Tibetan saint-sorcerer, will manifest his power. Kill himself, yet not die."

We at once understood what solemnity it was that thus attracted the Ortous-Tartars. A Lama was to cut himself open, take out his entrails and place them before him, and then resume his previous condition. This spectacle, so cruel and disgusting, is very common in the Lama-series of Tartary. The Boktè who is to manifest his power, as the Mongols phrase it, prepares himself for the formidable operation by many days fasting and prayer, pending which, he must abstain from all communication whatever with mankind, and observe the most absolute silence. When the appointed day is come, the multitude of pilgrims assemble in the great court of the Lamasery, where an altar is raised in front of the Temple-gate. At length the Boktè appears. He advances gravely, amid the acclamations of the crowd, seats himself upon the altar, and takes from his girdle a large knife which he places upon his knees. At his feet, numerous Lamas, ranged in a circle, commence the terrible invocations of this frightful ceremony. As the recitations of the prayers proceed, you see the Boktè trembling in every limb, and gradually working himself up into phrenctic convulsions. The Lamas themselves become excited. Their voices are raised. Their song observes no order, and at last becomes a mere confusion of yelling and outcry. Then the Boktè suddenly throws aside the scarf which envelops him, unfastens his girdle, and seizing the sacred knife, slits open his stomach, in one long cut. While the blood flows in every direction, the multitude prostrate themselves before the terrible spectacle, and the enthusiast is interrogated about all sorts of hidden things, as to future events, as to the destiny of certain personages. The replies of the Boktè to all these questions are regarded by everybody as oracles.

When the devout curiosity of the numerous pilgrims is satisfied, the Lamas resume, but now calmly and gravely, the recitation of their prayers. The Boktè takes, in his right hand, blood from his wound, raises it to his mouth, breathes thrice upon it, and then throws it into the air, with loud cries. He next passes his hand rapidly over his wound, closes it, and everything after a while resumes its pristine condition, no trace remaining of the diabolical operation, except extreme prostration. The Boktè once more rolls his scarf round him, recites in a low voice a short prayer: then all is over, and the multitude disperse, with the exception of a few of the specially devout, who remain to contemplate and to adore the blood-stained altar which the Saint has quitted.

TIBETAN NOVICE   A novice who is preparing for initiation into Tibetan mysticism may be instructed by magicians who call upon certain demons for the novice's protection.

TIBETAN NUMBERS   In Tibetan mysticism, numbers have metaphysical and religious implications. There are three precious things: Buddha, faith, community. There are ten space directions. Buddha, Lamaism, and the Law constitute the Three Gems.

TIBETAN OCCULTISM In Tibetan occultism, the male and female principles of cosmic energy are called fohat and sakti respectively.

T'IEN In Chinese religion, the supreme spiritual reality, the controlling principle in the universe, or Heaven. The Roman Catholic Church used the words T'ien Chu, 'Lord of Heaven,' to translate 'God' into Chinese.

TON A power ascribed to the gods by the Dakota Indians. It is the power to do supernatural things.

TORNAIT In Greenland, the Eskimos' belief is that various spirits, known as tornait or tartat or tungat, become helpers of the shaman or medicine man. In Alaska the tornait are Beings that are not the souls of visible beings but have strange forms of their own. They are usually evil and harmful. They are known as the Half-People, the Wanderers, the mountain Giants. These tornait, in groups or communities, are in turn controlled by superior, more potent agents.

TORTOISE SHELL DIVINATION As early as the Shang dynasty (1766-122 B.C.), diviners used the tortoise shell to foretell the future. The belly surface of the shell was incised with a hot stylus and heated until cracks appeared in it. The diviner then read the oracle. Later milfoil stalks arranged in a definite order replaced the tortoise shell. The symbols recorded in the I Ching, used in conjunction with the milfoil stalks, simplified the divination procedures.

TRAHERNE, THOMAS (c. 1637-1674) An English metaphysical poet. Author, among other works, of Centuries of Meditations.

TRAITE ELEMENTAIRE DE LA SCIENCE OCCULTE   This French title, Elementary Treatise on Occult Science, was composed by Papus, the pseudonym of Gérard Encausse, a French mystic who flourished in the nineteenth century. His interests included alchemy, astrology, and the Kabbalah. He was also the founder of a sect called Isis.

TRANCE   A state of hypnotic awareness. It is usual to distinguish several forms of trance: light, medium, deep, stuporous.

TRANCE MEDIUMS   In psychic phenomena some mediums, while in a trance state, are reputed to leave their own body, so that it may be inhabited for a time by another individual. This type of bodily transference occurs in the training of Tibetan initiates in Tibetan mysticism.

TRANSITOR   In astrology, a slow-moving major planet whose lingering aspect to a birth planet produces a displacement of equilibrium, which is then activated by an additional aspect from a Culminator, a faster-moving body such as the Sun or Moon, to the same or another planet, thereby precipitating the externalization.

TRANSLATION OF LIGHT   In astrology, the conveyance of influence which occurs when a transiting planet is found to be applying to an aspect of another, in which case some of the influence of the first aspected planet is imparted to the second aspected planet by a translation of light.

TRANSMUTATION   In astrology, the advantageous utilization, on the part of a controlled and developed character, of an astrological influence which otherwise might exert a destructive and disruptive force. The term is borrowed from alchemy.

355

TRANSMUTATION OF THE BODY The aim of alchemists is to restore man to his pristine state of innocence, grace, strength, perfection, and immortality. Their search for the Elixir of life continued through the centuries.

TREES The worship of trees has played an important part in the history of Europe. Tree worship is attested among the Celts, Slavs, Greeks, Romans, and Germans.

TREFOIL The three-leaved clover. It is the symbol of the Trinity.

TREMBLERS OF THE CEVENNES In the sixteenth century this Protestant group of convulsionaries spread from the Cevennes over most of Germany. They claimed to have visions, communicate with spirits, be insensitive to pain, and have the ability to perform miraculous cures.

TREVISAN, BERNARD The Italian alchemist was born at Padua in 1406. He traveled widely, bent on discovering the philosopher's stone. Toward the end of his long life, he is supposed to have had some measure of success.

TRIAD SOCIETY An ancient Chinese society, originally altruistic but later politically oriented. The esoteric society practiced elaborate initiation rituals involving the mingling of human blood and the blood of a cock. It is also known as the Hung Society.

TRIANGLE The Egyptian triangle, with a base of four parts, a perpendicular of three parts, and a hypotenuse of five parts was a symbol used by the Egyptian priests to typify universal nature. The base was equated with Osiris, Isis

356

was represented by the perpendicular, and the hypotenuse was their son Horus.

The first perfect odd number was three. Four was the square of two, the first even number. Five was the addition of three and two. The triangle with sides equal to 3,4,5 was applied in building the Pyramids.

TRIANGLE, MYSTICAL In mysticism, two triangles, super-imposed and forming a six-pointed star, represent the soul of man.

TRIGON In astrology, this term is applied to the three signs of the same triplicity.

TRIGRAMS Eight trigrams which combine to form sixty-four hexagrams or Kuas are the basis of the Chinese technique of divination. The sixty-four Kuas of the I-Ching express the complete range of situations in which man may find himself.

TRIMORION In astrology, an aspect in mundo which embraces three Houses, hence a mundane square, but which in some instances may actually extend to as much as 120 degrees. Hence in Primary Directions it was sometimes called the killing arc, since 120 years were considered the natural limit of life.

TRINE In astrology, this is a line drawn from the signs of the zodiac Aries, Sagittarius, Leo and then back to Aries. A triangle is thus formed which is called trine. Trine is a favorable figure.

TRINITIES In astrology, a classification of the twelve signs into four groups, representing the four seasons, is called the Trinities:

Intellectual (Spring)	Maternal (Summer)	Reproductive (Autumn)	Serving (Winter)
1. Aries	4. Cancer	7. Libra	10. Capricorn
2. Taurus	5. Leo	8. Scorpio	11. Aquarius
3. Gemini	6. Virgo	9. Sagittarius	12. Pisces

TRIPLICITY In astrology, the zodiacal signs are classified in groups of three, called triplicities, as follows:
Fire signs: Aries, Leo, Sagittarius
Air signs: Gemini, Libra, Aquarius
Earth signs: Taurus, Virgo, Capricorn
Water signs: Cancer, Scorpio, Pisces

TRISKAIDECAPHOBIA This Greek expression denotes fear of the number thirteen. It refers to the old traditional fear that many people experience when Friday falls on the thirteenth of the month. There are countless cases on record where men and women have met with unpleasant or dangerous encounters on the thirteenth. Popular logic has thus, in the course of the centuries, associated Friday the thirteenth with sinister possibilities. There is of course an unreasoning and perhaps mystical tone in this attitude.

In the U.S.A., for the last two decades, a society, consisting of thirteen members, has been actively opposed to the acceptance of thirteen as of malefic significance. It has also been suggested that a new calendar is now in order, which would eliminate the possibility of thirteen and Friday coinciding.

TRITHEMIUS (1462 - 1516) John Trithemius was a German abbot of Wurzburg and a friend of Agrippa von Nottesheim. Trithemius was a prominent scholar and wrote on magic and alchemy. There was a legend that he exorcised the dead Mary of Burgundy, wife of the Emperor Maximilian. Hesitant about the possible punishment as a result of publishing works on magic, he wrote in Latin in symbolic language, recognizable to initiates alone.

TROBRIAND MAGIC   The magic of the Melanesian community of the Trobriand Islands, a coral archipelago northeast of New Guinea, was studied by Malinowski. He used his research to demonstrate that magic fills a knowledge gap and provides an alternative way of giving expression to thwarted desires.

TRUTINE   In astrology, a term employed by Hermes in the process of rectification.

TSAMS   In Tibetan yoga, this term refers to an ascetic exercise in which the subject lives by himself, in continuous darkness, without any contact with the outside world.

TSONG   The symbol of the earth, corresponding to hexagon number 2 in the I-Ching. Tsong represents Yin.

TSONG-KA-PA   (1357 - 1419)   The Tibetan founder of the sect of Yellow Caps.

T'UAN   A brief statement accompanying each *kua* in the I Ching. The T'uan ('Judgments') are attributed traditionally to King Wen, one of the founders of the Chou dynasty (1150 - 249 B.C.).

TUNRAQS   The spirits controlled by an Eskimo shaman. He could dispatch them on an aggressive mission but risked having them fail to accomplish the mission and turn against him.

TURE A culture hero of the Azande, an African tribe living in the Sudan. Many of the stories told about him concern magical practices which are now lost.

TWELFTH HOUSE In astrology, this term refers to enemies. It is governed by the sign of Pisces.

TWELVE In mystic numerology, this number has special significance. It appears in mythology, folklore, and in esoteric concepts. The cosmos was divided into twelve signs called the Zodiac. In pagan cults, there were frequently groups of twelve: gods, followers, leaders. In Greek mythology, Hercules performed twelve labors. In the Bible, Jacob is recorded as having twelve sons. Mithra had twelve associates. King Arthur had his twelve knights. The year has twelve months. There are, too, the twelve days of Christmas. Mystically, for a number of reasons, twelve has been called 'the perfect number.'

TWENTY-ONE This number, a multiple of three and seven, is regarded in occultism as of powerful magical significance.

TWINS The belief that twin children possess magical powers is widespread. The Tsimshian Indians believe that twins can control the weather, call the salmon, and have their wishes fulfilled. The Kwakiutl and Nootka Indians associate twin children with the sky and believe that they can bring down the rain.

TYPTOLOGY A method of seeking communication with the spirits of the dead by means of rappings according to a predetermined code.

U

UDASINS   A Hindu sect that practiced abstinence, poverty, and chastity. Nowadays, the sect emphasizes human fraternity.

UFO   These abbreviations represent Unidentified Flying Objects, including Flying Saucers. The latter have been the subject of wide and variously interpreted discussions in many countries.

UMBRAL ECLIPSE   In astrology, this term is applied to an eclipse of the Moon, when the Moon definitely enters the earth's shadow. If the Moon is completely immersed in the earth's shadow a total eclipse results: otherwise, a partial eclipse. Applied to an eclipse of the Sun the term does not include a partial eclipse, but only those in which the Moon's disc is fully contained within that of the Sun, either total, annular, or annular-total.

UNFORTUNATE SIGNS   In astrology, the negative signs: Taurus, Cancer, Virgo, Scorpio, Capricorn, Aquarius.

UNICORN   During the Middle Ages, the unicorn was associated with the Holy Spirit and symbolized both the destructive and the creative manifestations of the divine power. In alchemy, the unicorn was used to represent Mercury and the Lion.

361

UNION OF OPPOSITES The alchemists' researches were directed toward achieving a union of opposites (for example, the symbiosis of temporal and spiritual power, the conjunction of the masculine and feminine principles, coitus). The conjunction of opposites was also illustrated by the androgyne, the unique being which combined within itself the masculine and feminine principles. True birth was assumed to take place in the hermetically sealed vase.

UNITAS FRATRUM This Latin expression means Society of Brethren. It was a fifteenth century organization of various religious sects. They formed an independent hierarchy of their own.

UNIVERSAL BROTHERHOOD Esoterically, Universal Brotherhood means the spiritual brotherhood of all beings. The doctrine implies that all men are inseparably linked by the very fabric of the universe and spring forth, with all other beings, from the spiritual Sun of the universe.

UNIVERSAL SELF In theosophy, the heart of the universe, the source of our being.

UNKNOWN FATHER In Gnostic mysticism, the Unknown Father was the demiurgos, second to the supreme divinity. The Unknown Father, in Gnostic tradition, was the author of Creation.

UPANISHADS The original source books of yoga. Also referred to as the Vedanta, or last part of the Vedas, they represent one of man's earliest attempts to arrive at methods of perceiving truth directly. The literal meaning of the expression is 'knowledge communicated from teacher to disciple.' The basic doctrine of these speculative treatises, some dating from the eighth century B.C., is that of the identity of the individual soul (atman) with the universal soul (Brahma).

UR In ancient Babylonia, this city was the principal seat of the worship of the Moon as a deity.

URAEUS Egyptian representation of the sacred asp, symbol of the serpent in its creative role and of the sovereignty of the pharaoh. It appeared on the headdress of the ruler, just above his forehead. The uraeus was supposed to defend the dead against evil spirits during the journey beyond the tomb.

URANIAN In astrology, this term is applied to a person of erratic and independent nature, with original and unorthodox ideas and viewpoints, due to a strong Uranus birth receptivity.

URANUS This planet is most remote from the earth.

UROBOROS A serpent which feeds on its own tail, depicted on Egyptian pottery, symbolizes the perpetual self-renewal of nature. The theme is found all over the world.

V

VALENS   Roman emperor flourished in the fourth century A.D. He had a court astrologer named Heliodorus, who predicted the future from observation of the stars. He also cast horoscopes.

VALENTINE, BASIL   A German prior and a Hermetic. He was the author of a number of treatises on alchemy.

VALENTINE, BASIL   Born at Mayence towards the end of the fourteenth century, he devoted his life to the search for the philosopher's stone. He contended that charitable deeds, mortification of the flesh, and prayer were prerequisites to the discovery of the stone.

VALENTINIANS   A Gnostic sect, followers of their founder Valentinus, who flourished in the second century A.D. Their principal sacrament was the bridal chamber where the heavenly marriage took place between Sophia, Wisdom, and the Redeemer.

VALENTINUS   One of the mystic sect of Gnostics. He flourished in the second century A.D. He taught that initiates would behold the marriage of Sophia, which is wisdom, and the Redeemer.

VAMPIRISM   A modern case of vampirism was reported in London in 1949. The accused, a man of substance and position, was executed. He had confessed to the murder of nine persons whose blood he had drunk.

VARAHA MUHIRA   A Hindu mystic who composed a treatise on astrology c. 500 A.D.

VEDANTA SOCIETY OF AMERICA   This society, which was organized in 1893, aims to reconcile religion and science and the philosophies of the East and the West.

VEDANTAS   The older Upanishads. Variously interpreted, they form the common doctrinal basis of Hinduism.

VEDAS   These are ancient Sanskrit texts describing the Hindu theogony and the relations between man and the supernatural universe.

VERGIL   In Eclogue 8, one of the bucolic poems by the Roman epic poet Vergil, a certain Moeris is described as a lycanthrope, who with the help of herbs and poisons can turn into a wolf and plunge into the woods.

VESPERTINE   In astrology, this term is applied to a planet which sets in the West after the Sun. The reverse is Matutine.

VETTIUS, VALENS   A writer on astrological subjects who belongs in the second century A.D.

VIA COMBUSTA   In astrology, the combust path. As employed by the ancients, the expression probably referred to a cluster of fixed stars in the early degrees of the constellation Scorpio. A birth Moon in that arc was considered to be as afflicted as if it were in an eclipse condition — at or near one of the Nodes.

VIBRATING UNIVERSE   A theory popular in nineteenth-century occultism, following the discovery of the motion of light, electricity, and magnetism. The theory assigns a basic rate of vibration to each number and reduces a person's name to a number which reveals his characteristic 'note.' A basic tenet is that a number sets up a vibration which should be kept in harmony with everyday life. Thus a man whose number is two ('companionship') should not choose the monastic life. George Washington's number is, appropriately, one ('leadership'). February 22, 1732, reduces as follows: 2/22/1732 becomes 24 plus 13, then 37, and 1.

VIBRATION   In occultism there are said to be two aspects, one esoteric or secret: the other exoteric or external.

VIEW OF DEATH   To the ancient Egyptians death was regarded as a temporary suspension of life, a condition which could be remedied by occult rites. Mummification was a corollary to this belief, and the practice included not only human beings but animals as well. In particular the cat was mummified, and the animal was conceived as participating later on in a blissful paradise of its own.

VIEWS ON MIRACLES   St. Augustine (354-430 A.D.), the famous Church Father and author of The City of God and Confessions, declared that miracles occurred by simple faith and piety, not by spells and incantations associated with the occult arts.

VILE (SAMOVILE)   Slavonic spirits that constantly watch over and control the destinies of men. Southern Slavs identify three varieties of spirits: *zracne vile*, evil spirits that inflict harm on people: *pozemme vile,* earth-dwelling spirits that give good counsel; and *dopovne vile*, or water spirits.

VIRGO In astrology, the Virgin. The sixth, northern sign of the zodiac. It represents the dual hermaphroditic form. In esoteric writings it symbolizes chastity and, on the intellectual plane, the realization of hopes. Kabbalistic, it symbolizes the solar plexus of the old man of the heavens. Thus it represents the assimilating and distributing functions of the human organism.

VIRGULA FURCATA A Latin term meaning a forked rod. This is the divining rod used by dowsers. It is so called by Agricola, the metallurgist who flourished in the sixteenth century. The divining rod, however, need not be forked.

VISIBLE GODS According to Julian the Apostate, the Roman emperor who turned to paganism, the planets were conceived as visible gods.

VOICE, SIGNS OF In astrology, this expression refers to Gemini, Virgo, Libra, Aquarius and the first half of Aquarius: so called because when one of these signs ascends and Mercury is strong, the person is regarded as having the capacity to become an orator.

VOID OF COURSE In astrology, this expression is applied to a planet which forms no complete aspect before leaving the sign which it is posited at birth. When the Moon is so placed it denies fruition to much of the good otherwise promised in the Figure. In Horary Astrology a planet so placed denies fruition to much of the good otherwise promised; hence one who abandons himself to aimless endeavor.

VOODOO An ancient occult system involving magic operations: prevalent mostly in the West Indies.

Voodoo rites make use of drums and bells as well as assons, ordinary gourds which have been pierced and fitted with a handle. Drums, made of skin and wood, are symbolic of resurrection. Priests and followers are revitalized by touching the drumskins. The shape of the asson suggests both male and female. The asson commands the occult powers of the ancestor-stars; the bells control the magic powers of the stars of the future.

The Baron Samedi is the Master of the Cemeteries. He is invoked during black magic ceremonies. His cross plays a part in funeral rites, the most famous of which is the ritual involving the zombies, corpses taken from graves and restored to life by sorcerers. The priests of the cult are called Hungan and the priestesses Mambo. Its two main rites are the radas, or initiation rite, and the petro, or worship of the dispenser of magic powers. In the rada rite, the initiate is required to have detailed knowledge of the cult. He must take an oath to venerate the powers of the hungans and their representatives. He must cross the waters to reach Ife to receive powers, which he must bring back, also by sea. A sheep as white as snow must be sacrificed while the initiate is crossing the water.

Voodoo is today the secret and national religion of Haiti. Fought by the Catholic Church since its importation from Africa, it has remained an obscure cult in parts of the West Indies and Brazil. The name may derive from the French words for Golden Calf (Veau d'or) or from an indigenous expression meaning pursuit of the unknown. Certain rites involve animal and human sacrifices. The cult has some adherents in the United States.

VOODOO SERPENT The giant Voodoo serpent organizes and controls everything. The sacred serpent is in possession of all the secrets of magic.

VULPINE NAMES The belief in the traditions that associate man with the ability to turn into a wolf is often manifested in old tribal names etymologically related to wolf-man. Such names are, anciently, Lycians, Lykaones, Lucanians. Many personal names, too, both in antiquity and in modern days, have vulpine reminiscences: for instance, Lucius, Lucianus, Autolycus. The first president of the Turkish Republic, Mustapha Kemal, was called Ata Turk: Grey Wolf.

W

WAKAN In American Indian religion, the impersonal power that animates the world. This extraphysical power, the embodiment of the elemental powers which, collectively, produce and maintain the order of the universe, is manifested physically in several ways — in prophetic utterances, visions, magic, etc. The American Indian term (also identified as *wakanda*) embraces concepts similar to *mana* in Polynesia.

WALPURGISNACHT This expression refers to the first night in May. At this time witches and demoniac creatures were wont to assemble to celebrate their gruesome orgies and Satanic rituals.

WATCHERS OF THE HEAVENS In astrology, this expression was applied by the Persians, about 3000 B.C., to the four Royal Stars, then to the angles of the zodiac: the Watcher of the East, then at the vernal equinox — Aldebaran: the Watcher of the North, which then marked the summer solstice — Regulus: the Watcher of the West, then at the autumnal equinox — Antares: the Watcher of the South, which then marked the winter solstice — Fomalhaut.

WEBSTER, JOHN (c. 1580 - 1625) In his drama The Duchess of Malfi, the Elizabethan playwright presents a character who, in a mad frenzy, feels himself to be a wolf: he howled fearfully, saying he was a wolf.

WELSH SEERS Giraldus Cambrensis (1146-c. 1220), the Welsh historian and geographer, in his Description of Wales, has the following account of soothsayers:

Among these Welsh people there are — and you will not find them elsewhere — certain men called Awenithion, that is, inspired. When consulted on some doubtful issue, they immediately go into a frenzy as though beside themselves and finally become prophetic. They do not however utter the desired answer forthwith: but through much devious circumlocution, through a spate of talk, trivial and meaningless rather than coherent, yet expressed altogether in ornate language, lastly in some verbal byway, the seeker who observes the reply carefully will find a clear answer. And so finally they are roused by others from this ecstatic state as though from a deep sleep, and are forcibly brought back to consciousness almost by violence. Now you will find two remarkable characteristics about them. After their reply, unless violently aroused and awakened, they do not usually become inspired after such a frenzy. Once awakened, they will recall nothing about what was uttered by them in their trance. Thus if they happen to be consulted on this point or any other and have no reply, they will explain in quite other, different terms: perhaps they speak through inspired and possessed spirits, though in ignorance. These gifts generally come to them in sleep through visions. For some believe that, as it were, sweet milk or honey is poured into them: while others think that a card with writing on it is placed on their mouths.

WEN King Wen is one of the founders of the Chou dynasty (1150-249 B.C.). The *T'uan* of the I Ching was attributed traditionally to him.

WEREFOX In Chinese thought, the werefox was similar to the European werewolf.

WEREWOLF, VARIANT NAMES FOR   In the Middle Ages, the werewolf was called guerulfus. In Old English the term werewolf itself meant man-wolf. In French, the equivalent is loup-garou. In Danish, vaerulf. In Swedish, varulf. In Greek, lukokantzari. Slavonic languages know the phenomenon as volkulaku, vokodlak, wilkodlak.

WESTCAR PAPYRUS   An Egyptian document devoted to magic and dating from the eighteenth century B.C.

WEST INDIAN POSSESSION   In the first decade of this century newspapers reported a case of a native who was allegedly possessed by two spirits.

WESTMINSTER ABBEY   When Westminster Abbey was being rebuilt the corpse of a cat was discovered between the walls. It was believed that the animal had been sacrificed to the Sun-God.

WHEATLEY, DENNIS   Contemporary English novelist who has written prolifically on occult and Satanic themes. Among his novels are: The Ka of Gifford Hillary, Strange Conflict, The Devil Rides Out, To the Devil — a Daughter.

WHEEL OF THE LAW   The Buddhist Wheel of the Law, in its mystical connotation, refers to the eight-fold path of Buddha teaching.

WHITE LOTUS   A Chinese secret society whose origins are contemporary with those of the ancient mysteries. The exact relation between the Hung Society and the White Lotus is unknown. Each may have been a different degree of a common rite, or they may have been separate societies.

WHOLE SIGNS   In astrology, this expression applies to Gemini, Libra, Aquarius, and, according to some astrologers, Taurus.

WIDOW'S SON   This expression is applied to Hiram Abif, reputedly the builder of Solomon's Temple.

WIERUS, JOHANN   A sixteenth century demonographer. Author of De praestigiis daemonum et incantationibus et veneficiis: on the practices of demons, on incantations, and poisons. He has an account of an Italian who was a versipellis, that is a werewolf, 'whose skin turned inside out.'

WIND   Primitive peoples try to control the wind by practicing imitative magic. The Yakut waves a special stick and utters a spell. Fuegians try to make the wind drop by throwing shells against it. The Lenuga Indians identify the rush of a whirlwind with the passage of a spirit.

WISCONSIN PHALANX   One of the most successful spiritualistic communities of the nineteenth century. It was founded near Ripon by Warren Chase in 1844 and survived until 1850.

WISE OF HEART   In the Zohar, the Book of Splendor, which is the essence of Hebraic mysticism, The Wise of Heart is a term applied to certain Kabbalistic adepts.

WITCH   In England a witch is defined as 'a person who hath conference with the Devil to consult with him or to do some act.'

WITCHCRAFT Since prehistoric times people have believed in a god incarnate in an animal or a human being. Palaeolithic paintings in a cave in southern France (Ariège) suggest that this god appeared to his worshipers in an animal disguise, clothed in the skin of a stag with antlers on his head. Christian commentators have invariably identified this god as the Devil. Assemblies of sabbaths of witches took place four times each year: on February 2 (Candlemas), May-eve (Roodmas), Aug. 1 (Lammas), and November eve (Hallowe'en). These seasonal divisions indicate the importance attached to the breeding of animals and the pre-agricultural origin of the cult. The celebrations began in the evening and lasted until dawn. Lesser celebrations took place at irregular intervals and were attended by leaders in each district. Twelve of these leaders and their chief or devil made up a Coven. One of their most important rites was the sacrifice, perhaps by fire, of the god at intervals of seven years.

WITCHCRAFT A LA MODE In Ceylon the 'witch doctor,' the kattadiya, is reputed to be an adept in the demoniac arts. He can summon the diabolic spirits and perform exorcism. The exorcism of malefic spirits requires special rites and, in particular, long formulaic chants, exhausting for the exorcist and, it is presumed, for the malevolent spirit. But now the kattadiya enlists the aid of modern techniques. He has a tape recorder and lets it do his work by chanting the prolonged exorcising conjurations, while the kattadiya, paid for his services and still refreshed, proceeds to the next village.

WITCHCRAFT IN ELIZABETHAN TIMES Shakespeare, speaking of current beliefs in witches, refers to "pale Hecate's offerings." Hecate was the triple goddess who in Hell presided over the occult arts.

WITCH-CULT The Old Religion survived in England until at least the eighteenth century and vestiges of it can be found in France and Italy today. It consists of a belief in a god incarnate in an animal or a person. Sacred dances, feasts, rituals, and ceremonies to promote fertility were supervised in many instances by priests who were drawn from the peasant class and were only outwardly Christians.

WITCH DOCTOR This term, as used popularly, is anthropologically erroneous. In Africa and elsewhere, the correct description is a ritual specialist.
A popular magazine carries an advertisement from Quito, South America. It announces a witch doctor endowed with the powers of a secret miracle drug. By means of this drug the future is an open book to this witch doctor.

WITCHES In remote historical times women who were reputed to practice witchcraft were regarded as having been votaries and priestesses dedicated to the mystery cults of Isis, or Hecate, or the Phrygian Cybele, the Mighty Mother of the Gods.

WITCHES AND CATS In medieval legend, the witch, bound for the assembly of the Sabbat, is often represented as riding on a cat, her familiar. A panel in Lyons Cathedral depicts a witch riding on a goat and carrying her cat.

WIZARDS AT THE SABBAT It was a belief that wizards participated at the Satanic witches' Sabbats in spirit-bodies in the form of animals.

WORK OF MERCY A mystic sect that was founded in France in the nineteenth century.

376

WORLD OF EMANATION   In Hebraic mysticism the highest of the four Kabbalistic worlds, between the Infinite and the earthly sphere.

WORTHY ONES   The Worthy Ones were a Hebraic esoteric sect of whom little else is known.

WRAITH   An apparition or 'double' closely resembling its prototype and generally supposed to be an omen of death.

X

XYLOMANCY A method of divination by casting sticks or twigs on the ground and interpreting their position.

Y

YAH Also Yahu. A mystic designation for God. The term is found on a Moabite stele of the ninth century B.C. It denotes: I am who I am.

YAMABUSI This Japanese term refers to an ancient mystic sect of monks known as Hermit Brothers.

YANG The positive, male principle, also associated with goodness and light. Yang and yin are terms in a dualism that permeates Chinese speculative thought, magic, and divination.

YANG-HSIAO A continuous undivided line used with the divided line called *yin-shiao* to form the trigrams of the I Ching. Yang-Hsiao is the symbol of the male or positive principle.

YIDAMS In Tibetan mysticism, yidams are powerful beings, giving protection to their devotees. They are regarded as occult agents with diabolic associations: or as phenomenal projections of a person's inherent energy. If a person of impure spirit seeks initiation, a Lama may command the yidams to tear the novice to pieces. Yidams may be evoked by silent conjuration.

YIH KING A Chinese expression denoting Book of Changes. This is the title of an ancient Chinese treatise on occult philosophy. Also, I Ching and Y Ching.

YIN The negative, female principle, also associated with darkness and evil.

YIN-HSIAO A divided line, used in combination with the undivided line called yang-hsiao to form the trigrams of the I Ching. It symbolizes the female or negative principle.

YIN AND YANG The two fundamental forces at the base of all divination, according to the ancient Chinese system. The bright, male, positive, beneficent principle (yang) contrasts with the dark, female, negative, evil principle (yin).

YOGA In Hinduism, yoga ('union') includes various physical disciplines designed to enable the ascetic to gain control over specific forces, to possess occult powers, and to achieve union with Brahma. Eight stages of yoga are generally enumerated: (1) yama, or restraint; (2) niyama, or religious observances of various kinds; (3) asana, or particular postures; (4) pranayama, or methods of controlling breathing; (5) pratyahara, or withdrawal of consciousness from external objects; (6) dharana, or mental concentration; (7) dhyana, or abstract contemplation; and (8) samadhi, or union with Brahma.

YOGA-LEVITATION In yoga, levitation applies to walking over water, over thorns, or remaining suspended in the air. To achieve levitation, asserts Patanjali, who flourished around the second century B.C., mastery is required over one of the vital airs named udana, which resides at the throat centre.

YOGA PHILOSOPHY Yoga philosophy has a number of purposive aspects. It is spiritual, stressing the independent, self-originating spirit in man. It is also, in its aims and precepts, intellectual and emotional and, further, postulates a body of ethics.

382

YUGA   In Hindu cosmogony, one of the four ages of the world. The golden age, the Krita Yuga, lasts 1,728,000 years; the second age, the Treta Yuga, is darker than the first and lasts 1,296,000 years; the third age, the Dvapara Yuga, is darker still and lasts 864,000 years. The last age, the Kali Yuga, began in 3102 B.C. and will endure 432,000 years. The total period (4,320,000 years) is a Manvantara. Its close is signaled by a pralaya, inaugurating the 'night of Brahma,' which lasts a thousand cycles, and ends when Brahma awakens to renew the cycle of the ages. A night and a day of Brahma constitute a Kalpa.

Z

ZACHAIRE, DENIS French alchemist who flourished in the sixteenth century. He reputedly transmuted quicksilver into gold.

ZACUTO, MOSES Born in Amsterdam in 1625: died in Mantua in 1697. He was a Hebrew scholar and exegete. He wrote on Kabbalistic subjects.

ZARBIES Instruments of mutilation used in ritual tortures practiced by the Helveti dervishes in Albania.

ZEN This term is Japanese, but it stems from the Sanskrit dhyana, which denotes meditation. Zen is an Oriental system of mental tranquillity or stillness. It is directed to the attainment of total release from attachment to the material, objective, external world. The movement dates back some 1500 years in China. Zen is now in force largely in Japan and Korea, where it assumes practical applications.

ZENITH In astrology, this term applies mathematically to the Pole of the Horizontal. The point directly overhead, through which pass the Prime Vertical and Meridian circles. Every place has its own zenith, and the nearer a planet is to that zenith, the more powerful is its influence. The expression is sometimes loosely applied to the cusp of the Tenth House, which strictly speaking is only the point of the zodiac or ecliptic path through which the meridian circle passes.

ZEUS LYCAEUS The concept of lycanthropy appears in the appellation of the Greek supreme divinity, Zeus Lycaeus. According to Plato, in the worship of Zeus Lycaeus a man was offered in sacrifice to the god and whoever partook of the sacrificial flesh became a wolf. The cult of Zeus Lycaeus was founded by Lycaon, whose name is associated with wolf. He sacrificed a child to Zeus and was himself turned into a wolf.

ZILTO A magician at the court of King Wenceslaus of Bohemia. He is supposed to have swallowed a rival magician.

ZIMZUM In Hebraic Kabbalistic mysticism, this term denotes the primal act of Creation.

ZINZENDORF, COUNT LOUIS DE In the eighteenth century he founded at Herrnhut near Bohemia a mystic Fraternity whose tenets were based on continuous prayer.

ZODIAC In astrology, a branch of the occult arts, the examination of the sky, the stars, the planets, the zodiacal signs, their relations to each other and their movements were studied with mathematical precision in order to find what influences were exerted by the celestial bodies on the conduct and fate of man: when these influences were most potent or weakest.

The signs of the zodiac mark the twelve compartments of heaven. The six northern signs are:

Aries   Cancer
Taurus   Leo
Gemini   Virgo

To each of these names is assigned a mystic symbol.
The six southern signs are:

Libra   Capricorn
Scorpio   Aquarius
Sagittarius Pisces

The zodiac was divided into two sections of Sun and Moon. Each half consists of six signs. The signs of the Moon of Night are: Aquarius, Pisces, Aries, Taurus, Gemini, Cancer. The signs of the Sun or Day are: Leo, Virgo, Libra, Scorpio, Sagittarius, Capricorn.

By means of scrupulous calculations the astrologer could determine the degree of influence exerted by the planets in relation to the zodiac. The issues to be determined astrologically concerned life; wealth; inheritance; land; wife, city, children, parents; health, sickness; marriage; death religion, travel; honors, character; friends; enemies, captivity.

ZODIAC ASPECTS   In astrology, those measured in degrees along the Ecliptic. When used in connection with Primary Directions the Promittor's place is taken without latitude in contrast to the usual method used with mundane aspects wherein one takes cognizance of the latitude the significator will have when it arrives at the longitudinal degree at which the aspect is complete.

ZODIACAL DIRECTIONS   In astrology, those formed in the zodiac by the progressed motion of Ascendant, Midheaven, Sun, Moon, to aspects with the planets. These may be: Direct, in the order of the signs: or Converse, against the order of the signs.

ZODIACAL METALS   In astrology, zodiacal metals are those of the planetary Rulers, as follows:
Aries-Scorpio: Iron
Taurus-Libra: Copper
Gemini-Virgo: Mercury
Cancer: Silver
Leo: Gold
Sagittarius-Pisces: Tin
Capricorn-Aquarius: Lead

387

ZODIACAL PARALLELS In astrology, any two points within the zodiac that are of equal declination are said to be in zodiacal parallel with each other. If both are North or both South declination they were anciently termed antiscions. Modern astrologers attribute astrological significance only to those points between two bodies in parallel on the same side of the equator.

ZODIACAL QUALITIES Astrologically, the signs of the zodiac have individual properties and characteristics which reflect on human beings involved in astrological computations. Taurus, for instance, is feminine, cold, dry. Gemini is masculine, hot, moist. Cancer is feminine, nocturnal, cold. Leo is diurnal and bestial. Sagittarius is fiery and mutable. Virgo is earthy, quiet. Capricorn is earthy, solid. Libra is airy, restless. Aquarius is airy, inventive. Scorpio is secretive, passionate. Pisces is nervous, confused. Aries is creative, full of movement.

ZODIACAL SIGNS In astrology, the zodiacal signs and the planets are always present but not all of them are visible. Some lie above and others below the horizon.
The antiquity of the study of the zodiacal signs is attested by the rock-painting near Cadiz and the maps of the heavens in stone-engravings in Galicia, Spain.

ZODIAC AND CHARACTER The signs of the zodiac are assumed to exert strong influences on personal traits, abilities, and potentialities. In a general sense, for instance, Aries is associated with mental ability. Taurus implies physical force. An adaptable nature is under the patronage of the Gemini. Cancer, on the other hand, stresses conservative tradition. Leo is exuberant and dominating. Virgo is critical. Libra is equated with justice. Daring men with initiative look toward Scorpio as their protector. Sagittarius denotes a dynamic personality. Intellectual capacity is conditioned by Capricorn. Humane traits belong to Aquarius, while a humble modesty hides behind Pisces.

ZODIAC AND PLANET The twelve zodiacal signs are each considered to be under the direction of a particular planet: as the Sun, that rules the sign of Leo.

ZODIAC, MEANING OF This astrological term is derived from zoe, the Greek for life, and diakos, which denotes a wheel.

ZODIACUS VITAE This Latin expression means The Zodiac of Life. In astrology, it was an old school book by Marcellus Palingenius Stellatus that was widely used in Shakespeare's day. The earliest edition extant, now in the British Museum, is dated 1574.

ZOHAR In Hebrew, the meaning of this term is The Book of Splendor. It is the most important work of the Kabbala, the Judaic mystical philosophical system.
The Zohar was first published in 1558, at Cremona, and numerous editions have appeared since then in many countries.
The authorship was ascribed to Tannaite scholars belonging in the first century A.D. Along with the Zohar is the Book Bahir, which is also Kabbalistic. Together they form the chief corpus of Kabbalistic literature. The Book Bahir stresses letter-mysticism, the interpretation of sounds. Among other subjects discussed are the mystical significance of the human organism, creation, light and its emanations, reincarnation. The Book Bahir is written in Hebrew: the Zohar, in an Aramaic dialect.
The Zohar presents a mystical interpretation of creation, man, the concept of evil, demons, the transmigration of the soul, and the Messiah.

ZOMBIES According to those who have been initiated into the cult of Voodoo, Zombies are corpses which have been taken from their graves and restored to life by sorcerers.

389

ZOON This Greek term, meaning animal, has a diminutive form, zodion. In English, zodion takes the form of Zodiac.

ZOROASTRIANISM In the ancient mystery cult of Zoroaster, the cosmos is peopled with demons of various character: Yatus, Nasus, malefic creatures and monsters.

ZOSIMUS THE PANOPOLITE Greek writer who flourished in the third or fourth century A.D. He is the author of an alchemical treatise that is the oldest extant work on this subject.

ZRACNE VILE Evil spirits believed by southern Slavs to inflict injuries on mortals. These air-dwelling spirits are implacable in their wrath.